P9-CFG-406

Donated to the
Fauquier County Public Library
From
The Piedmont Lace Guild

According to S. Annie Frost, author of The Ladies' Guide to Needlework *(1877), "There is no occupation so essentially feminine, at the same time so truly ladylike, as needlework in every branch, from the plain, useful sewing that keeps household and person neat and orderly, to the exquisite, dainty fancy work that adds beauty to every room." In keeping with the renewed interest in Victoriana, we have compiled a gathering of needlecraft projects for you to make for your home. These projects are soft and light with a romantic style that is in harmony with the current definition of Victorian.*

70 PARLOR ARTS

92 GENTLEMAN'S DOMAIN

102 A ROMANTIC RETREAT

130 THE CHILDREN'S CORNER

Victorian Workbasket

In Queen Victoria's day, a woman's workbasket was her constant companion and most cherished possession. In it she kept her needlework tools and treasures gathered over the course of a lifetime: Grandmother's silver thimble, the pincushion pieced by a childhood friend, Mother's embroidered needle case, and a fine set of whalebone spools, carved by a lovesick suitor. Each trinket had a useful task to perform and a special tale to tell—and all were as dear and familiar as old family friends.

SMITH
STUDIO

Needlework accessories were among the mundane household items upon which stitchers lavished special care and attention, creating a vast array of sewing tools and trinkets that are as treasured today as they were a century ago.

Pincushions offered opportunities to practice and perfect various stitchery skills. These fanciful whimsies were popular gifts for young girls to stitch and exchange as tokens of friendship and affection—even Queen Victoria fashioned a pin pillow for her favorite governess. The potpourri of pincushions pictured on page 7 (embellished with crochet, tatting, needlepoint, embroidery, and button appliqué) are similar to those that young Victorian stitchers might have made while learning to stitch.

The sumptuous beaded set of "needle friends"—needle book, scissors sheath, and pincushion—pictured *below,* graced with beaded wreaths and sprigs and Gothic initials, is worked on black linen and trimmed with borders and tassels of polished seed pearls.

The Victorian mania for embellishment extended to more ephemeral items as well. When printed paperback books became more widely available in the 1840s, embroidered book or journal covers (destined to dress up the penny dreadfuls, as paperback adventure novels were called then) and bookmarks, like the cross-stitch lily-of-the-valley motif, *opposite,* were considered nice gifts for friends.

Instructions for these projects are on pages 12–23.

By the turn of the century, a little book entitled *Encyclopedia of Needlework* had become the most popular sewing guide ever published on either side of the Atlantic. First issued in 1890, it is still in print—and in demand—today.

"The hand that can do good plain sewing will soon learn to do any sort of fancy work," insists the author, Thèrése de Dillmont, in her book, where she counsels young seamstresses to master practical sewing before attempting more ornamental stitchery.

Believing, as she did, that practice is the surest path to perfection, Mme. de Dillmont surely would have applauded the handsome darning sampler *opposite.* Stitched with varicolored threads on linen, the sampler boasts a simple cross-stitch alphabet framed by blocks of intricate darning weaves, each worked in different mending patterns, including twill, herringbone, and damask.

Once the intricacies of "plain sewing" were mastered, an adventuresome seamstress might have turned her hand to a fancywork project like paper embroidery. By following patterns published in magazines of the day, or by using preprinted cards (purchased for as little as a penny apiece in the 1880s), Victorians quickly turned bits of perforated paper into dainty keepsakes like the cross-stitch floss box, *below.* Such simple-to-stitch projects yield instant results.

Instructions for the projects shown here are on pages 24–27.

ABCDE
FGHIJ
KLMN
OPQRS
TUVW
XYZ
SINGER

NEEDLEPOINT PINCUSHION

Shown on page 7.
Pincushion measures 3½ inches square.

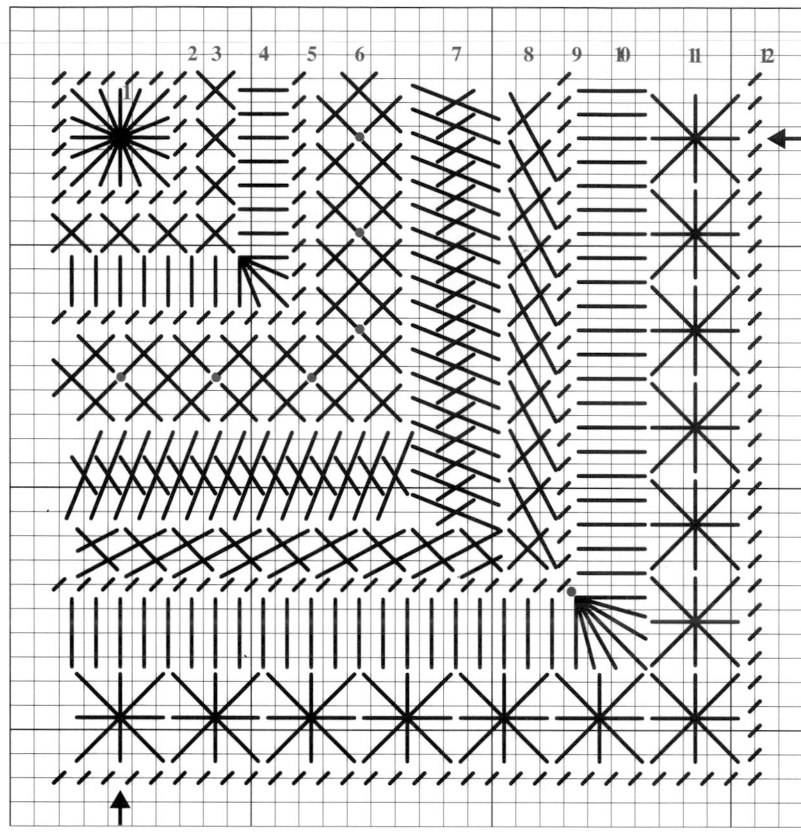

NEEDLEPOINT PINCUSHION

MATERIALS

6-inch square of 14-count needlepoint canvas
25 yards of Paternayan 3-strand yarn in peach (No. 865)
Size 22 tapestry needle
24 pearl beads measuring 2.5 mm in diameter
1 yard of ⅛-inch-wide ivory rayon cording; fiberfill
Ivory sewing thread
6-inch square of peach felt

INSTRUCTIONS

Note: For better coverage of the canvas, separate the three strands of yarn; recombine them in the number of strands indicated *below* for each stitch.

STITCHING: Follow the red numbered steps on the chart *above right* and the numbered steps *below.* When following the stitch diagrams, *opposite,* come up from under the canvas on the odd numbers and go back into the canvas on the even numbers.

1. Beginning in the center of the canvas, use two strands of yarn to work a double leviathan stitch over four canvas threads.

2. Work continental stitches using one strand of yarn over one canvas thread. See page 69 for the stitch diagram.

3. Work cross-stitches using two strands of yarn over two threads of canvas.

4. Work the Gobelin stitches using two strands of yarn over two threads of the canvas.

5. Work continental stitches using one strand of yarn over one canvas thread.

6. Using two strands of yarn, work rice stitches over four canvas threads.

7. Work knotted stitches with two strands of yarn over four canvas threads.

8. Work Greek stitches using two strands of yarn over two canvas threads.

9. Work continental stitches with one strand of yarn over one canvas thread.

10. Work Gobelin stitches over three canvas threads using two strands of yarn.

11. Use two strands of yarn to work Smyrna cross-stitches over four canvas threads.

12. Work continental stitches with one strand of yarn over one canvas thread.

FINISHING: Referring to the needlepoint blocking tip on page 14, block the stitched piece.

Sew pearls to the blocked piece following the red dots in the rice stitch (Step 6) and in the corners of the continental stitch (Step 9) for placement.

Place needlepoint and felt together with right sides facing. Machine-stitch between the Smyrna cross-stitches and the last row of continental stitches, completing the seaming on three sides only. Trim seams and turn right side out.

Stuff pincushion firmly with fiberfill. Turn the edges of the side opening in and hand-sew the side closed, leaving a small opening in one corner.

Form a 6-inch loop in one end of the ivory cording and tie an overhand knot to make a 4-inch loop. Insert the short tail of the cording into the small corner opening. Hand-sew the remaining length of the cording along the needlepoint and felt seams, stitching the cording around all four sides. Trim the excess cording, leaving a ½-inch tail. Insert the tail into the corner opening; sew the corner opening closed.

Referring to the tassel instructions on page 42, make a 3-inch-long tassel with peach yarn. Sew the tassel into the corner opposite the corded loop.

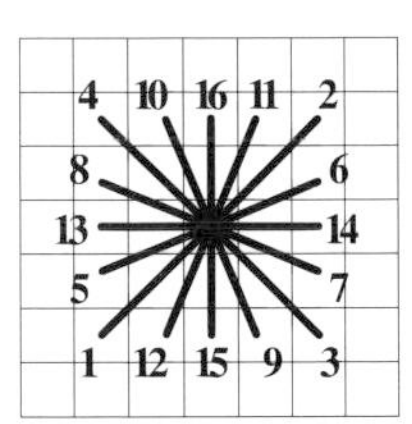

1. DOUBLE LEVIATHAN STITCH

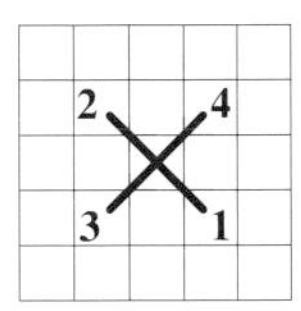

3. CROSS-STITCH

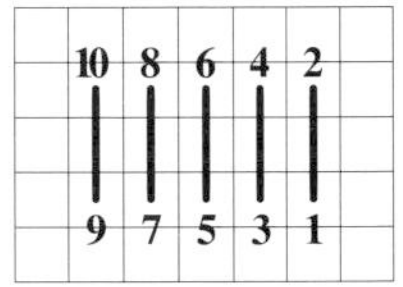

4. GOBELIN STITCH

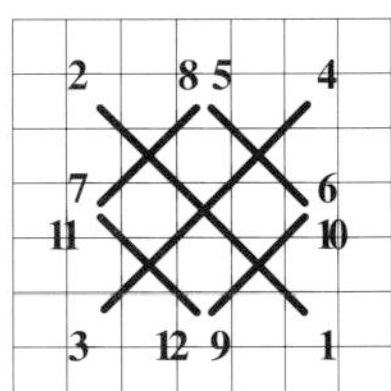

6. RICE STITCH

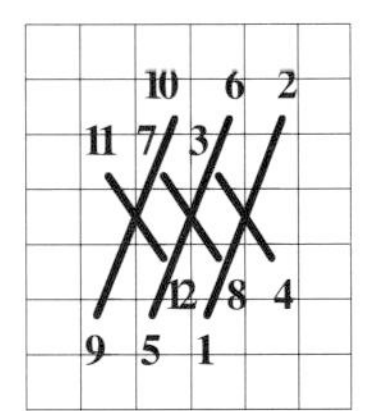

7. KNOTTED STITCH

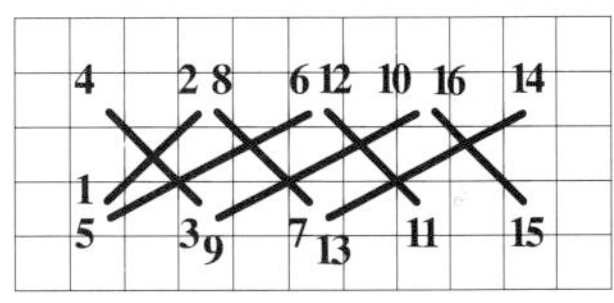

8. GREEK STITCH

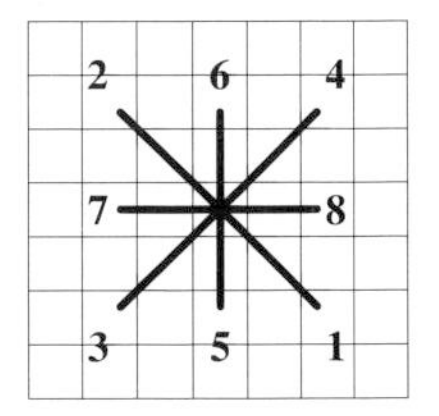

11. SMYRNA CROSS-STITCH

TATTED PINCUSHION

Shown on page 7.
Pincushion measures 5½ inches in diameter.

MATERIALS

For the tatted cover

DMC Cebelia crochet cotton, Size 30 (563-yard ball): 1 ball of beige (No. 619); tatting shuttle
Spray starch

For the pincushion

10x18-inch piece of purple velvet
Matching sewing thread
Sewing needle
Fiberfill
5½-inch-diameter circle of cardboard for base of pincushion (optional)

Abbreviations: See page 48.

INSTRUCTIONS

For the tatted cover

ROUND 1: Wind 3 yards of thread onto the shuttle; 2 yards of thread will be used from the ball. Leave 9-inch beginning tails.

Step 1: R of 4, p, 4, p, 4, p, 4; clr, rw.

Step 2: Ch of 4, p, 4, p, 4, p, 4, p, 4; tighten ch by pushing sts close tog, rw.

Step 3: R of 4, join to last p of previous r, 4, p, 4, p, 4; clr, rw.

Step 4: Ch of 4, p, 4, p, 4, p, 4, p, 4; tighten ch, rw.

Step 5: Rep steps 3 and 4 alternately until there are 8 rs and 8 chs.

Step 6: R of 4, join to last p of previous r, 4, p, 4, join to *first* p of first r, 4; clr, rw.

Step 7: Ch of 4, p, 4, p, 4, p, 4, p, 4; tighten ch.

Cut the ending tails 9 inches long. Tie two square knots with the beginning and ending tails. Thread one tail through the needle and stitch back through the tatted sts to secure; cut off excess thread. Rep with the other three tails.

ROUND 2: Wind 7½ yards of thread onto the shuttle; no thread will be used off the ball. Leave a 9-inch beginning tail.

Step 1: R of 6, join to second p from the left of any ch of Rnd 1, 6; clr, rw; leave ⅜-inch thread sp between rs.

Step 2: R of 2, p, 2, p, 2, p, 2, p, 2, p, 2, p, 2, p, 2; clr, rw; leave ⅜-inch thread sp between rs.

Step 3: R of 6, join to next p to the right in the same ch of Rnd 1, 6; clr, rw; leave ⅜-inch thread sp between rs.

Step 4: Rep Step 2.

Step 5: R of 6, join to the second p from the left in the next ch to the right in Rnd 1, 6; clr, rw; leave ⅜-inch thread sp.

Step 6: Rep steps 2 and 3 alternately until 18 small rs have been joined to the 9 chs of Rnd 1—18 rs with ps extended from the perimeter.

Leave a 9-inch ending tail and finish as in Rnd 1.

ROUND 3: Wind 10 yards of thread onto the shuttle; 11 yards of thread will be used off the ball. Leave 9-inch beginning tails.

Step 1: R of 2, p, 2, p, 2, p, 2, p, 2, p, 2, p, 2, p, 2, p, 2; clr, rw.

Step 2: Ch of 4, p, 4, p, 4, p, 4; tighten ch, rw.

Step 3: R of 6, join to last p of previous r, 6; clr, rw.

Step 4: Ch of 4, p, 4, p, 4, p, 4; tighten ch, rw.

Step 5: R of 6, join to fifth p of second previous r, 6; clr, rw.

Step 6: Ch of 4, p, 4, p, 4, p, 4, join to fourth p of second previous r, 4, p, 4; tighten ch, rw.

Step 7: R of 6, join to center p of any large r of Rnd 2, 6; clr, rw.

Step 8: Ch of 4, p, 4; tighten ch, rw.

Step 9: R of 2, p, 2, p, 2, p, 2, p, 2, p, 2, p, 2, p, 2, p, 2; clr, rw.

Step 10: Ch of 4, p, 4, join to center p of third previous ch, 4, p, 4; tighten ch, rw.

Step 11: R of 6, join to last p of previous r, 6; clr, rw.

Step 12: Ch of 4, p, 4, p, 4, p, 4; tighten ch, rw.

Step 13: R of 6, join to fifth p of previous r, 6; clr, rw.

continued

Step 14: Ch of 4, p, 4, p, 4, p, 4, join to fourth p of second previous r, 4, p, 4; tighten ch, rw.

Step 15: R of 6, join to center p of the next large r to the right of Rnd 2, 6; clr, rw.

Step 16: Rep steps 8 through 15, 15 times more.

Step 17: Ch of 4, p, 4; tighten ch, rw.

Step 18: R of 2, p, 2, p, 2, p, 2, p, 2, p, 2, p, 2, p, 2; clr, rw.

Step 19: Ch of 4, p, 4, join to the center p of the third previous ch, 4, p, 4; tighten ch, rw.

Step 20: R of 6, join to last p of the previous r, 6; clr, rw.

Step 21: Ch of 4, p, 4, p, 4, p, 4; tighten ch, rw.

Step 22: R of 6, join to the fifth p of the second previous r, 6; clr, rw.

Step 23: Ch of 4, p, 4, join to the middle p of the first ch of Rnd 3; 4, p, 4, join to fourth p of the previous r, 4, p, 4; tighten ch, rw.

Step 24: R of 6, join to the last free large r of Rnd 2, 6; clr, rw.

Step 25: Ch of 4, p, 4; tighten ch.

Leave 9-inch ending tails. Tie in two square knots and finish as for Rnd 1. Pin the finished tatting to a padded ironing board with rustproof pins and spray lightly with starch to block the top of the cover. Allow the tatting to dry before continuing to Rnd 4.

ROUND 4: Wind 6 yards of thread onto the shuttle; no thread will be used from the ball. Leave a 9-inch beginning tail.

Step 1: R of 6, p, 6; clr, rw; leave ½-inch thread sp.

Step 2: Join at joined chs at any point of Rnd 3; leave ½-inch thread sp.

Note: Joins at pairs of chs will slide. When making each small r measure 1 inch from the previous small r to ensure the proper spacing.

Step 3: R of 6, p, 6; clr, rw; leave ½-inch thread sp.

Step 4: Join at the next pair of joined chs to the right in Rnd 3; leave ½-inch thread sp.

Step 5: Rep steps 3 and 4 alternately until thread has been joined at all joined chs of Rnd 3 and there are 18 small rs at the perimeter.

Cut the thread, leaving a 9-inch ending tail; tie it to the beginning tail in a square knot and finish as for Rnd 1.

ROUND 5: Wind 8 yards of thread onto the shuttle; no thread will be used from the ball. Leave a 9-inch beginning tail.

Step 1: R of 2, p, 2, p, 2, p, 2, p, 2, p, 2, p, 2, p, 2; clr, rw, leave ½-inch thread sp.

Step 2: Join to any p of the small r of Rnd 4; leave ½-inch thread sp.

Step 3: R of 2, p, 2, p, 2, p, 2, p, 2, p, 2, p, 2, p, 2; clr, rw, leave ½-inch thread sp.

Step 4: Join in the p of the next small r to the right in Rnd 4; leave ½-inch thread sp.

Step 5: Rep steps 3 and 4 alternately until 18 joins have been made to Rnd 4 and there are 18 large perimeter rs with ps.

Cut the thread, leaving a 9-inch ending tail; tie it to the beginning tail in a square knot and finish as for Rnd 1.

ROUND 6: Wind 6 yards of thread onto the shuttle; no thread will be used from the ball. Leave a 9-inch beginning tail.

Step 1: R of 6, p, 6; clr, rw; leave ½-inch thread sp.

Step 2: Join to the center p of any r of Rnd 5; leave ½-inch thread sp.

Step 3: R of 6, p, 6; clr, rw; leave ½-inch thread sp.

Step 4: Join to the center p in the next large r to the right in Rnd 5; leave ½-inch thread sp.

Step 5: Rep steps 3 and 4 alternately until joins have been made to all large rs of Rnd 5 and there are 18 small rs at the perimeter.

Cut the thread, leaving a 9-inch ending tail; tie it to the beginning tail in a square knot and finish as for Rnd 1.

For the pincushion

Note: Cutting directions, *below,* for the fabric pieces include ¼-inch seam allowances. Sew all pieces together with the right sides facing.

From velvet, cut one 1½x17½-inch velvet boxing strip for the sides; cut two 6-inch-diameter velvet circles for the top and bottom of the pincushion.

Sew the short sides of the boxing strip together to make a tube.

To assemble the top of the pincushion, sew one circle and the boxing strip together. For the bottom, sew together the second circle and the opposite side of the boxing strip, sewing halfway around; turn right side out. Stuff the pincushion firmly with fiberfill. Insert a 5½-inch-diameter circle of cardboard into the bottom of the cushion for added stability; hand-sew the opening closed.

Stretch the tatted cover over the pincushion. Sew the picots on the last round to the bottom edge of the cushion.

BLOCKING NEEDLEPOINT

Blocking finished needlepoint restores the canvas to its original shape.

Use a pine board that's at least 4 inches larger in both width and length than the stitched area. Cover the board with gingham fabric; use the checks to square the canvas.

Sprinkle the needlepoint canvas with water until the yarn feels slightly damp on both sides. Center and tack the needlepoint facedown to the blocking board. (Use rustproof tacks or pins.) Start tacking in the centers of opposite sides; work out to the corners, pulling as you go. Repeat the tacking on the remaining two sides. Make sure the edges align with the gingham checks.

After the canvas has dried thoroughly, remove it from the board.

FAN-SHAPE PINCUSHION

Shown on page 7.
Pincushion measures approximately 9 inches across at the widest part and holds a 6-inch-long scissors.

MATERIALS

18-inch square of ecru velour
16-inch square of mat board
1½ yards of ½-inch-wide ecru braid
1½ yards of ⅛-inch-wide ecru cord
One ½-inch ecru ribbon rose
One ¼-inch ecru ribbon rose
Two ¼-inch white ribbon roses
1 yard of ¼-inch-wide ecru satin ribbon
Assorted mother-of-pearl, plastic, and metal buttons
Assorted pearl beads
Ecru sewing thread; sewing needle
Tracing paper; nonpermanent fabric marker; fiberfill
Straight pins; crafts knife
White crafts glue; Fray Check liquid
Hot-glue gun and glue sticks

INSTRUCTIONS

Fold the tracing paper in half. Place the fold of the paper atop the fold lines of the patterns *below* and on page 16; trace and cut out the patterns.

Fold the fabric with right sides together; align the fold line of the fan pattern and the straight grain of the fabric. Trace around the fan pattern. Cut out two fans, adding a ½-inch seam allowance to each. On the right side of one of the fans mark the blue topstitching lines.

On the wrong side of the other fan mark the red slash lines with the nonpermanent marker. Turn the fabric over and put Fray Check on the marked slash lines. Allow Fray Check to dry completely. Cut along each slash line, taking care not to cut outside the area covered with Fray Check.

Place fan shapes together with the right sides together. Machine-stitch the two fans together. Clip the curves.

Carefully turn the fan right side out through one of the slashed openings.

With the marked side up, machine-stitch along the blue topstitching lines.

Stuff each divided section firmly through the slashed openings in the back of the fan; hand-sew the openings closed.

Trace around the fan back pattern atop the mat board; cut out the fan back with the crafts knife.

Trace around the fan back fabric pattern with the nonpermanent fabric marker atop the wrong side of the velour.

continued

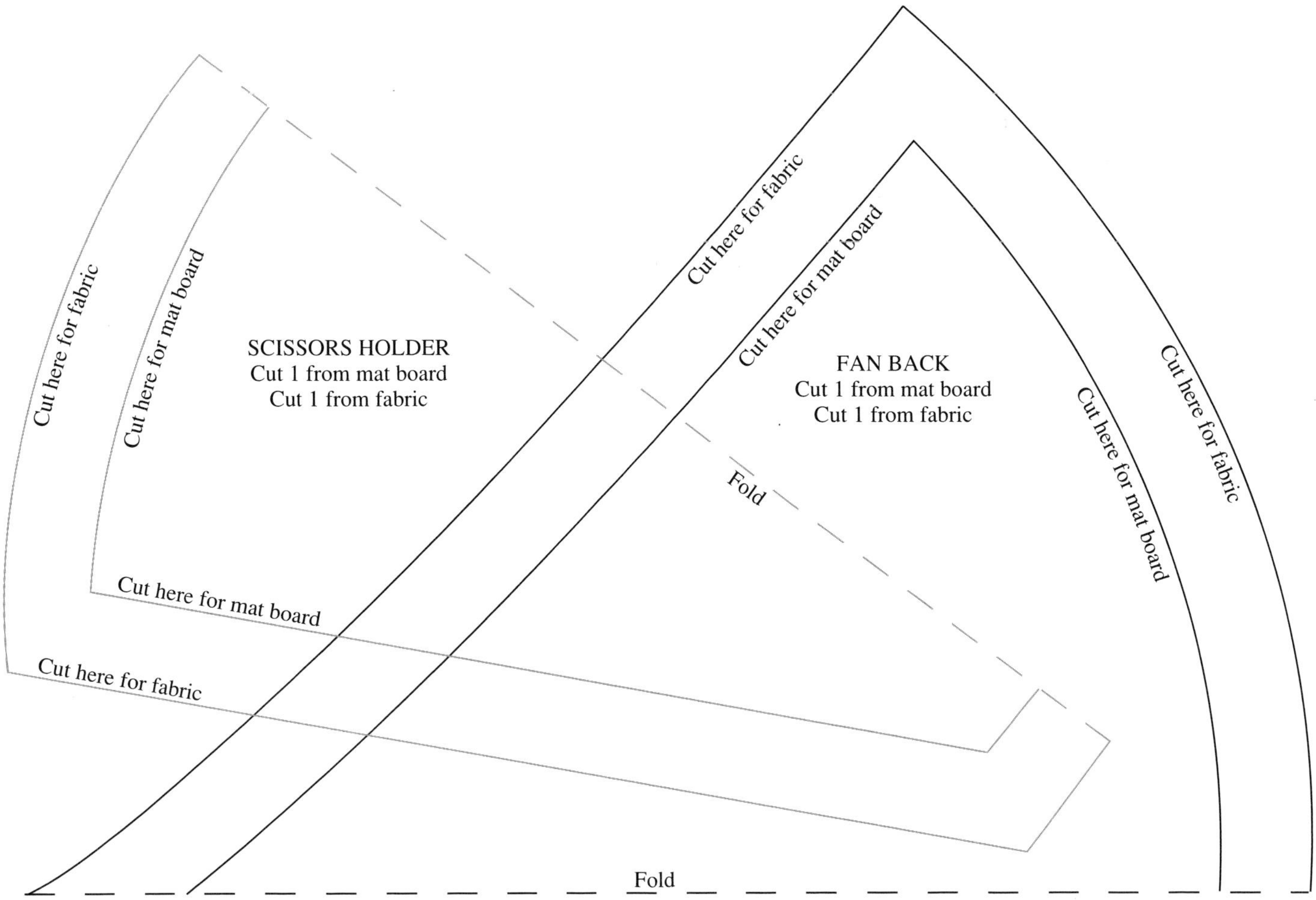

FAN PINCUSHION PATTERNS

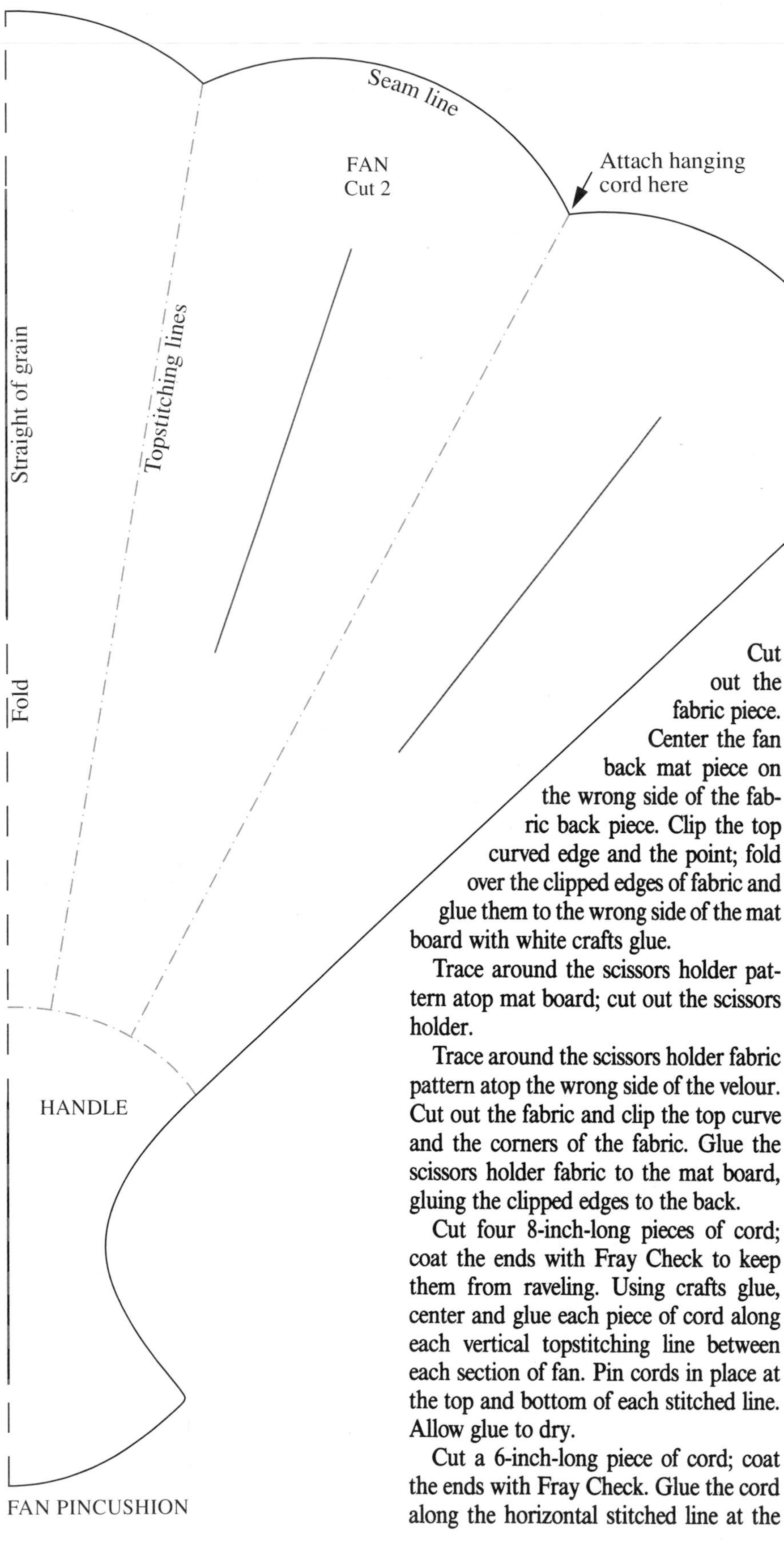

Cut out the fabric piece. Center the fan back mat piece on the wrong side of the fabric back piece. Clip the top curved edge and the point; fold over the clipped edges of fabric and glue them to the wrong side of the mat board with white crafts glue.

Trace around the scissors holder pattern atop mat board; cut out the scissors holder.

Trace around the scissors holder fabric pattern atop the wrong side of the velour. Cut out the fabric and clip the top curve and the corners of the fabric. Glue the scissors holder fabric to the mat board, gluing the clipped edges to the back.

Cut four 8-inch-long pieces of cord; coat the ends with Fray Check to keep them from raveling. Using crafts glue, center and glue each piece of cord along each vertical topstitching line between each section of fan. Pin cords in place at the top and bottom of each stitched line. Allow glue to dry.

Cut a 6-inch-long piece of cord; coat the ends with Fray Check. Glue the cord along the horizontal stitched line at the handle, covering and pinning the cord over the ends of the 8-inch cords. Allow the glue to dry.

Remove all the pins and turn the fan over. Glue the cord ends to the back of the fan.

With the right side up, glue braid around the outside edge of the fan, starting and ending the braid at the right side of the handle. Cover the seam line and the cords with braid. Pin the glued braid securely to the fan at ½-inch intervals and at each cord juncture.

Turn the fan wrong side up. Cut a 20-inch piece of cord for the hanger. Use a generous amount of glue to attach both ends of the cord to the back of the fan along the cord ends already glued between sections 1 and 2 and between sections 4 and 5. Allow the glue to dry. Remove the pins.

With the wrong side of the fan facing up, place the fabric-covered fan back in position and lightly mark around the outside edges of the back; remove the fan back. Place hot glue on the raised areas of the fan that will be covered by the fan back; with the fabric-covered side of the fan back facing out, glue the fan back to the fan. Press down firmly. Allow the glue to dry.

Hot-glue the side edges only of the fabric-covered scissors holder to the back of the fan. *Do not glue the top or bottom edges of the scissors holder.*

Tie the ¼-inch-wide satin ribbon around the narrow part of the fan handle, placing the knot at the center back. Add glue to the knot to secure it; allow the glue to dry. Tie overhand knots at 3-inch intervals along the tails of the ribbon and then tie a large bow in back where the knot was glued. Glue the bow at the knot to keep it from slipping.

With the right side of the fan facing up, use crafts glue to glue ribbon roses to the right side of the fan handle.

Referring to the photograph on page 7, hot-glue assorted buttons to fill the second and fourth panels of the fan. Fill in the button panels as desired with the assorted pearls.

CROCHETED PINCUSHION

Shown on page 7.
Pincushion measures 3⅝ inches in diameter.

MATERIALS

For the crocheted cover

DMC Cebelia crochet cotton, Size 10, (282-yard ball): 1 ball of lavender (No. 210)
Size 7 steel crochet hook
Large-eye tapestry needle

For the pincushion

12-inch square of purple velvet
Matching sewing thread
Sewing needle
Fiberfill
3½-inch-diameter cardboard circle for the bottom support (optional)

Abbreviations: See page 99.

INSTRUCTIONS

For the crocheted cover

Beg at center, ch 6, join with sl st to form ring.

Rnd 1: Ch 3, work 23 dc in ring; join to top of beg ch-3—24 dc.

Rnd 2: Ch 4, (dc in next dc, ch 1) 23 times; join to third ch of beg ch-4.

Rnd 3: Sl st to next ch, sc in same ch-1 sp, (ch 5, sc in next ch-1 sp) 23 times; end ch 3, dc in beg sc.

Rnd 4: Ch 3, dc in next ch-5 sp, ch 7, **in next ch-5 lp work first half of dc leaving last 2 lps on hook, work another dc in next ch-5 lp, work off all lps—2-dc cluster made;** (ch 7, 2-dc cluster in next two ch-5 lps) 10 times; end ch 3, trc in top of beg ch-3.

Rnd 5: Ch 3, work 4 dc in next lp; **5 dc, ch 3, and 5 dc in next ch-7 lp—shell made;** (shell in next ch-7 lp) 10 times; 5 dc in next lp, ch 1, hdc in top of beg ch 3.

Rnd 6: Ch 10, dc in next ch-3 lp, ch 3, dc in same lp, (ch 7, dc in next ch-3 lp, ch 3, dc in same lp) 10 times; end ch 7, dc in top of hdc.

Rnd 7: Ch 3, dc in third ch of ch-10 lp, work 5 dc in same lp, * 2 dc in ch-3 lp, 7 dc in next ch-7 lp; rep from * around; join with sl st to top of beg ch-3—108 sts.

Rnd 8: Ch 3, sk first dc, dc in next 2 dc; **keeping last lp on hook, work dc in each of next 2 dc, yo, draw through all lps on hook—dec made;** dc in next 2 dc; * dec over next 2 dc; dc in next 3 dc, dec over next 2 dc, dc in next 2 dc; rep from * around; join with sl st to top of beg ch-3—84 sts.

Rnds 9–11: Ch 3, sk first dc, dc in each dc around; join to top of beg ch-3.

Rnd 12: Ch 3, sk first dc, dc in each dc around; at the same time dec 4 sts evenly spaced; join with sl st to top of beg ch-3—80 sts.

Rnd 13: Ch 1, sk first dc, * **sc in 9 dc, ch 5, sl st in first ch of ch-5—picot made;** rep from * around; join with sl st to beg ch-1; fasten off.

For the pincushion

Note: Cutting directions, *below,* for the fabric pieces include ¼-inch seam allowances. Sew all pieces together with right sides facing.

From velvet, cut one 1¾x12-inch velvet boxing strip for the sides; cut two 4-inch velvet circles for the top and bottom of the pincushion.

Sew the short sides of the boxing strip together to make a tube.

To assemble the top of the pincushion, sew one circle and the boxing strip together. For the bottom, sew together the second circle and the opposite side of the boxing strip, sewing halfway around; turn right side out. Stuff the pincushion firmly with fiberfill. Insert a 3½-inch circle of cardboard into the bottom of the cushion for added stability; hand-sew the opening closed.

Turn the crocheted cover *wrong side out* and stretch it over the pincushion. Tack the picots on the cover to the bottom of the pincushion.

CRAZY QUILTED SHOE PINCUSHION

Shown on page 7.
Pincushion measures 7x8½ inches.

MATERIALS

6-inch squares of 18 different velveteen, satin, moiré taffeta, metallic, polished, or cotton print fabrics
8x10-inch piece of satin for the back
8x10-inch piece of cotton batiste for the base
Contrasting sewing thread
Assorted embroidery flosses
Embroidery needle
Assorted pearl cottons
Fiberfill
Three small metallic shank buttons
¼ yard of narrow lace
½ yard of 1-inch-wide satin ribbon
Tracing paper

INSTRUCTIONS

Trace the shoe pattern on page 18 onto tracing paper; cut out the pattern. Trace the shoe pattern onto batiste for the crazy patchwork base. *Do not cut out the shoe shape.*

Draw around the pattern onto satin fabric for the back. Cut out the shoe back from the satin, adding a ½-inch seam allowance. Set aside the back.

Using a contrasting thread, machine-stitch around the shoe base using the marked line as a guide.

Refer to the instructions for crazy quilting on pages 80 and 81 to sew fabric patches to the batiste. Use 2- to 3-inch three- or four-sided pieces of fancy fabrics for the patchwork.

continued

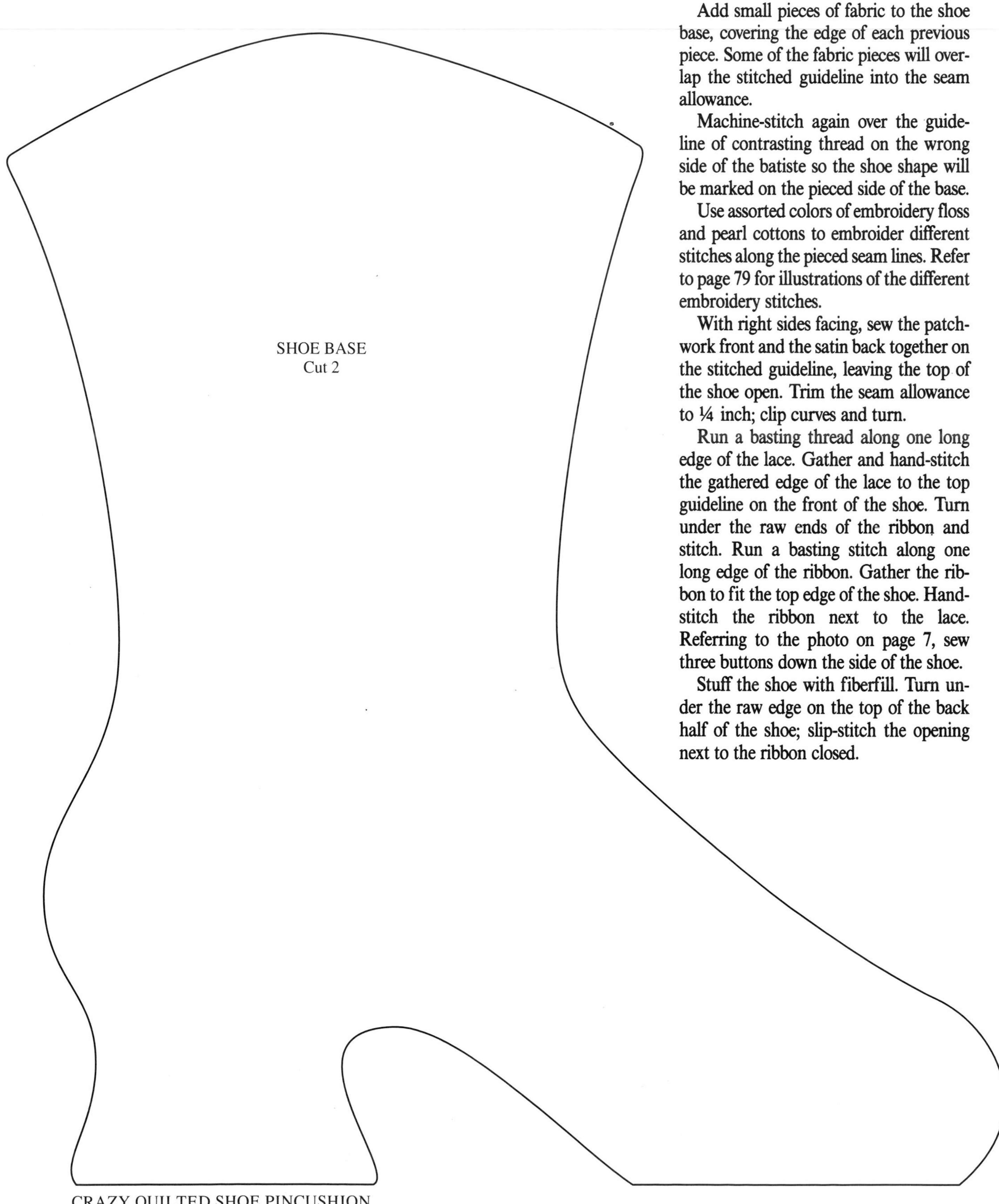

CRAZY QUILTED SHOE PINCUSHION

Add small pieces of fabric to the shoe base, covering the edge of each previous piece. Some of the fabric pieces will overlap the stitched guideline into the seam allowance.

Machine-stitch again over the guideline of contrasting thread on the wrong side of the batiste so the shoe shape will be marked on the pieced side of the base.

Use assorted colors of embroidery floss and pearl cottons to embroider different stitches along the pieced seam lines. Refer to page 79 for illustrations of the different embroidery stitches.

With right sides facing, sew the patchwork front and the satin back together on the stitched guideline, leaving the top of the shoe open. Trim the seam allowance to ¼ inch; clip curves and turn.

Run a basting thread along one long edge of the lace. Gather and hand-stitch the gathered edge of the lace to the top guideline on the front of the shoe. Turn under the raw ends of the ribbon and stitch. Run a basting stitch along one long edge of the ribbon. Gather the ribbon to fit the top edge of the shoe. Hand-stitch the ribbon next to the lace. Referring to the photo on page 7, sew three buttons down the side of the shoe.

Stuff the shoe with fiberfill. Turn under the raw edge on the top of the back half of the shoe; slip-stitch the opening next to the ribbon closed.

BEADED SEWING SET

Shown on page 9.
Both the needle case and pincushion are 4 inches square; the scissors sheath is 5¼ inches long.

MATERIALS

For the scissors sheath

8-inch square of black 28-count linen
8-inch squares of black broadcloth and fusible lightweight black interfacing
One 8-mm bead with a large hole

For the pincushion

8-inch square and 5-inch square of black 28-count linen
Four 8-mm beads with large holes
Fiberfill
Fusible interfacing

For the needle case

10-inch square of black 28-count linen
One black snap fastener
7-inch square of red felt
One 8-mm bead with a large hole
Pinking shears

For all projects

Bead needles
Black bead thread
Size 11 seed beads in the following colors: iris finish in red, green, apricot, and amber; silver lined in dark red and dark green; pearl finish in ecru and yellow
Black sewing thread
Sewing needle
White tailor's chalk
Tracing paper
White paper tape

INSTRUCTIONS

For the scissors sheath

Note: The scissors sheath pattern, *below,* is finished size; add a ½-inch seam allowance when cutting it out of fabric.

Fold tracing paper in half and align the fold of the tracing paper with the dashed fold line of the pattern; cut out the completed pattern. Place the pattern atop black linen with the upper right corner of the front on the straight grain. Draw around the pattern with white chalk. Draw a fold line where indicated by the dashed line. Cut out the scissors sheath. Cover the edges of the fabric with white paper tape to keep the fabric from raveling while stitching.

Measure ½ inch down and 1 inch in from the chalk line on the right side. Begin stitching the design there. Work only the first half of a cross-stitch over two threads of fabric, attaching a bead with each stitch. See the chart on page 20 to work the beaded cross-stitch on the scissors sheath.

Remove paper tape from the edges of the fabric after the design is complete. Lay the piece on a thick towel with the bead design down and steam.

Using the stitched piece as the pattern, cut a lining from broadcloth and one from fusible interfacing.

Fuse the interfacing and broadcloth lining together following the manufacturer's instructions.

Place the lining and beaded piece with right sides together and sew only across the top of the sheath along the seam line. Zigzag-stitch in the seam allowance next to the seam. Trim seam allowance close to zigzag stitching.

Turn right side out and steam.

Fold the sheath on the fold line with the lining facing out. Sew the sheath closed along the side and across the bottom. Zigzag-stitch in the seam allowance next to the seam. Trim seam allowance close to zigzag stitching.

Turn the scissors sheath right side out and press on a thick towel with the beaded design down.

PICOT BEAD EDGING: Anchor the bead thread securely at the top fold line with a whipstitch over two threads of fabric on both sides of the seam.

Attach one ecru bead with each whipstitch, spacing the beads and whipstitches two threads apart.

* Stitch four beads on four whipstitches, **string 4 beads on next whipstitch and draw up firmly—picot made;** repeat from * around top of scissors case to first bead strung. Anchor the thread securely. Do not cut the thread.

TASSEL: * Run the needle through an 8-mm bead, string 50 ecru beads, run needle back through the 8-mm bead, draw

continued

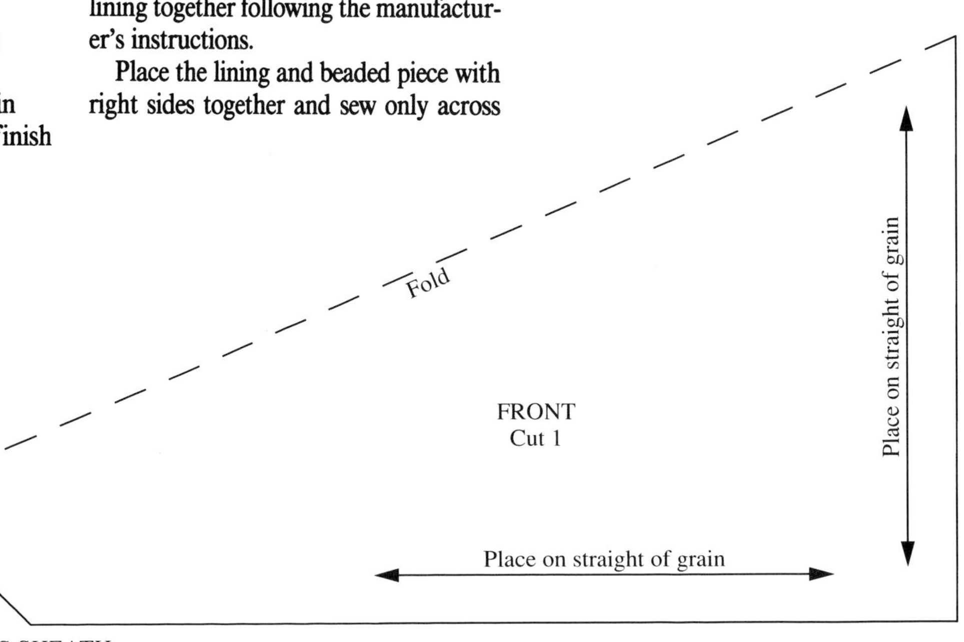

SCISSORS SHEATH

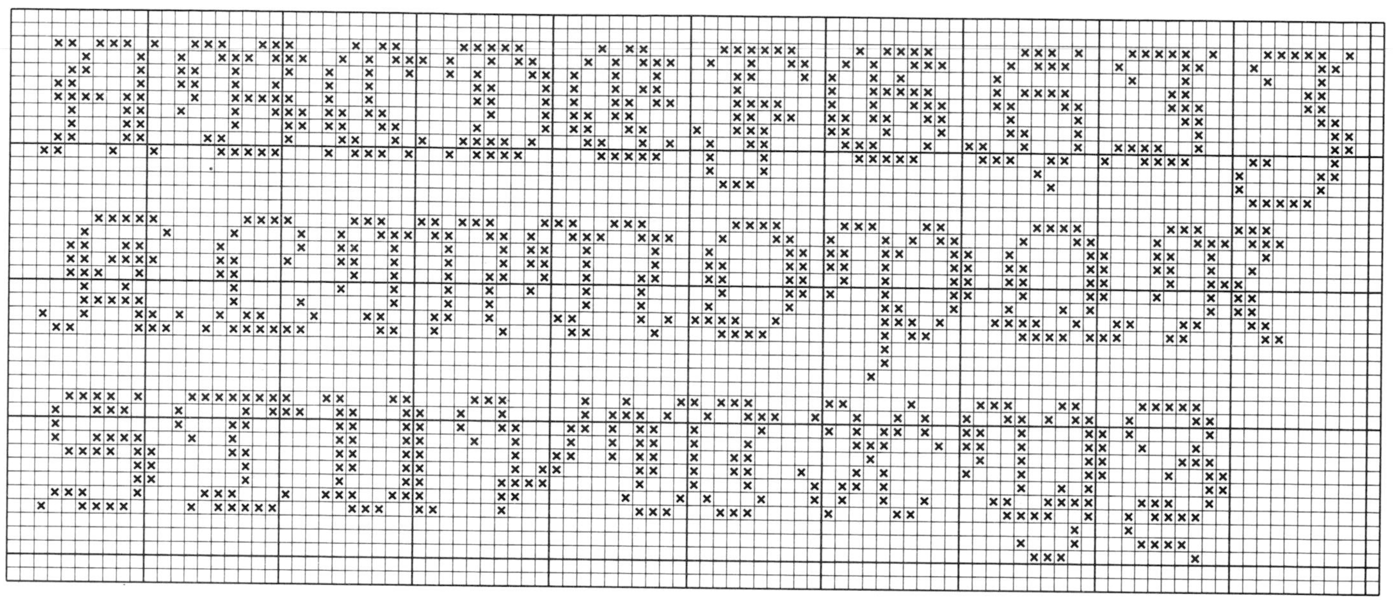

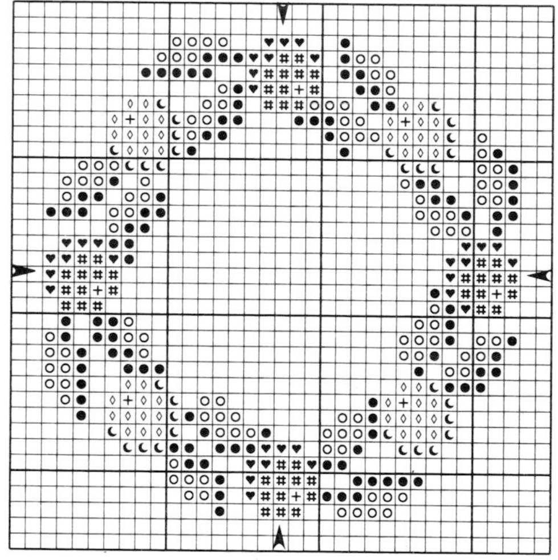

PINCUSHION AND NEEDLE CASE

BEADED SEWING SET

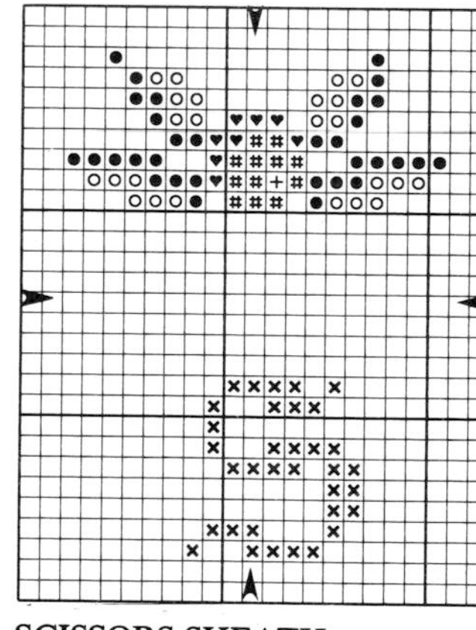

SCISSORS SHEATH

BEADS	
⌗⌗	red iris
♥♥	dark red silver lined
××	amber iris
○○	green iris
●●	dark green silver lined
◊◊	ecru pearl
☾☾	apricot iris
++	yellow pearl

up thread firmly and take a small stitch in the fabric, repeat from * until there are four loops of 50 beads. Knot and secure the thread in fabric.

For the pincushion

Cover the edges of the fabric with white paper tape to keep the fabric from raveling while stitching. Center and work the beaded design, *left,* in the middle of the 8-inch square of linen fabric.

Remove the paper tape from the edges of the fabric after the design is complete. Lay the piece on a thick towel with the bead design down and steam.

Trim the beaded piece to a 5-inch square.

Cut two 5-inch-square pieces of fusible interfacing. Fuse a piece of interfacing to the wrong side of the beaded design and the bottom linen piece.

Place the beaded piece and bottom piece with right sides together; using ½-inch seams, sew around 3½ sides, leaving an opening for turning. Zigzag-stitch in the seam allowance next to the seam. Trim seam allowance close to zigzag stitching. Turn right side out and press.

Stuff firmly with fiberfill and hand-sew the opening closed.

Work the picot bead edging and the tassel following the directions on page 19 and *opposite* for the scissors sheath. Work the picot bead edging around all four sides of the pincushion and stitch a tassel in each corner.

For the needle case

Cut the linen in half; set one piece aside. Baste a contrasting thread around the linen ½ inch from the edges to define the seam line. Run a second contrasting basting thread vertically through the center of the linen to define the fold line.

Cover the edges of the fabric with the white paper tape to keep the fabric from raveling.

Center and work the bead design, *opposite,* in the right-hand section.

Remove the tape and contrasting thread from the edges of the fabric after the design is complete. Lay both linen pieces facedown on a thick towel and steam.

Place linen pieces with right sides together; using ½-inch seams, sew around 3½ sides, leaving an opening for turning.

Zigzag-stitch in the seam allowance next to the seam. Trim the seam allowance close to the zigzag stitching. Turn the piece right side out; sew the opening closed.

Cut the felt in half. Use pinking shears to pink around all four sides of both pieces of felt.

Open the needle case flat and lay it with the design side down. Center the felt pieces, one on top of the other, on the inside of the needle case cover.

Sew through the felt and needle case cover along the center basting threads on the cover. Remove the basting threads.

Sew the snap fastener to the inside of the case at the center of the side edge.

Work the picot bead edging around the top, bottom, and open sides of the *front* of the needle case. Stitch a tassel in the center edge of the side where the snap is located. Follow the picot bead edging and tassel directions for the scissors sheath on page 19 and *opposite.*

Lily-of-the-Valley Book Cover and Bookmark

Shown on page 8.
Book cover fits a 5¾x8¼x¾-inch blank journal. The bookmark measures 1¾x11¾ inches.

MATERIALS

For the book cover

One hardcover, blank journal measuring 5¾x8¼x¾ inches
22x16-inch piece of 30-count seafoam green linen
12¾x8⅜-inch piece fleece batting
15⅜x8⅛-inch piece of white synthetic suede

For the bookmark

15x4-inch piece of 30-count seafoam green linen
1⅞x7¾-inch piece of white synthetic suede

For both

Size 24 or 26 tapestry needle
One skein *each* of DMC embroidery floss in the colors listed on the color keys; one skein of pistachio green lt (No. 368) floss

INSTRUCTIONS

For the book cover

Following the diagram on page 23, measure and baste all guidelines on the linen with a contrasting thread.

Work counted chain stitch using two strands of No. 367 floss along the basted lines marked in red on the diagram. Refer to the diagram *below* to work this stitch.

Refer to the diagram on page 23 for placement on the book cover of the lily-of-the-valley design; the actual design is on page 22. Begin stitching the top right side of the leaf located in the center of the design on the right side of the cover as indicated on the diagram by the arrows. Use two strands of floss over two threads to work cross-stitches. Use one strand of floss over two threads for backstitches. Both stitches are illustrated in diagrams on page 69.

continued

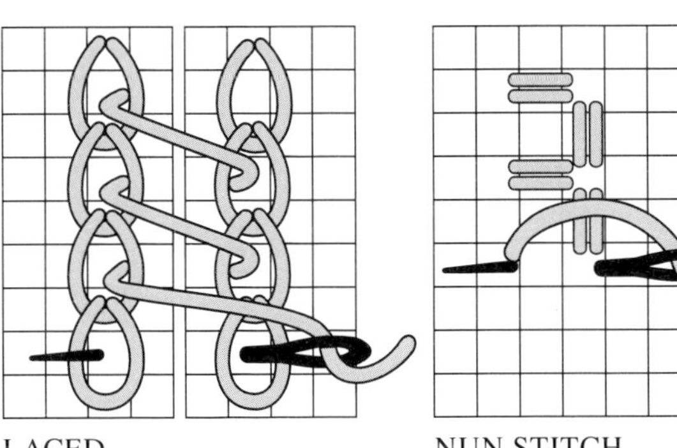

LACED CHAIN STITCH

NUN STITCH

COUNTED CHAIN STITCH

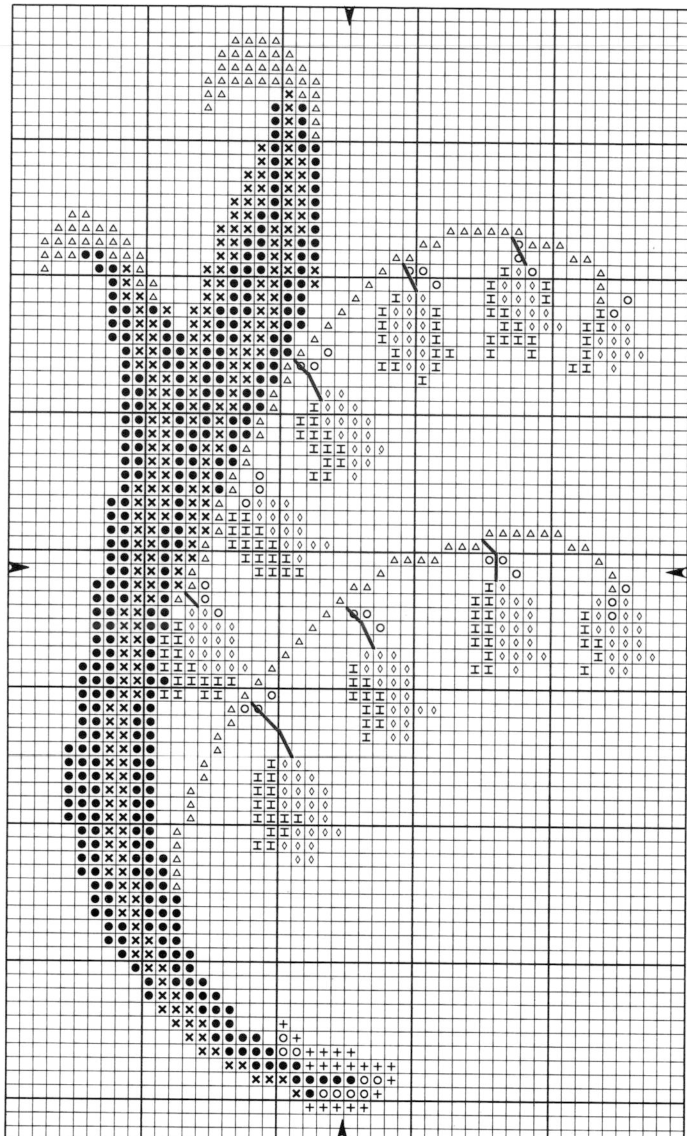

LILY-OF-THE-VALLEY BOOK COVER

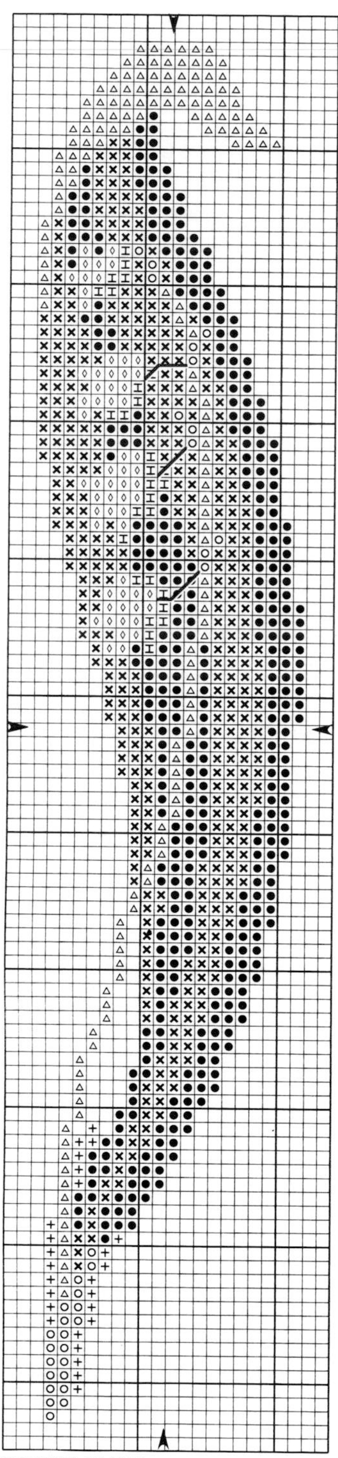

BOOKMARK

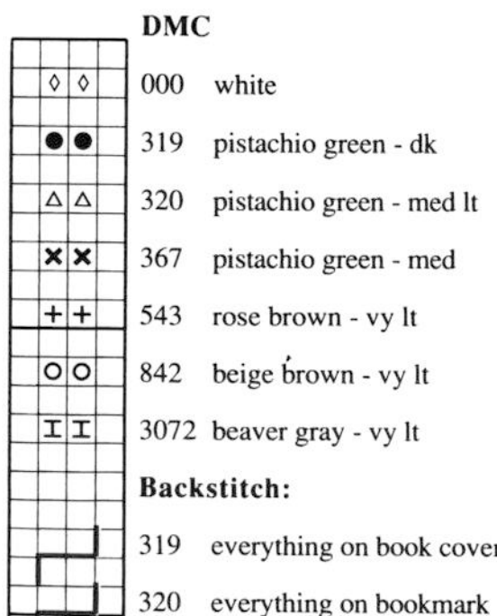

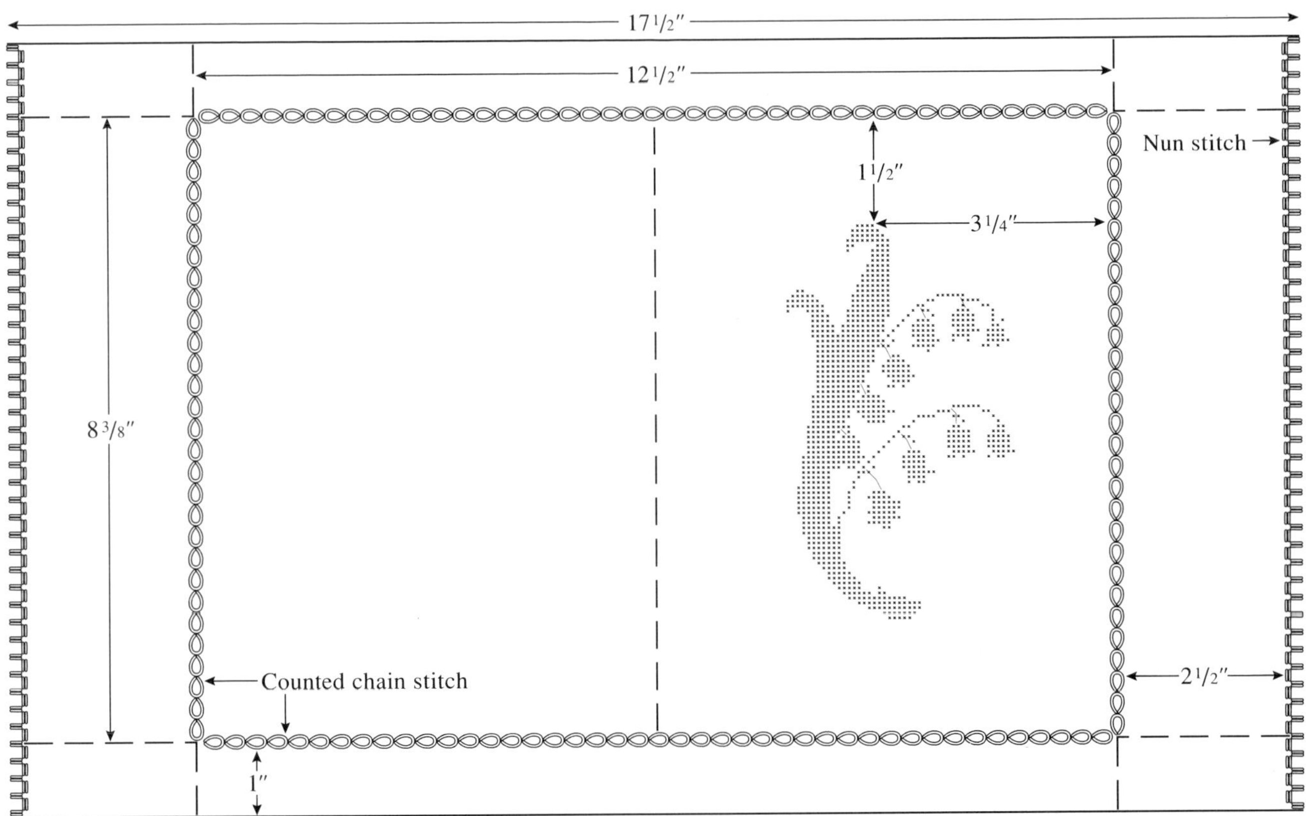

LILY-OF-THE-VALLEY BOOK COVER

When the design is complete, lay the cover on a thick towel with the design side down and press well.

Measure 2½ inches out from the counted chain stitch on the short sides. Work nun stitches along this line on both short sides with two strands of No. 368 floss. Refer to page 21 for a diagram of this stitch.

Trim the excess linen fabric close to the nun stitches, taking care not to cut the stitching.

Fold long sides to the wrong side along the counted chain stitch and press well.

Place linen design facedown and lay batting on top of linen. Fold the linen over on top of the batting at the counted chain stitch pressing line at the top and bottom of the book cover. Overlap the counted chain stitch with batting by ¼ inch on either side; pin batting in place.

Cover batting with synthetic suede and slip-stitch along all four sides.

Turn the short sides under along the counted chain stitch; press fold.

Using two strands of No. 367 floss, lace the chain stitches together where they meet along the top and bottom corners forming pockets in which to slide the book cover. Refer to page 21 for a diagram to lace chain stitches.

For the bookmark

Measure 4 inches down from the top of the linen strip and 1¾ inches in from the right side; begin stitching the top of the leaf at the arrow on the chart, *opposite.* Work backstitches with one strand of floss over two threads.

Work nun stitches with two strands of No. 368 floss around all four sides of bookmark, leaving eight threads between the design and the nun stitch on the long sides and 10 threads between the design and nun stitch on the short sides.

Press well. Trim excess linen next to the nun stitches along the long sides, taking care not to cut the stitching.

Measure and mark 2 inches beyond nun stitches on short sides. Cut along the marked line on the short sides. Remove the horizontal threads from the cut edge to the nun stitches to form fringe.

Place the bookmark facedown on a terry towel and press well.

Trim synthetic suede to fit just inside the nun-stitch border.

Slip-stitch the synthetic suede to the back of the bookmark.

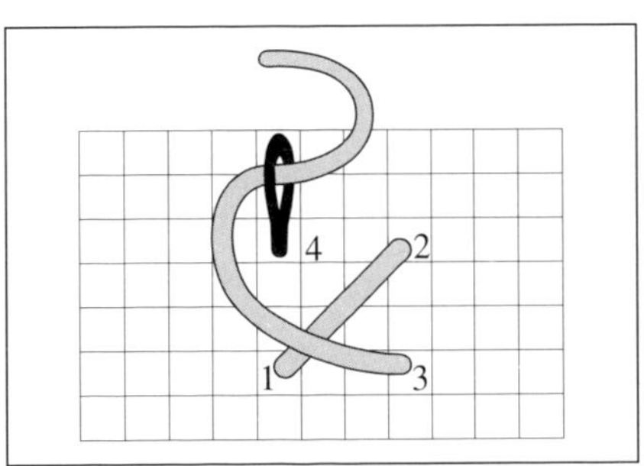

CROSS-STITCH

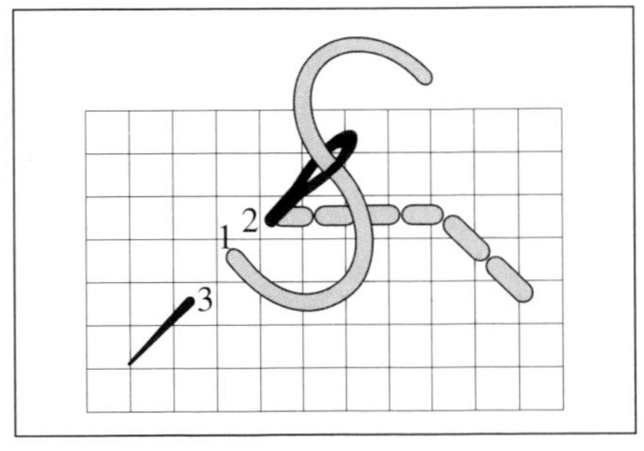

BACKSTITCH

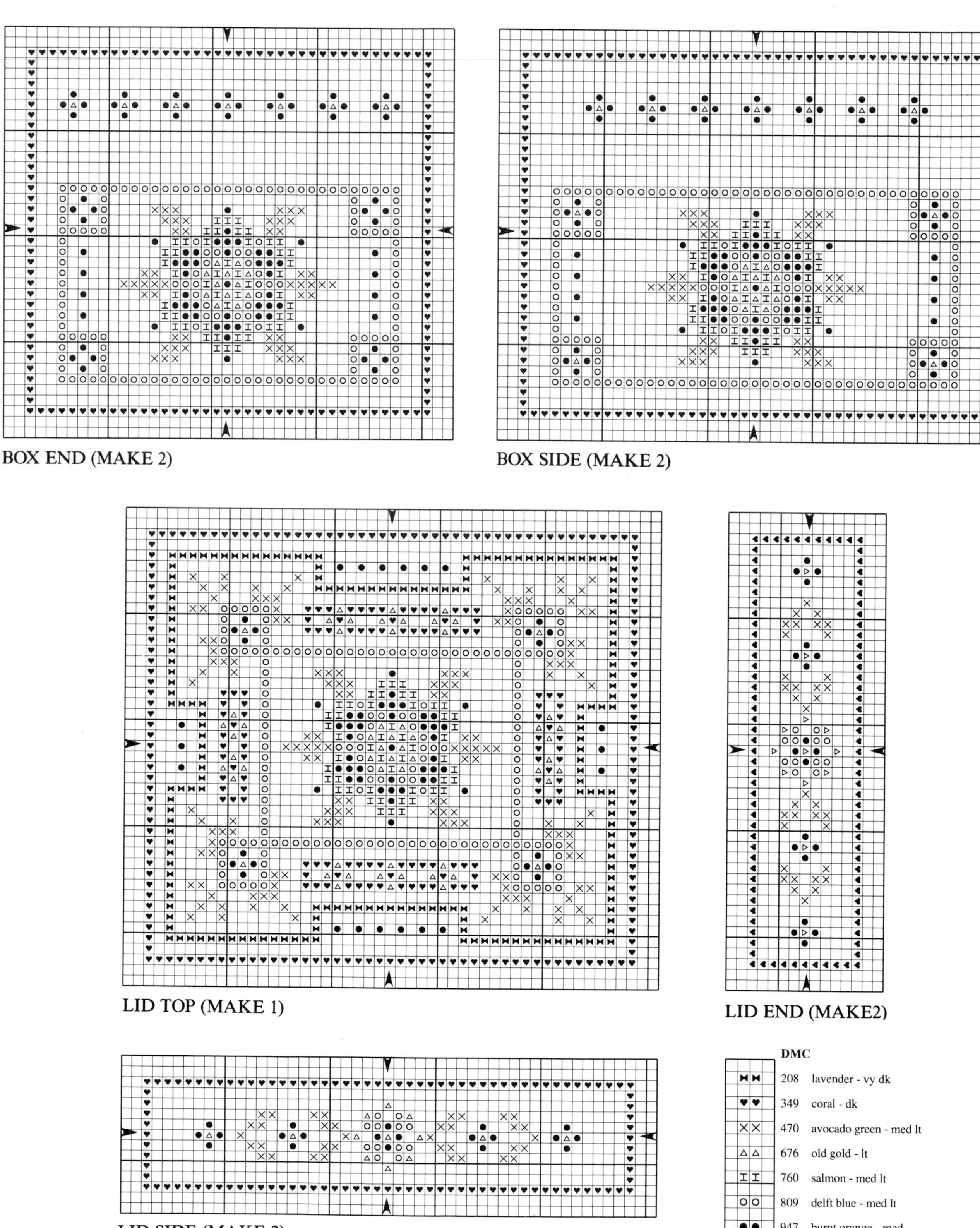

BOX END (MAKE 2)

BOX SIDE (MAKE 2)

LID TOP (MAKE 1)

LID END (MAKE2)

LID SIDE (MAKE 2)

STITCHED PAPER BOX

STITCHED PAPER BOX

Shown on page 10.
Box measures approximately 3⅝x3⅛x2¾ inches.

MATERIALS

Two 8x11-inch sheets of ivory perforated paper
One skein *each* of DMC embroidery floss in colors listed on the color key
Size 24 or 26 tapestry needle
Black poster board to line box
White crafts glue

INSTRUCTIONS

STITCHING: Refer to the charts, *opposite,* for the box's lid top, lid sides, and bottom sides. Use two strands of floss to work cross-stitches over one square of paper. Make two each of the bottom and lid side and end pieces. Make one lid top.

After all pieces have been stitched, cut them out, cutting two squares beyond the last row of stitching. For the unstitched bottom of the box, cut one piece of perforated paper measuring 49x43 squares.

Cut black poster board to fit behind all of the box pieces so that the box will be fully lined; set aside.

ASSEMBLY: Use four strands of No. 208 floss and whipstitch around the first row of edge squares on the lid top and the lid sides. Stitch only the top edges of the sides to begin with so that the lid lies flat. When all five pieces are joined along one edge, whipstitch the edges of the four lid sides together. Then whipstitch around the bottom of the lid sides.

Assemble the bottom of the box in the same way.

Trim poster board as needed to fit inside the box without bending. Lightly glue the poster board pieces inside the box, being careful not to get glue on the floss on the outside of the box.

DARNING SAMPLER

Shown on page 11.
The actual stitched area of the sampler measures 8⅞x11⅛ inches.

MATERIALS

18x20-inch piece of 18-count even-weave fabric—for the sampler on page 11 we used tan (No. 307) Davosa cloth from Zweigart
One skein *each* of DMC Flower thread in colors listed on the color key
Size 24 tapestry needle
Embroidery hoop (optional)
White paper tape

INSTRUCTIONS

Before beginning to stitch the sampler, you need to know a few technical weaving steps in order to complete the darning patterns.

Start each darning square by stitching the warp threads onto the fabric. To stitch the warp onto the fabric, begin on the back of the top or bottom of one corner, bring the thread through to the front of the fabric, and stitch over and under the number of fabric threads indicated. When you get to the center area that will be woven, bring the warp threads to the front and over the entire length of the woven area and back through the fabric to the back. When you get to the end of the first warp thread, take the thread to the back, being careful not to pull the warp thread tight, take the thread over one fabric thread, and bring the warp to the front of the fabric. Repeat for all of the warp threads. Warp threads always run in a vertical direction.

The darn is created by weaving the weft threads, which run horizontally, over and under the warp threads. To weave the weft through the warp, follow the design on the chart and stitch the horizontal stitches in the same manner as you laid the warp. When you come to the center area to be woven, use the tapestry needle to carry the weft thread over or under the number of threads indicated on the chart. The over-and-under spacing of each successive row of weft is what creates the pattern.

STITCHING: *Note:* Before you begin stitching, tape the edges of the fabric to prevent them from raveling. If desired, use an embroidery hoop while stitching.

The complete chart for the sampler appears on pages 26 and 27. The one shaded row represents the overlap of the two sections; do not rework this shaded portion of the chart. The sampler has 10 darning pattern blocks and a cross-stitch alphabet and border. Blocks 1, 2, 3, 5, 9, and 10 are woven as an actual darn would be.

The other four blocks imitate darning in appearance but are not woven. The Flower thread is woven over and under the fabric threads so that the fabric threads become the warp.

Blocks 4 and 8 are woven horizontally over and under the fabric. When one color is on top of the fabric the other color is underneath.

Each line of the grid on the design blocks indicates the number of fabric threads the Flower thread is to be woven over or under. Each design block also has heavier lines that represent the warp and weft stitches. Three strands of Flower thread make up each heavy line indicated on the chart. If the chart indicates that you need to take the weft thread under two threads, you actually take it under the next six threads. Work the border and alphabet in cross-stitch using one strand of Flower thread over one fabric thread.

Measure 4½ inches in from the left side of the fabric and 4½ inches down from the top of the fabric and begin stitching the top left corner of the cross-stitch border there.

When stitching is complete, press the back of the fabric with a damp cloth. Frame the sampler, leaving 1½ inches around all four sides of the stitched area.

DARNING SAMPLER

COLOR KEY
- Teal (2595)
- Red (2815)
- Burgundy (2902)
- Dark blue (2797)
- Yellow (2742)
- Pumpkin (2354)
- Purple (2394)
- Blue-green (2597)
- Gray (2413)
- Dark green (2958)
- Lavender (2395)
- Celery (2502)

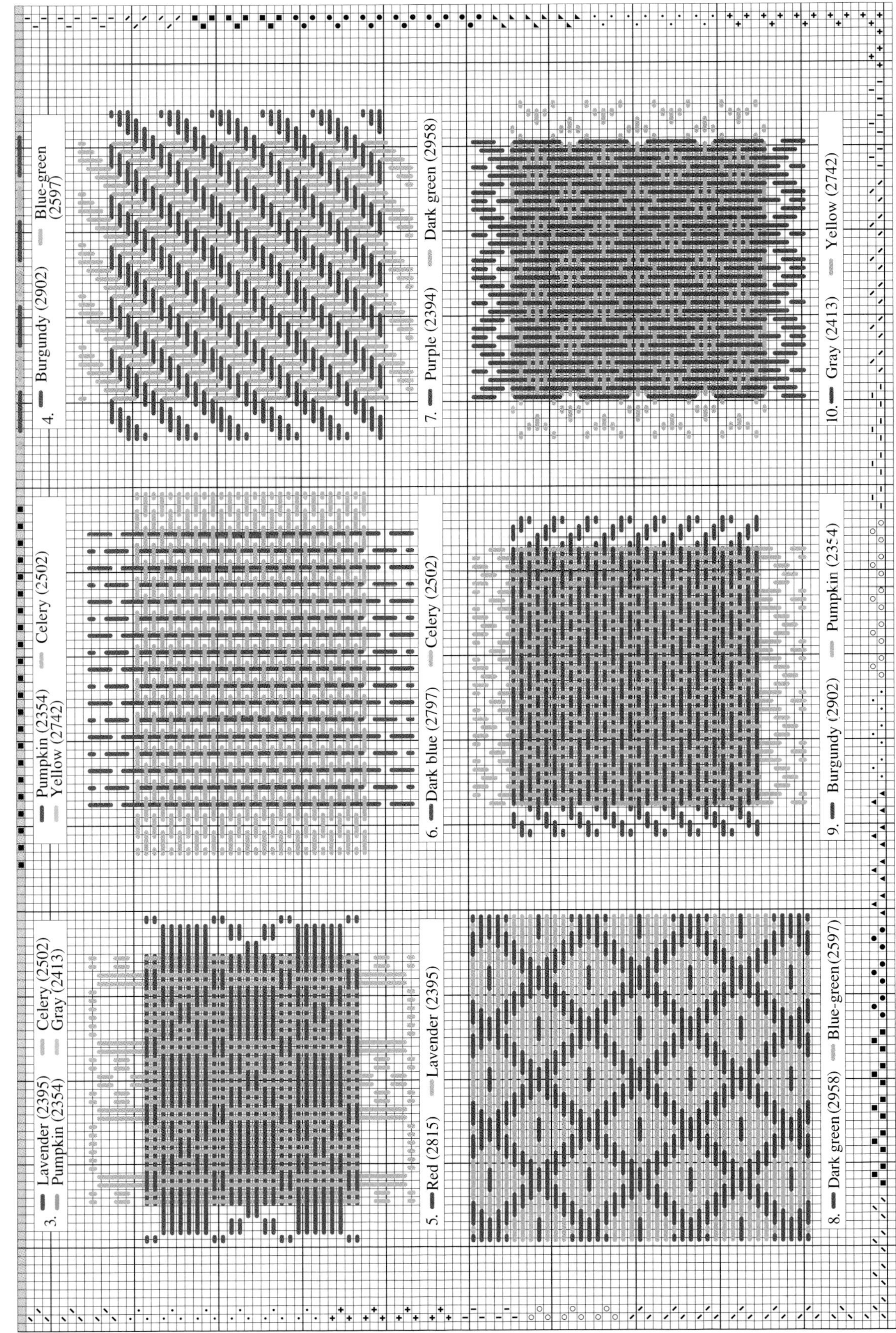

3. Lavender (2395) Pumpkin (2354) Celery (2502) Gray (2413)
4. Burgundy (2902) Blue-green (2597)
Pumpkin (2354) Yellow (2742) Celery (2502)
5. Red (2815) Lavender (2395)
6. Dark blue (2797) Celery (2502)
7. Purple (2394) Dark green (2958)
8. Dark green (2958) Blue-green (2597)
9. Burgundy (2902) Pumpkin (2354)
10. Gray (2413) Yellow (2742)

A Passion for Detail

At the height of the Victorian era there existed an almost insatiable appetite for ornamentation, a sensual delight in the interplay of pattern, texture, and color that extended to even the smallest details of home decor. No surface was left uncovered, no curtain hung without its trims and tassels, no chair put in place without its complement of cushions, and ribbons of lace edged everything.

VEGETABLE GROWING
My Secret Places

Along with a commitment to color and pattern in household furnishings, the Victorians had a particular passion for white work. White-on-white laces and richly textured embroideries had an aura of aristocratic elegance and purity that proved irresistible. Battenberg lace (like the envelope pillow at the top of page 29) and bold monogram embroidery, laced with garlands and flowers (also pictured on page 29), enjoyed a kind of renaissance in the 1880s, remaining popular up until the outbreak of World War I.

Hardanger, a somewhat more restrained form of white work, was introduced to this country by Norwegian immigrants and was much in vogue at the turn of the century. Boldly patterned trim, such as the geometric lace edging on the china cabinet, *opposite,* or more lyrical lengths of heavy crocheted lace, add an architectural element to the simplest of shelves and cabinets. Such trim can be used effectively to turn nondescript pieces of furniture into "vaguely Victorian" treasures complete with gingerbread trim. To be most effective, edging should be at least an inch and a half wide, and have sufficient weight to drape well.

Flirty tassels and crocheted pulls, like those *at right,* graced many a tieback and window shade in 19th-century parlors across America. Made from remnants of crochet cotton and embroidery floss, they were economical grace notes—finishing touches that lent an air of elegance to the front parlor or best bedroom in many a middle-class dwelling. Today, these little frills can add a charming note to lamp pulls, curtain rods, pillow tops, and even drawer handles.

Instructions for these projects begin on page 36.

Yards of handmade lace—crocheted, tatted, or knotted—seemingly trimmed every scrap of linen in the better homes of yesteryear. Lace-edged towels and pillow slips, like those pictured *opposite* and *below,* were not just for company, but graced every room in the house, from parlor to pantry, bedroom to bath.

Indeed, as portrayed by the *Delineator* magazine in October 1884, making lace was a full-time job for the ideal homemaker: "Pretty household appointments flew from under her deft fingers like opening blossoms, and the linen closet rejoiced in their addition to its snowy stores."

Whether you have time to produce an entire snowy store of lacy linens or not, a lace-trimmed towel or two and a pair of lace-edged pillowcases for company best add a touch of polish to any setting.

The pillowcases, *below,* are trimmed with borders of tatted lace, both narrow and wide. The four hanging towels, *opposite,* are adorned with knitted edgings (left to right: wide V-shape, leaf pattern, narrow V-shape, and fan design); the towel on the dresser top has a scalloped filet crochet edging.

If carefully cleaned and kept in proper repair, strips of handmade lace can be salvaged and transplanted from a worn-out towel or pillow slip to a new one for years to come.

Instructions for all projects shown here are on pages 45–47.

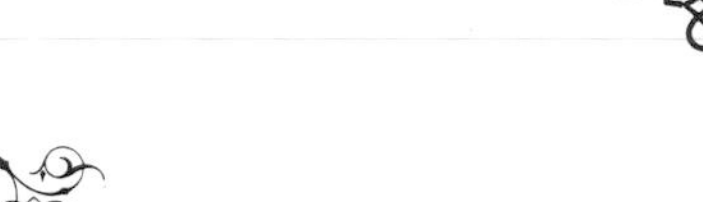

No shelf or mantel or tabletop in a Victorian home could be considered "dressed" without its cluster of keepsakes, its flock of mementos and family pictures. Although photography had been part of the American scene since daguerreotypists first began shooting family portraits in the 1840s, it was not until George Eastman introduced his hand-held camera in the 1880s that photography became a national hobby. Suddenly, a modest grouping of formal family portraits had to compete for display space with a host of informal snapshots celebrating every mood and occasion, every expedition, and every rite of passage in the family's landscape. Pictures not on display were stashed in elaborate photo albums that were laid on parlor tables for visitors to peruse at their leisure.

As collections of photographs multiplied, instructions for crafting picture frames from all manner of materials—from velvet plush to varnished twigs—began to appear in leisure magazines. The quartet of softly padded fabric frames, *right,* trimmed with snatches of ribbons, lace, and satin rosebuds, recall the lush handmade frames of the Victorian era.

Instructions for these frames begin on page 47. Similar frames can be created from other fabrics and unusual trims that specifically are selected to suit your own decor or to complement the individual photographs you have on hand. Use white satin trimmed with antique lace and tiny pearl buttons salvaged from Grandmother's wedding dress to frame her bridal portrait; use tea-dyed calico and scraps of eyelet to frame a picture of your mother on her first day at school; try gray flannel and scraps of tie silk for the sober portrait of a young executive. And, flowered chintz will set off Great-Aunt Effie to perfection.

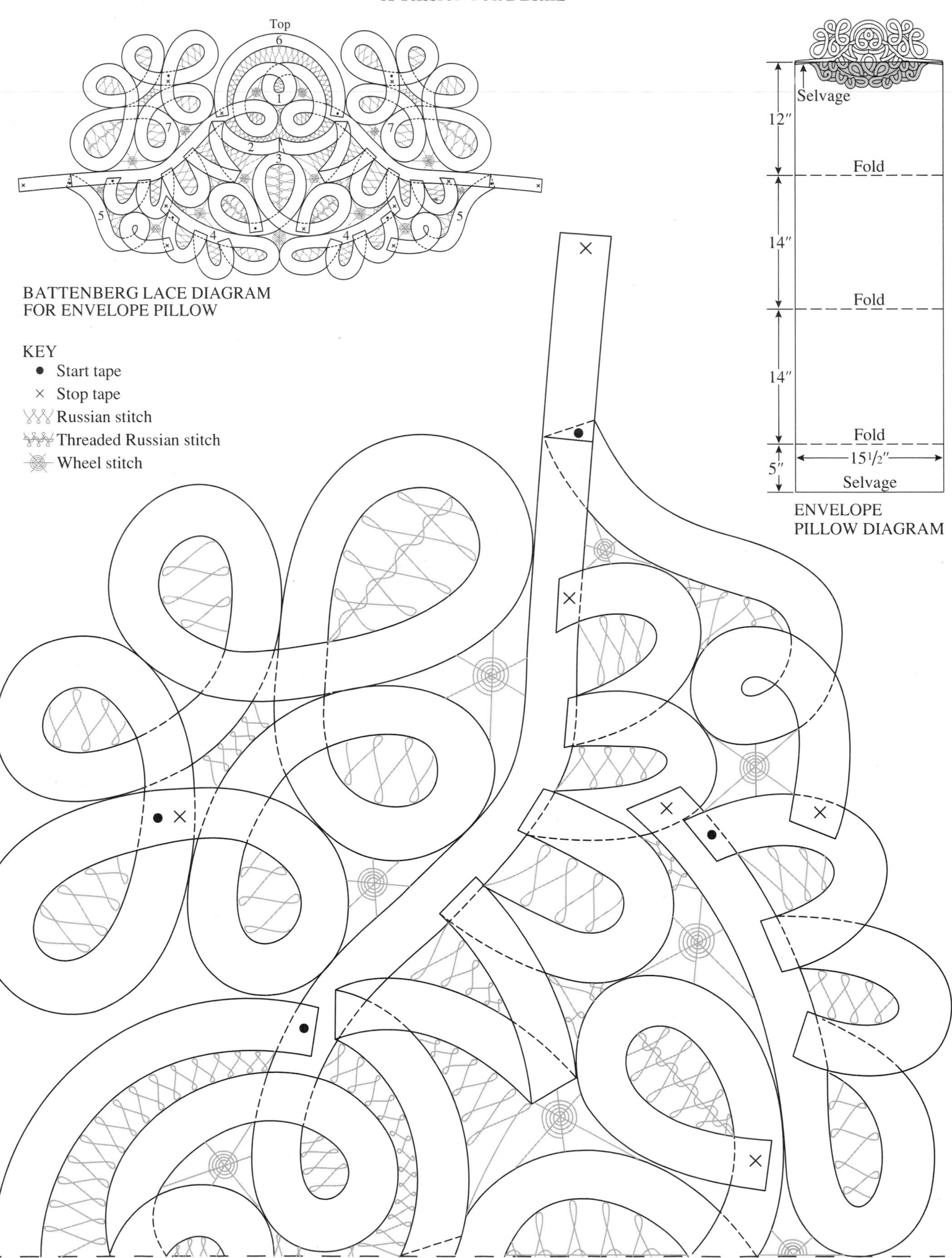

BATTENBERG LACE DIAGRAM
FOR ENVELOPE PILLOW

HALF OF BATTENBERG LACE PATTERN

BATTENBERG LACE ENVELOPE PILLOW

Shown on page 29.
Pillow measures 14 inches square.

MATERIALS

7 yards of 8-mm ecru lace tape
10x14-inch piece of interfacing
Large, heavy, plastic food storage bag
Permanent black marker
DMC Cordonnet Special crochet cotton, Size 50 (286-yard ball): 1 ball of ecru
Fine hand-sewing thread; sewing needle
Contrasting thread for basting
Size 26 tapestry needle for working filling stitches
15½x45-inch piece of white cotton fabric; 14-inch-square pillow form
Large decorative button (optional)
Tracing paper

INSTRUCTIONS

Note: Preshrink the lace tape and fabric before beginning. To preshrink the tape, soak the tied bundle in warm water. When you remove the tape from the water, set it on a white towel and press some of the water out. Allow the tape to dry. Do not wring the water out as this will wrinkle the tape.

Trace the half pattern for the lace, *opposite, bottom,* completing the second half of the lace as in the diagram, *opposite, top.*

Split open the sides of the plastic bag. Trace the solid black lines from the pattern onto the plastic bag. Baste the plastic to the piece of interfacing, making sure the ink side is facing the interfacing. Pull about 10 inches of heavy cord out from one edge of the tape so the tape curls.

BASTING THE LACE: Pin the tape to the plastic pattern in numerical order according to the numbers on the lace diagram, starting and stopping the tape at the designated points. Cut the tape at the stopping positions. The side facing you is the wrong side of the lace, so keep the ends on top. Leave the ends long enough to turn under once the piece is finished.

After the tapes are pinned into position, baste the tapes to the plastic. Baste around the outside edges of the tapes first, then the inside edges.

Use fine sewing thread to whipstitch tape edges wherever they touch or overlap another portion of tape. When moving from one area to the next, whipstitch along the edge of the tape to the next junction. When stitching is complete, knot the thread and hide the knots at tape intersections.

WORK FILLING STITCHES: Following the red stitch markings on the pattern, use the tapestry needle and a single strand of Size 50 thread to work the stitches in the open spaces between tapes. Refer to the diagrams *below* to work the Russian stitch, the threaded Russian stitch, and the wheel stitch.

MAKING THE PILLOW: Referring to the pillow diagram, *opposite, top right,* center lace on the right side of one selvage end of the white fabric. Zigzag-stitch the top edge of the design to the fabric. Trim away fabric behind the lace as indicated by the gray tint on the diagram.

Zigzag-stitch both long edges; turn under a ½-inch-wide hem. With wrong sides together, fold the other selvage in 5 inches. Make a second fold *with right sides together,* 14 inches from the first fold. Beginning at the edge of the lace and fabric, stitch a ¼-inch-wide seam line; stop at the bottom of the folded portion of the pillow. Repeat for the other side. Turn right side out.

Insert the pillow form, tucking it under the 5-inch flap.

If desired, attach a large decorative button to the lower half of the pillow front (below the lace flap) and sew a crocheted button loop to the bottom of the flap as in the embroidered B pillow shown on page 29.

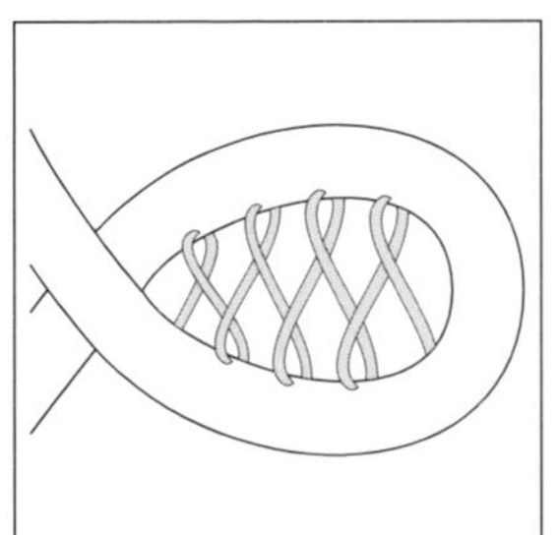

RUSSIAN STITCH

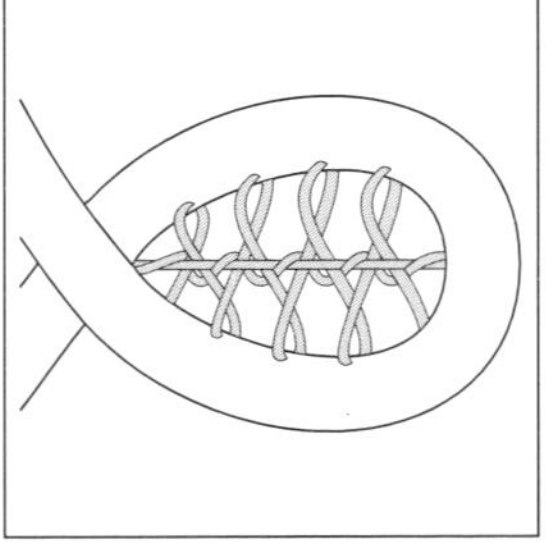

THREADED RUSSIAN STITCH

WHEEL STITCH

BATTENBERG LACE STITCH DIAGRAMS

EMBROIDERED FLORAL MONOGRAM

Shown on pillows on page 29.
The diamond-shape frame is 6¾x7¼ inches; the other two frames are about 6¼x5½ inches.

MATERIALS

Linen fabric—we used sandstone, tea-dyed 40-count linen for the R pillow and ivory 40-count linen for the B pillow from Wichelt Imports Inc.; we used natural 36-count linen from Charles Craft for the T pillow
Two skeins of DMC embroidery floss in a shade darker than the fabric color—we used dark cream (No. 738) for the R pillow, cream (No. 739) for the B pillow, and khaki (No. 3790) for the T pillow
Embroidery needle
Embroidery hoop
Nonpermanent marker

INSTRUCTIONS

Before embroidering your linen, decide what item you are going to monogram.

continued

We selected pillows (see page 29).

After you've decided what you will make, figure out how much fabric you will need and where you will place the monogram.

The frame and letter patterns on pages 38–42 are stitched using a variety of embroidery stitches. The letters we used on our pillows are located in the center of the frame in which they were used. Refer to pages 69 and 79 for embroidery stitch diagrams.

Trace the frame and letter of your choice onto the linen fabric using the nonpermanent marker. Position linen in the embroidery hoop before stitching.

EMBROIDERY: Separate the floss into strands. Use one strand for the satin stitch and the long-and-short stitch. Use two strands for the lazy daisy stitch, French knots, and buttonhole stitch. Use three strands for the stem stitch. Some stitches lend themselves better to certain areas of the frames and letters. Refer to the photograph on page 29 for stitching ideas.

When stitching is complete, remove any markings that show on the fabric. Lay the design facedown on a soft towel and press.

Finish embroidered linen into pillows as shown or as desired.

EMBROIDERED FLORAL MONOGRAM ALPHABET

EMBROIDERED FLORAL MONOGRAM ALPHABET

EMBROIDERY FLOSS TASSELS

Shown on page 31.

Tassel, including the cord, is 10 inches long.

MATERIALS

Seven skeins of embroidery floss
Tapestry needle
6-inch square of cardboard
Masking tape
Plastic soft-tooth hairbrush—for floss tassels only

INSTRUCTIONS

These instructions can be adapted to make tassels of any size using other threads or yarn.

Cut a 12-inch length of six-strand floss and set aside. Using six skeins, wrap all six strands of floss around the piece of cardboard. Tightly tie the 12-inch length of floss through the wrapped bundle, catching all of the threads. Remove the tied bundle from the cardboard. Cut the bundle in half opposite the tie.

From the remaining floss, cut six 6-strand pieces, each 36 inches long. Put one end of all six 6-strand pieces together and tie an overhand knot. Tape the knot to the edge of a table or countertop. Twist the six 6-strand pieces together clockwise until they start to kink. Fold the twisted strands in half, letting them slowly twist back on each other in a counterclockwise direction. Remove the tape. Tie an overhand knot at the end of the twisted cord loop; trim off the ends near the knot.

Insert half of the tied bundle through the cord loop, centering the tie of the bundle over the knot of the cord. Allowing both ends of the bundle to hang from the cord, tightly tie a 1½-yard length of six-strand floss approximately 1 inch below the top of the bundle. Wrap the floss around the bundle, working toward the top for ½ inch. Thread the end of the wrapping threads into the needle. Insert

EMBROIDERED FLORAL
MONOGRAM ALPHABET

the needle into the bundle and push it to the top. Bring the needle out at the top of the bundle and wrap the base of the twisted cord for ¼ inch. Insert the needle into the cord and down into the bundle to finish off the wrapping.

Use the hairbrush to gently brush and separate the strands of floss. Trim the bottom of the tassel so the ends are even.

HARDANGER SHELF EDGING

Shown on page 30.
The finished edging measures approximately 24½ inches long.

MATERIALS

For two 24-inch edgings

30x15-inch piece of ecru 22-count hardanger fabric
DMC pearl cotton: 1 ball *each* of ecru Size 12, Size 8, and Size 5
Size 24 tapestry needle
Ecru sewing thread
Sharp scissors

INSTRUCTIONS

Cut the hardanger fabric in half lengthwise. Follow the chart, *far right,* to work the hardanger design.

Work the buttonhole stitch with Size 8 pearl cotton, starting in the upper left corner and working down the left edge, across the bottom, up the right edge, and across the top. For the 24-inch edging shown in the photograph on page 30, work the buttonhole stitch for seven complete scallops along the bottom edge.

Refer to the diagrams, *near right,* to work the different stitches. Refer to page 69 for a cross-stitch diagram.

Work seven heart motifs of Kloster blocks with the Size 5 pearl cotton. Cut out the openings in the heart as indicated on the chart by the gray areas, then work the woven bars over the remaining threads with the Size 12 pearl cotton.

Cross-stitch the six bows with one strand of Size 8 pearl cotton.

Note: Work more scallop repeats for a longer edging. Each additional scallop will make the edging approximately 3½ inches longer.

When the edging is completed, lay it facedown on a thick towel and press it with a damp cloth. With your sewing machine set for a short stitch, straight-stitch in the ditch of the buttonhole stitch. Sew completely around the edging. With scissors, cut around the edging; take extra care not to snip the threads of the machine stitching or the buttonhole stitch. Press the edging again.

Use tiny brads to mount the edging onto the edge of a wooden shelf. Do not use double-stick tape. It will leave a residue on your hardanger that eventually will yellow the fabric.

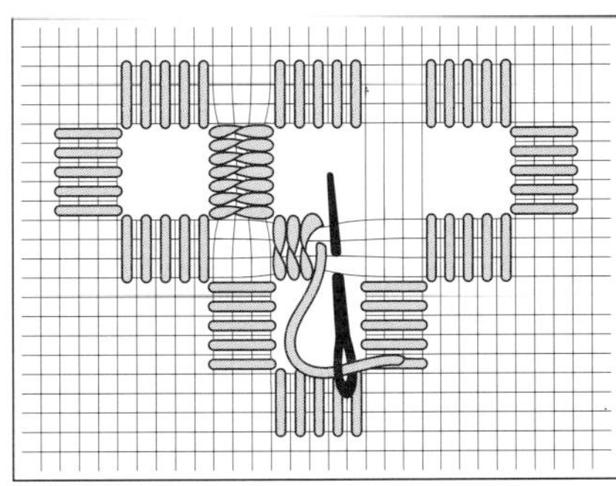

KLOSTER BLOCKS AND WOVEN BARS

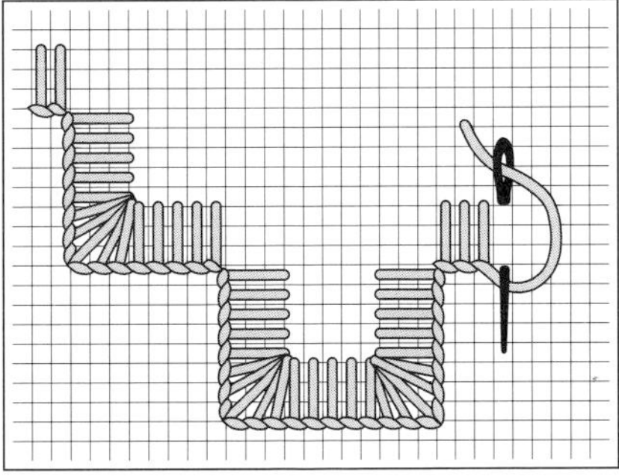

BUTTONHOLE STITCH

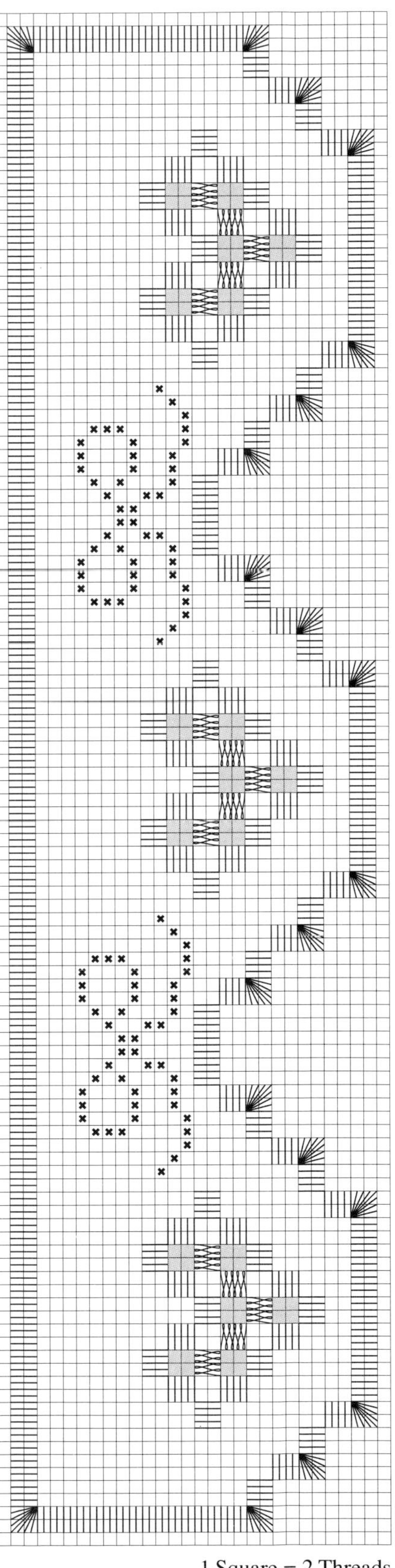

1 Square = 2 Threads

HARDANGER EDGING

CROCHETED SHADE PULLS

Shown on page 31.
Tassel pull is 4 inches long, the flower pull is 3 inches in diameter, the pineapple pull is 4½ inches long, and the triple-ring pull is 3 inches long. (All measurements exclude the cords.)

MATERIALS

For the triple-ring pull

J. & P. Coats Knit-Cro-Sheen (225-yard ball): 1 ball of ecru

One *each* of plastic bone rings in the following diameters: ½, ⅝, and ¾ inch

For the tassel pull

J. & P. Coats Knit-Cro-Sheen (225-yard ball): 1 ball of almond pink (No. 35)

3½x5-inch piece of cardboard to make the tassel

For the pineapple pull

J. & P. Coats Knit-Cro-Sheen (225-yard ball): 1 ball of ecru-gold metallic (No. 61G)

One 1⅛-inch-diameter plastic bone ring

For the flower pull

J. & P. Coats Knit-Cro-Sheen (225-yard ball): 1 ball of orchid pink (No. 101)

One ¾-inch-diameter plastic bone ring

For all shade pulls

Size 9 steel crochet hook

Abbreviations: See page 99.

INSTRUCTIONS

For the triple-ring pull

Large Ring: Using ecru thread, work 48 sc in the ¾-inch-diameter plastic ring; join to beg sc. Fasten off.

Medium Ring: Work 19 sc in the ⅝-inch-diameter plastic ring; sl st in any sc on the Large Ring; work 20 more sc in Medium Ring; join to beg sc. Fasten off.

Small Ring: Work 16 sc in ½-inch-diameter plastic ring, sk 19 st on Medium Ring (after the join to the Large Ring), sl st in next sc on Medium Ring; work 15 more sc in Small Ring; join to beg sc. Fasten off.

EDGING: Sk 1 sc on left side of Large Ring (after join to Medium Ring), attach thread to next sc, sc in same sc, sc in next 2 sc, **[ch 3, sc in 3rd ch from hook—picot (p) made,** sc in next 3 sc] 14 times; sk 2 sc on Medium Ring, (sc in next 3 sc, p) 4 times; sc in next 3 sc, sk 1 sc on Small Ring, (sc in next 3 sc, p) 4 times; sc in next 2 sc, make a chain 13 inches long, sc in last sc made, sc in next 2 sc, (p, sc in next 3 sc) 4 times; sk 2 sc on Medium Ring; (sc in next 3 sc, p) 4 times; sc in next 3 sc; join to beg sc. Fasten off.

For the tassel pull

THE CAP: Using almond pink thread and starting at center, ch 10; join with sl st to form ring.

Rnd 1: Ch 3, 23 dc in ring; join with sl st in top of beg ch-3.

Rnd 2: Sc in same place as sl st, sc in each dc around; join with sl st to beg sc.

Rnds 3–10: Sc in each sc around; join.

Rnd 11: Sl st in next sc, sc in next sc, * sk 1 sc, 5 dc in next sc, sk 1 sc, sc in next sc; rep from * around; join. Fasten off.

THE TASSEL: Cut a 10-inch strand of thread and lay it across the length of the cardboard. Wind a single strand of thread around the cardboard 200 times. Pick up both ends of the 10-inch strand and tie securely (top). Remove cardboard and cut the loops at the other end. Cut a strand of thread and wind it tightly around the thread bundle about ⅜ inch from the top and fasten securely.

THE CORD: Cut 12 strands of thread, each measuring 24 inches long; combine them into a bundle. Holding both cut ends, twist these strands tightly in a clockwise direction until they kink; double these strands in half and give them a twist counterclockwise; knot free ends.

Sew the cord to the top of the tassel. Slip the cap over the tassel.

For the pineapple pull

THE TASSEL: *Row 1:* Using ecru-gold metallic thread, work 21 sc in the plastic ring; ch 3, turn.

Row 2: Dc in first sc, ch 2, and 2 dc—beg shell made; ch 2, sk 2 sc, dc in next 15 sc, ch 2, sk 2 sc, in next sc make 2 dc, ch 3, and 2 dc; ch 5, turn.

Row 3: In next sp make **2 dc, ch 2, and 2 dc—shell over shell made;** ch 2, (dc in next dc, ch 1) 14 times; dc in next dc, ch 2, shell over next shell; ch 5, turn.

Row 4: Shell over next shell, ch 3, sk next ch-1 sp, sc in next ch-1 sp, (ch 3, sc in next ch-1 sp) 13 times; ch 3, shell over shell; ch 5, turn.

Row 5: Shell over next shell, ch 3, sk next ch-3 sp, (sc in next ch-3 lp, ch 3) 13 times; shell over next shell; ch 5, turn.

Row 6: Shell over next shell, ch 3, sk next ch-3 sp, (sc in next ch-3 lp, ch 3) 12 times; shell over next shell; ch 5, turn.

Rows 7–16: Work as Row 6, dec 1 ch-3 lp on each row until 1 ch-3 lp rem.

Row 17: Shell over next shell, ch 4, sc in ch-3 lp, ch 4, 2 dc in next shell, ch 1, sl st in sp of last shell made, ch 1, 2 dc in same shell as last 2 dc; ch 5, turn; sl st in joining of shell. Fasten off.

THE CORD: Cut 12 strands of thread 24 inches long; combine them into one bundle. Pass one of the cut ends of the bundle through the plastic ring. Holding both cut ends, twist strands in a clockwise direction until they kink; double the strands in half next to the plastic ring and twist counterclockwise; knot free ends.

For the flower pull

Rnd 1: Using orchid pink thread, work 48 sc in the ¾-inch-diameter plastic ring; join with sl st in first sc.

Rnd 2: Sc in same place as sl st, sc in next 4 sc, * ch 3, sk 1 sc, sc in next 5 sc; rep from * around; end with ch 3; join with sl st in first sc.

Rnd 3: Sl st in next sc, sc in same sc, sc in next 2 sc, * ch 3, sc in next ch-3 lp, ch 3, sk 1 sc, sc in next 3 sc; rep from * around; join with sl st in first sc.

Rnd 4: Sl st in next sc, sc in same sc, * (ch 3, sc in next ch-3 lp) twice; ch 3, sk 1 sc, sc in next sc; rep from * around; join with sl st in first sc.

Rnd 5: Sl st in next ch-3 lp, sc in same lp, * ch 3, in next ch-3 lp make dc, ch 3, and dc; ch 3, sc in next ch-3 lp, ch 1, sc in next ch-3 lp; rep from * around, ending with ch 1; join with sl st in first sc.

Rnd 6: * 3 sc in next ch-3 sp, ch 3, in next ch-3 sp make 2 sc, ch 3, and 2 sc; ch 3, 3 sc in next ch-3 sp, sc in next ch-3 sp; rep from * around; join with sl st in first sc. Fasten off.

CORD: Cut two strands of thread 1 yard long; twist these strands tightly. Now double these strands and twist in the opposite direction. Insert one end of twisted cord through one of the ch-3 lps of Rnd 6; combine ends and tie into a knot.

KNITTED LEAF EDGING

Shown on a towel on page 32.
Edging measures about 1¼ inches wide. Make 18 inches of lace for every 21 inches of finished lace you desire. (Lace will stretch 3 inches in blocking.)

MATERIALS

Clark's Big Ball 3-cord crochet cotton, Size 10 (200-yard ball): 1 ball of ecru
Size 0 knitting needles

Abbreviations: See page 99.

INSTRUCTIONS

Cast on 9 sts.

Row 1: Sl 1, p 1, k 3, k 2 tog, (yo, k 1) twice—10 sts, counting each yo as 1 st.

Row 2 and all even rows: K 1, p across to within last 2 sts, k 2.

Row 3: Sl 1, p 1, k 2, k 2 tog, (k 1, yo) twice; k 2—11 sts.

Row 5: Sl 1, p 1, k 1, k 2 tog, k 2, yo, k 1, yo, k 3—12 sts.

Row 7: Sl 1, p 1, k 2 tog, k 3, yo, k 1, yo, k 4—13 sts.

Row 9: Sl 1, p 1, k 1, yo, sl 1, k 1, psso; k 5, sl 1, k 2 tog, psso—11 sts.

Row 11: Sl 1, p 1, k 1, yo, k 1, sl 1, k 1, psso, k 3, k 2 tog—10 sts.

Row 13: Sl 1, p 1, k 1, yo, k 2, sl 1, k 1, psso; k 1, k 2 tog—9 sts.

Row 15: Sl 1, p 1, k 1, yo, k 3, sl 1, k 1, psso, k 1—9 sts.

Row 16: Rep Row 2.

Rep rows 1–16 for pat. Work in pat for desired length. Bind off. Block to measurement. Sew in place.

WIDE TATTED PILLOW EDGING

Shown on page 33.
Edging measures approximately 2 inches wide.

MATERIALS
For one pillowcase

DMC Cordonnet Special, Size 20 (174-yard ball): 2 balls of white
Tatting shuttle
Large-eye tapestry needle
White sewing thread; sewing needle
One pillowcase

Abbreviations: See page 48.

INSTRUCTIONS

ROUND 1: Wind the tatting shuttle full of thread. Use thread from the ball for chaining. Leave 9-inch beginning tails.

Step 1: R of 5, p, 4, p, 3, p, 4, p, 5; clr, rw.

Step 2: Ch of 5, p, 6; tighten by moving stitches close to r, rw.

Step 3: R of 5, join to last p of previous r, 4, p, 3, p, 4, p, 5; clr, rw.

Step 4: Rep steps 2 and 3 alternately until a length double the width of the pillowcase has been made; join last p of last r to first p of first r to complete the rnd.

Cut thread leaving 9-inch ending tails; tie in square knots with beginning tails. Thread each tail through the tapestry needle and stitch back through tatted sts.

ROUND 2: Leave 9-inch beginning tails.

Step 1: With chs of Rnd 1 up, join to any p of Rnd 1; ch of 5, p, 5; join to next ch to right on Rnd 1.

Continue chaining and joining in same manner until all chs of Rnd 1 have been joined into.

Cut thread leaving 9-inch ending tails; tie in square knots with beginning tails. Stitch tails back through tatted sts.

ROUND 3: Work same as for Rnd 2.

ROUNDS 4 and 5: *Note:* Rep rnds 1 and 2 independent of the work already completed. Rnd 6 will connect rnds 4 and 5 to rnds 1–3. Finish rnds 4 and 5 as before.

ROUND 6: Join to any p of any ch of Rnd 5, ch 5, join to any p of Rnd 3; 5, p, 5, join to next p to right in Rnd 5. Continue alternating sts and joins to rnds 3 and 5. Cut ending tails; tie and finish rnd as before.

FINISHING: Block tatting flat; allow to dry. Hand-sew the blocked edging to the open edges of the pillowcase.

KNITTED FAN EDGING

Shown on a towel on page 32.
Edging measures approximately 3 inches wide. Make 18 inches of lace for every 21 inches of finished lace you desire. (Lace will stretch 3 inches in blocking.)

MATERIALS

J. & P. Coats Knit-Cro-Sheen (225-yard ball): 1 ball of ecru
Size 1 knitting needles

Abbreviations: See page 99.

INSTRUCTIONS

Cast on 17 sts.

Row 1: K 17 sts.

Row 2: K 1, **[yarn over needle twice—double yarn over (yo) made;** *being careful not to drop the double yo,* p 2 tog] 5 times; double yo, k 6—24 sts, counting each

continued

double yo as 2 sts.

Row 3: Sl 1, k 6, (p 1, k 2) 5 times; p 1, yo, k 1—25 sts, counting yo as 1 st.

Row 4: Sl 1, k 24 sts.

Row 5: Sl 1, k 22, yo, k 2—26 sts.

Row 6: K 3, double yo; p 2 tog, k 13, p 2 tog, double yo; k 6—28 sts.

Row 7: Sl 1, k 6, p 1, k 16, p 1, yo, k 3—29 sts.

Row 8: Sl 1, k 28 sts.

Row 9: Sl 1, k 24, yo, k 4—30 sts.

Row 10: K 5, (double yo, p 2 tog) twice; k 11, (p 2 tog, double yo) twice; k 6—34 sts.

Row 11: Sl 1, k 6, p 1, k 2, p 1, k 14, p 1, k 2, p 1, yo, k 5—35 sts.

Row 12: Sl 1, k 34 sts.

Row 13: Sl 1, k 10, (double yo, k 1) 14 times; k 4, yo, k 6—64 sts.

Row 14: Bind off 6 sts, (p 1, yo) 4 times; (sl 1 st as if to p; drop double yo off needle) 14 times; sl 1 st; sl first 15 sts on RH needle back onto LH needle; *being careful not to drop previous double yo,* p these 15 sts tog; (yo, p 1) 4 times; k 6—24 sts rem.

Rep rows 3–14 for pat. Work in pat for desired length; bind off. Block to measurement and sew in place.

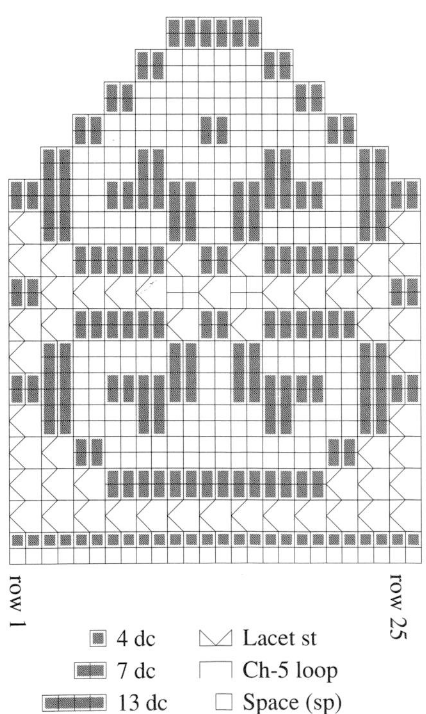

FILET CROCHET EDGING

FILET CROCHET EDGING

Shown on a towel on page 32.
Edging measures 5 inches across its widest point.

MATERIALS

DMC Cordonnet Special cotton thread, Size 50 (286-yard ball): 1 ball makes 18 inches

Size 14 steel crochet hook

Abbreviations: See page 99.

Gauge: 19 dc = 1 inch; 8 rows = 1 inch.

INSTRUCTIONS

See page 157 for information on the filet crochet technique.

Beg along narrow edge, ch 77.

Row 1: Dc in eighth ch from hook and in next 3 ch; **ch 3, sk 2 ch, sc in next ch, ch 3, sk 2 ch, dc in next ch—lacet st made;** make 3 lacets, dc in next 6 ch, (make 2 lacets, dc in next 6 ch) twice; ch 3, turn.

Row 2: Sk first dc, [dc in 6 dc, (ch 5, dc in next dc) twice] twice; dc in next 6 dc, (ch 5, dc in next dc) 4 times; dc in 3 dc, ch 2, dc in top of turning ch; ch 5, turn.

Row 3: Dc in next 4 dc; **ch 3, sc in center ch of ch-5 lp, ch 3, dc in next dc—lacet st over ch-5 lp made;** (work lacet st over next ch-5 lp) twice; 5 dc in ch-5 lp, dc in 7 dc, 5 dc in ch-5 lp, dc in next dc, work lacet st over next ch-5 lp; make lacet; work lacet st over next ch-5 lp; 5 dc in ch-5 lp, dc in 6 dc; dc in top of turning ch; **(yo hook, draw up lp at base of last dc made; yo, draw through 1 lp on hook—base ch for next dc; complete st as for dc)** 6 times—6 sts inc at end of row; ch 3, turn.

Rows 4–25: Refer to chart, *left,* and work as established. Rep rows 2–25 for desired length plus 2 to 3 inches to allow for shrinkage. Wash and press edging. Use sewing thread to sew edging to a towel or other desired item.

NARROW TATTED PILLOW EDGING

Shown on page 33.
Edging measures approximately ⅝ inch wide.

MATERIALS

For one pillowcase

DMC Cordonnet Special, Size 30 (216-yard ball): 1 ball of white

Tatting shuttle

Large-eye tapestry needle

White sewing thread

One pillowcase

Abbreviations: See page 48.

INSTRUCTIONS

Wind the tatting shuttle full of thread. Use thread from the ball for chaining. Leave 9-inch beginning tails.

Step 1: R of 3, p, 3, p, 3, p, 3, p, 3, p, 3; clr, rw.

Step 2: Ch of 3, p, 3, p, 3; tighten by moving stitches close to r, rw.

Step 3: R of 3, join to next to last p of previous r, 3, p, 3, p, 3, p, 3, p, 3; clr, rw.

Step 4: Ch of 3, p, 3, p, 3, p, 3, p, 3, p, 3, tighten; join to middle p of previous r, 3, p, 3, p, 3; tighten, rw.

Step 5: R of 3, p, 3, join to free p between joins of previous r; 3, join to middle p of second previous r; 3, p, 3, p, 3; clr, rw.

Step 6: Ch of 3, p, 3; tighten, rw.

Step 7: R of 3, p, 3, p, 3, p, 3, p, 3, p, 3; clr, rw.

Step 8: Ch of 3, join to second p of second previous ch; 3, p, 3; tighten, rw.

Step 9: Rep steps 3 through 8 for desired length or twice the width of the pillowcase. Join last p of next to last ch to first p of first ch before completing this rnd with ch of 3, p, 3.

Cut thread leaving 9-inch ending tails; tie in square knots with beginning tails. Thread tails through the tapestry needle; stitch back through sts.

Wide Knitted V-Shape Edging

Shown on a towel on page 32.
Edging measures about 3½ inches wide. Make 18 inches of lace for every 21 inches of finished lace you desire. Lace will stretch 3 inches in blocking.

MATERIALS

J. & P. Coats Knit-Cro-Sheen (225-yard ball): 1 ball of ecru
Size 1 knitting needles

Abbreviations: See page 99.

INSTRUCTIONS

Cast on 26 sts.

Row 1: K 26 sts.

Row 2: Sl 1, k 1, k 2 tog, yo, k 1, yo, k 2 tog, k 6; yo, k 3 tog, yo, k 6, yo, k 2 tog, yo, k 2—27 sts, counting each yo as 1 st.

Row 3 and all odd rows except Row 13: P across to within last 2 sts; k 2.

Row 4: Sl 1, k 1, k 2 tog, yo, k 1, yo, k 2 tog, k 5, k 2 tog, yo, k 1, yo, sl 1, k 1, psso; k 5, k 2 tog, yo, k 1, yo, k 2—28 sts.

Row 6: Sl 1, k 1, k 2 tog, yo, k 1, yo, k 2 tog, k 4, k 2 tog, yo, k 3, yo, sl 1, k 1, psso; k 4, (yo, k 2 tog) twice; yo, k 2—29 sts.

Row 8: Sl 1, k 1, k 2 tog, yo, k 1, yo, k 2 tog, k 3, k 2 tog, yo, k 5; yo, sl 1, k 1, psso; k 3, (k 2 tog, yo) twice; k 1, yo, k 2—30 sts.

Row 10: Sl 1, k 1, k 2 tog, yo, k 1, yo, k 2 tog, k 2, k 2 tog, yo, k 7, yo, sl 1, k 1, psso; k 2, (yo, k 2 tog) twice; k 2, yo, k 2—31 sts.

Row 12: Sl 1, k 1, k 2 tog, yo, k 1, yo, k 2 tog, yo, k 3 tog, yo, k 9, yo, sl 1, k 2 tog, psso; (yo, k 2 tog) twice; yo, k 5—31 sts.

Row 13: P 5, k 1, sl 5 p sts (now on RH needle), one by one over the k st; p 23 sts, k 2—26 sts.

Rep rows 2–13 for pat. Work in pat for the desired length; bind off. Block to measurement and sew in place.

Narrow Knitted V-Shape Edging

Shown on a towel on page 32.
Edging measures approximately 2 inches wide. Make 18 inches of lace for every 21 inches of finished lace you desire. Lace will stretch 3 inches in blocking.

MATERIALS

J. & P. Coats Knit-Cro-Sheen (225-yard ball): 1 ball of cream (No. 42)
Size 0 knitting needles

Abbreviations: See page 99.

INSTRUCTIONS

Cast on 17 sts.

Row 1: K 17 sts.

Row 2: K 1, (yo, k 2 tog) 3 times; yo, k 2, (yo, sl 1, k 1, psso) 3 times; k 2—18 sts, counting each yo as 1 st.

Row 3: K 2, p 16 sts.

Row 4: (K 1, sl st from RH needle back onto LH needle) twice; **k 1, k 2 tog, pass k 1 over k 2 tog—ch-3 lp made;** (yo, k 2 tog) twice; yo, k 4, (yo, sl 1, k 1, psso) twice; k 3—17 sts.

Row 5: K 2, p 15 sts.

Row 6: K 1, (yo, k 2 tog) twice; yo, k 6, (yo, sl 1, k 1, psso) twice; k 2—18 sts.

Row 7: K 2, p 16 sts.

Row 8: Ch-3 lp, yo, k 2 tog, yo, k 2, k 2 tog, yo, sl 1, k 1, psso; k 2, yo, sl 1, k 1, psso; k 3—16 sts.

Row 9: K 2, p 6; in next st make p 1 then k 1; p 7—17 sts.

Rep rows 2–9 for pat. Work in pat for the desired length; bind off. Block to measurement and sew in place.

Fabric-Covered Picture Frames

Shown on pages 34 and 35.
The three larger frames measure approximately 8x10 inches; the small frame measures 5x7 inches.

MATERIALS

For one 8x10-inch frame

⅓ yard satin, moiré taffeta, or velvet fabric for the frame cover
8x10-inch piece of mat board
8x10-inch purchased mat frame with opening
5x10-inch piece of ¼-inch-thick foam-core board for back of frame and stand
12x20-inch piece of fleece
1 yard fusible webbing paper
10x12-inch batiste lining fabric (optional)

For one 5x7-inch frame

¼ yard satin, moiré taffeta, or velvet fabric for the frame cover
5x7-inch piece of mat board
5x7-inch purchased mat frame with oval opening
4x7-inch piece of ¼-inch-thick foam-core board for back of frame and stand
11x18-inch piece of fleece
½ yard fusible webbing paper
7x9-inch batiste lining fabric (optional)

For all frames

Tacky crafts glue
Assorted antique laces, ribbons, and ribbon roses

INSTRUCTIONS

Note: These instructions can be adapted to make any size frame using other sizes of purchased mat frames. Cut the fabrics accordingly.

continued

LARGE FRAME FRONT: *Note:* To make the small frame pictured on pages 34 and 35, adapt the measurements in the instructions *below* to the 5x7-inch mat board and mat frame.

Cut two layers of fleece the same size and shape as the mat frame. Glue the two layers of fleece to the front of the frame. Cut one 8x½-inch piece of foam-core board; cut two 9½x½-inch pieces of foam-core board. Glue the strips of foam-core board to the sides and bottom of the wrong side of the frame. The top edge is left open for inserting a photo.

Cut a 9x11-inch rectangle of the fabric for the frame covering. Center the front of the frame on the wrong side of the fabric. Glue the raw edges of the fabric to the back side of the frame, mitering the edges at the corners. For the window opening, cut the fabric diagonally from corner to corner, making an X cut. Trim the excess fabric from the points on the X. Slightly stretch the raw edges toward the wrong side of the frame and glue.

Note: If the fabric used to cover the frame is a light color or sheer, use fusible webbing paper to fuse batiste lining fabric to the wrong side of the fabric. Then proceed with the above instructions.

For the beige satin frame

Cut four pieces of antique lace that will fit over the corners. Glue the lace pieces over the four corners of the frame front.

Cut four ⅝-inch-wide pieces *each* of dusty rose and beige satin ribbon, each long enough to cross a corner. Glue the dusty rose pieces to the frame front, covering the edge of the lace. Glue the beige pieces across the corners, covering the edges of the dusty rose ribbons.

Cut a ⅝-inch-wide piece of lace long enough to go around the inside of the center oval opening. Glue the lace around the inside edge of the opening.

Make two beige and one dusty rose satin ribbon bows; cluster and glue bows to the top right corner of the frame. Glue ribbon roses to the center of the bows.

For the white velvet frame

Cut four wide lace pieces that are each long enough to diagonally cover a corner. Glue lace across the corners of the frame.

Cut a piece of lace that is long enough to go around the inside of the rectangular opening. Glue lace around the inside of the opening, pleating it in the corners. Glue ribbon roses at the corners.

For the white moiré taffeta frame

Cut four plain satin ribbon pieces long enough to cover each of the four sides of the frame front; glue the ribbons vertically and horizontally approximately ¼ inch from the outside edges of the frame. Cut four more ribbon pieces from a different texture or color the same length as the previous ribbon; glue the pieces vertically and horizontally along the sides of the frame, covering the edges of the satin ribbons already glued to the frame.

Make four bows from each of the two ribbons. Glue one of each bow in each corner of the frame. Glue a ribbon rose on top of the bows in each corner.

Glue a narrow piece of lace around the inside of the rectangular opening so that approximately ¼ inch of the lace shows in the opening.

For the small velvet frame

Glue narrow lace around the outside edges of the frame and inside the oval opening.

Glue two lace heart motifs in the lower right-hand corner of the frame. Make a bow from ½-inch-wide ribbon and glue it in the center of the lace hearts. Glue three ribbon roses over the center of the bow.

LARGE FRAME BACK: Cut a 9x11-inch rectangle of fabric to cover the frame back. Following manufacturer's instructions, attach fusible webbing to the wrong side of the fabric. Center the 8x10-inch mat board on the fusible webbing side of the fabric and fuse. Fuse the raw edges of the fabric to the back side of the mat board, mitering the edges at the corners.

From foam-core board, cut a 2¼x6½-inch table support for the 8x10-inch frame or a 2x5-inch table support for the 5x7-inch frame. Score the back of the support approximately 1¼ inches from one narrow end. Bend the scored portion back to make a hinge. Cover the non-scored side with tape for reinforcement.

From the same fabric that covers the frame, cut a piece that is ½ inch larger than the support. Attach fusible webbing to the wrong side of the fabric. Lay the support on the center of the fusible webbing side of the fabric, scored side up, and fuse. Pull the fabric edges around the foam-core board and fuse. Cut another piece of fabric with fusible webbing on back slightly smaller than the dimensions of the support. Fuse this piece to the back side of the longer portion of the support below the scored hinge.

Fuse the fabric to the frame back with fusible webbing paper. Center and glue the top of the stand to the frame back. Cut and glue a 3½-inch length of ribbon between the frame back and the support.

FINISHING: Glue the decorated frame front to the frame back along the three sides with the foam-core board spacers. Leave the top open for inserting a photo.

TATTING ABBREVIATIONS

ch(s) .... chain(s)
clr .... close ring
dnrw .... do not reverse work
p(s) .... picot(s)
r(s) .... ring(s)
rep .... repeat
rnd .... round
rw .... reverse work
sp .... space
st(s) .... stitch(es)
tog .... together

GUIDE TO TATTING

Tatting is a knotting technique that is done using a shuttle as the carrier for the thread. The knots are formed over the circle of thread that is held in the left hand. And in most cases (all cases in this book), these knots must slide along that circle. The knots in tatting are called double stitches. There are two halves to a double stitch.

Wind your tatting shuttle in a counterclockwise direction with the appropriate thread; leave 24 inches of thread free from the shuttle.

The following diagrams will guide you in learning to tat.

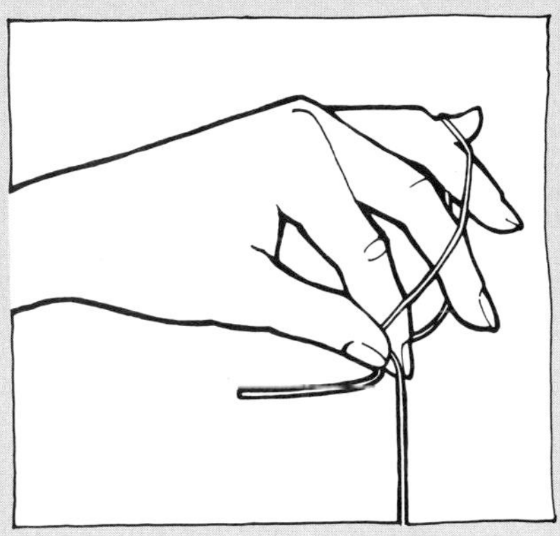

1. Loosely wrap your left hand once with the thread. Grasping the thread between your thumb and index finger, lift the other three fingers of your left hand—this is called the circle thread. Leave a 6-inch thread tail hanging from your fingers.

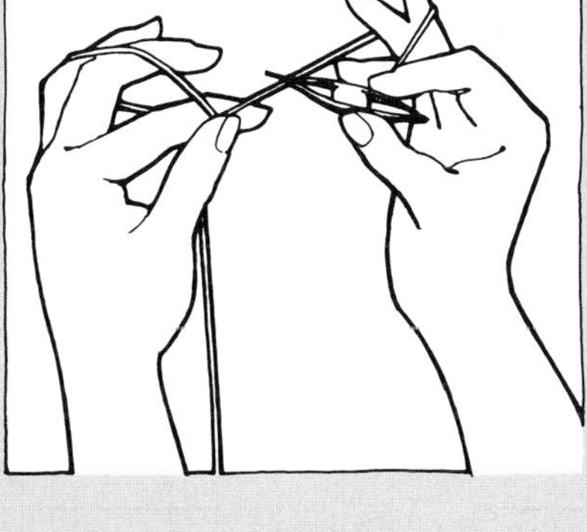

2. With the shuttle in your right hand and the point of the shuttle facing your left hand, hold 12 inches of thread taut—this is called the shuttle thread. Pass the shuttle under the shuttle thread, then under the circle thread between the index and middle fingers.

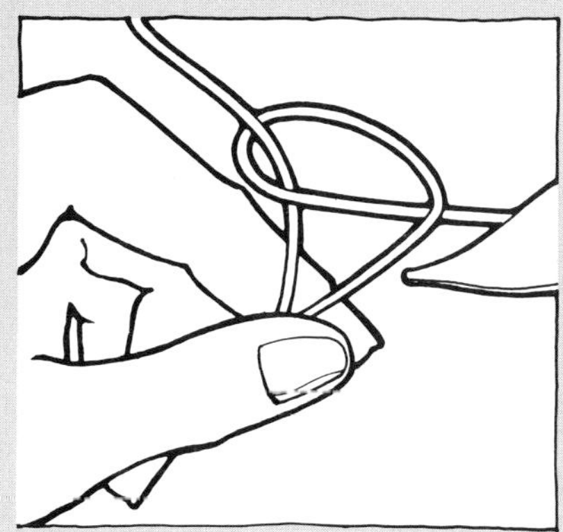

3. Pass the shuttle up and over the circle thread and down under the shuttle thread. Close the fingers on your left hand so that the circle thread becomes loose. Pull your right hand out parallel from your left hand, making the thread taut again.

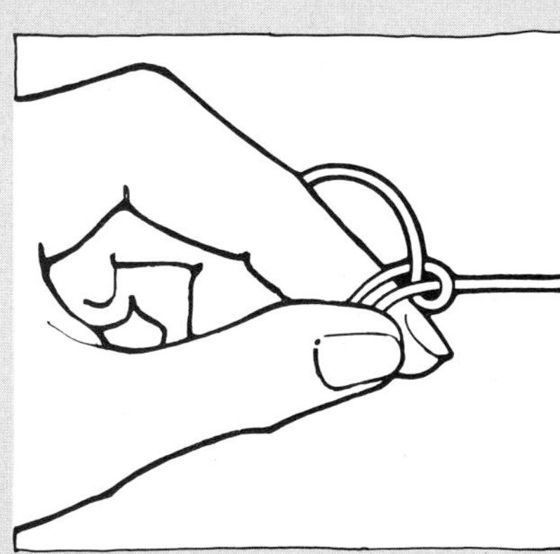

4. Lift the middle finger of your left hand to slowly move the first half of the double stitch into place. Position the first half of the knot in the groove of your index finger; slightly cover it with your thumb to hold it in place.

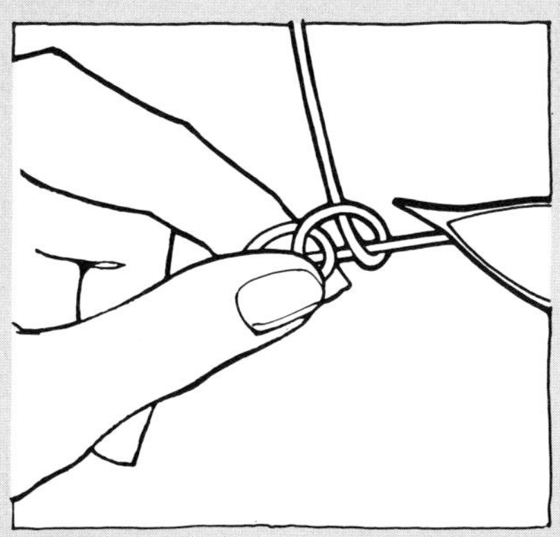

5. To complete the second half of the double stitch, pass the shuttle over the top of, and back under, the circle thread. Close the fingers on your left hand so that the circle thread is loose. Pull your right hand out parallel from your left hand, making the thread taut again. Repeat Step 4.

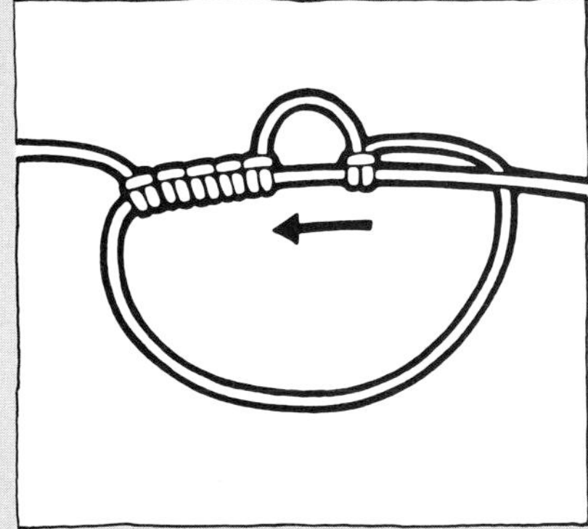

6. To make a picot, use your thumb to cover a space in the circle thread. Make a complete double stitch, and slide it up next to the last stitch made.

To close the ring, remove the tatted circle from your hand; hold the last stitches tatted and pull the shuttle thread until the ring closes.

An Invitation to Tea

"There are few hours in life more agreeable than the hour dedicated to the ceremony known as afternoon tea," wrote Henry James in his delicious novel, The Portrait of a Lady *(1880), and few would disagree. For wherever the setting and whatever is served, if the tea is hot and fresh and plentiful, then the soul will be soothed and the tongue loosed. What could be more delightful?*

Toward the close of the last century, renewed interest in the ancient art of counted thread embroidery, or cross-stitch, swept the country, and that interest has continued unabated until this day. *Godey's Lady's Book* and other needlework publications of the period were filled with pretty cross-stitch patterns. Tea set designs (a tray cloth and matching napkins) were popular offerings. The design pictured on page 51, a basket filled with roses, pansies, and a host of forget-me-nots, is especially appealing. For a contemporary touch with a Victorian flair, add the bow-tie napkin rings worked on plastic canvas.

The charming teatime picture *below* also is worked in cross-stitch. When the basic design is complete, a smattering of decorative stitches adds dimension to the picture.

Filet crochet also came into its own at the turn of the century. Floral motifs like the basket design on the antimacassar and the lily pattern on the tea cozy, *opposite,* always have been favored themes.

Many Victorian stitchers were adept at translating designs from one technique to another. Because cross-stitch, filet crochet, and needlepoint are based on charted patterns in which a single square on the pattern represents a single stitch, a savvy stitcher easily could turn a cross-stitch design into a filet crochet project (and vice versa). If you'd like to try such a translation, the winsome teapot doily design, *below,* is an easy pattern with which to experiment. Instructions for these projects begin on page 58.

Dining alfresco was an exciting novelty in the mid-1800s, and fashionable Victorians delighted in impromptu tea parties held on the terrace, in the garden, or beneath a picturesque arbor whenever weather and landscape permitted.

Though the setting became more informal as the century wore on, the table still was laid with as much care as ever. The pristine white cloth, *left,* bedecked with "natural" motifs of birds and blossoms, would have provided an elegant, pastoral backdrop for such open-air festivities. Worked in delicate filet crochet, the 4½-inch-wide border and triangular insertions depicting roses and robins (see the inset, *below)* can be easily adapted to suit any size project. Instructions for the edging and cloth are on pages 65–67.

Frosty pitchers of tea laced with lemon and mint and platters of dainty cucumber sandwiches are the perfect refreshments for a hot summer's day. Although iced tea is a comparatively recent and uniquely American contribution to tea-table canon, cucumber sandwiches are as traditional and as quintessentially English as Queen Victoria herself, who was said to adore them. Elegant enough to complement fancier fare, these dainty delights are wonderfully simple to make. Use a fancy-shape cookie cutter to cut thin rye or wheat bread. Spread the bread with soft cream cheese, top with thin cucumber slices, and sprinkle with fresh dill.

Novelty needlework projects, especially those in which different stitchery techniques or unusual materials were combined, became the rage in the 1890s, and stitchery magazines vied with one another to offer the most unusual designs. A cleverly designed cloth like this one, *opposite,* in which rows and rows of rickrack are combined with dainty crocheted medallions, might have graced the table of a fashion-conscious turn-of-the-century young matron getting ready for her first formal tea.

The sherbet-hued coasters in lilac and rose, *at right,* are another artful combination of rickrack and crochet. They are especially easy to stitch and most effective for a festive table setting. Instructions for these projects are on pages 67–69.

Today, as in days gone by, the menu for a party is always a matter of some concern for the hostess. Meat sandwiches, for example, were added in Victoria's day to distinguish high tea from other teas. But then, as now, it seems fancy cakes and confections were what guests remembered best. Ladies of the day were advised to make cookies and cakes from scratch using the finest ingredients. Serving tips for a formal tea table included piling little iced cakes on plates or pedestals.

But for those who had limited time and resources, Mr. Jessup Whitehead offered the following reassurance in his *Steward's Handbook* (1893): Whether homemade or store bought, "a pyramid of assorted little cakes will be more immediately attractive and give more satisfaction than an elaborately ornamented cake on which two to three days' work has been put."

As for the tea itself, further reassurance came from that doyenne of household management, Isabella Beeton, who said in 1861, "There is very little art in making good tea: if the water is boiling, and there is no sparing of the fragrant leaf, the beverage will almost invariably be good."

Cross-Stitched Flower Basket

Shown on page 51.
Design area measures 7x5⅛ inches when stitched over two threads on 36-count linen. Design is 124x92 stitches.

MATERIALS

- 15x18-inch piece of 36-count ivory linen
- One skein *each* of DMC embroidery floss in colors listed on the color key
- Size 26 tapestry needle
- White paper tape
- Wooden tray with 11x6⅜-inch nonglare glass opening—available from Anne Brinkley Designs (see page 158 for the address)

INSTRUCTIONS

The flower basket chart is shown *opposite.*

Tape the raw edges of the fabric to prevent the threads from raveling. Use two strands of floss to work cross-stitches and one strand of floss to work backstitches over two threads of fabric. The stitch diagrams on page 69 illustrate how to work these stitches.

Note: If you prefer to work on Aida cloth over one thread, you can stitch this design on 18-count fabric and end up with the same size design.

Measure 5 inches up and 8 inches in from the bottom left corner of the linen. Begin stitching the bottom left side of the basket here.

Once the cross-stitching is complete, work the backstitching with No. 3371.

Remove the tape and press the finished stitchery on the back using a damp cloth and a warm iron.

Following the tray manufacturer's instructions, mount the stitched piece in the tray under the glass top.

Cross-Stitched Linen Napkins

Shown on page 51.
Napkins measure approximately 11 inches square.

MATERIALS
For two napkins

- Two 12-inch squares of 36-count ivory linen
- One skein *each* of DMC embroidery floss in colors designated with an * on the color key
- Size 26 tapestry needle
- Blue sewing thread
- White paper tape

INSTRUCTIONS

The napkin design is part of the flower basket chart, *opposite.* Refer to the photo on page 51 for guidance.

Tape the raw edges of the fabric to prevent the threads from raveling. Use two strands of floss to work cross-stitches and one strand of floss to work backstitches over two threads of fabric. The stitch diagrams on page 69 illustrate how to work these stitches.

Once the cross-stitching is complete, work the backstitching with No. 3371.

When the stitching is complete, remove the tape and press the wrong side of the napkins.

With blue thread, surge the napkin edges or turn them under ¼ inch twice on all four sides and machine-topstitch ⅛ inch from the outside edges.

Plastic Canvas Napkin Rings

Shown on page 51.
Bow measures 4½x2 inches.

MATERIALS
For two napkin rings

- 8¼x11-inch piece of 14-count plastic canvas
- Size 24 tapestry needle
- One skein *each* of DMC embroidery floss in the following colors: antique blue lt (No. 932), antique blue med (No. 931), and antique blue dk (No. 930)
- Hot-glue gun and glue sticks

INSTRUCTIONS

Use the bow from the flower basket chart, *opposite.*

Use six strands of floss to work continental or basket-weave stitches over one mesh of plastic canvas. The stitch diagrams on page 69 illustrate how to work these stitches.

In a separate area of the plastic canvas, stitch a 1x4-inch rectangle for the ring using No. 932.

When the stitching is complete, cut around the stitched areas leaving a plastic edge. With six strands of No. 930, whipstitch around the edges of the bow to hide the plastic and whipstitch around the band using No. 932. Sew the narrow ends of the band into a ring. Glue the ring to the back of the bow.

Symbol	DMC	Color
◇	223	shell pink - med lt
J	224	shell pink - lt
#	225	shell pink - vy lt
□	320	pistachio green - med lt *
✜	333	periwinkle - dk *
Ж	347	salmon - dk *
●	351	coral - med *
S	369	pistachio green - vy lt *
■	433	brown - med
L	434	brown - lt
+	436	tan
Z	445	lemon - lt *
✢	470	avocado green - med lt *
∾	472	avocado green - vy lt *
⋈	553	violet - med *
@	554	violet - lt *
▬	561	malachite - dk *
♦	562	malachite - med *
♠	725	topaz - med
△	726	topaz - lt *
◊	727	topaz - vy lt *
B	733	olive green - med *
∩	760	salmon - med lt
O	775	baby blue - lt *
•	930	antique blue - med dk
⠿	931	antique blue - med
G	932	antique blue - med lt
▲	937	avocado green - med dk *
I	3078	golden yellow - vy lt *
×	3325	baby blue - med lt *
★	3371	black brown *
♥	3608	fuchsia - med *
▮	3712	salmon - med
☾	3721	shell pink - med dk
Backstitch:		
(line)	801	everything*
French knot:		
●	351	flower centers

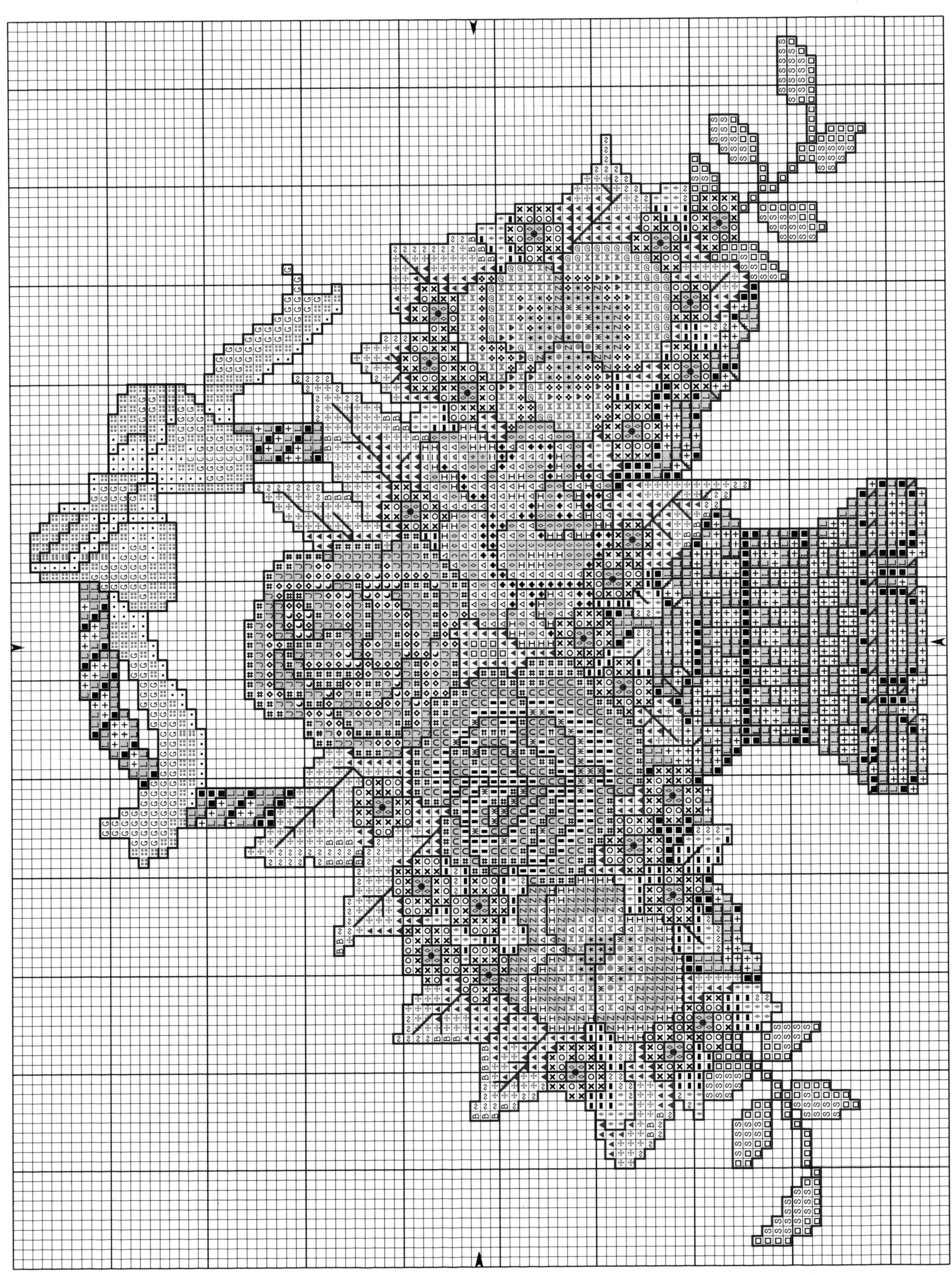

CROSS-STITCHED FLOWER BASKET

CROCHETED ANTIMACASSAR

Shown on page 52.
Antimacassar measures 17¾ inches wide and 13¾ inches long.

MATERIALS

Clark's Big Ball crochet cotton, Size 30 (350-yard ball): 2 balls of ecru
Size 12 steel crochet hook

Abbreviations: See page 99.
Gauge: 6 sp = 1 inch; 6 rows = 1 inch.

INSTRUCTIONS

Note: To make the antimacassar, follow the chart *below* and work from the top of the design (the straight edge) toward the bottom. This piece is worked using the filet crochet technique (see page 157 for more information).

Beginning along the top edge, ch 288.

Row 1: Dc in fourth ch from hook, and in next 41 chs; ch 2, sk 2 ch, dc in next 88 chs; ch 2, sk 2 ch, dc in next 16 chs; ch 2, sk 2 ch, dc in next 88 chs; ch 2, sk 2 ch, dc in next 43 chs; ch 3, turn.

Row 2: Sk first dc, dc in next 3 dc, **(ch 2, sk 2 dc, dc in next dc—ch-2 sp made)** 13 times; 2 dc in ch-2 sp, dc in next dc; **(ch 5, sk next 5 dc, dc in next dc—ch-5 sp made;** ch-2 sp) 9 times; ch-5 sp, 2 dc in ch-2 sp; dc in next dc, ch-5 sp, ch-2 sp, ch-5 sp; 2 dc in next ch-2 sp, dc in next dc; (ch-5 sp, ch-2 sp) 9 times, ch-5 sp, 2 dc in ch-2 sp, dc in next dc; make 13 ch-2 sps; dc in next 2 dc, dc in top of turning ch; ch 3, turn.

Rows 3–33: Follow the chart *below.*

Row 34: Sk first dc, dc in next 3 dc, ch 2, dc in next dc, 2 dc in ch-2 sp, dc in next 7 dc, ch 2, dc in next dc; (ch 2, sk 2 dc, dc in next dc) 3 times; ch 2, dc in next 4 dc, ch 2, dc in next dc, ch 5, dc in next dc, ch 2, dc in next dc, 2 dc in ch-2 sp, dc in next dc, (ch 2, sk 2 dc, dc in next dc) twice; ch 5, sk 5 dc, dc in next dc, ch 2, sk 2 dc, dc in next dc; ch 2, dc in next dc, ch 2, dc in next 13 dc; ch 2, dc in next 4 dc, 2 dc in ch-2 sp, dc in next dc, ch 2, dc in next 19

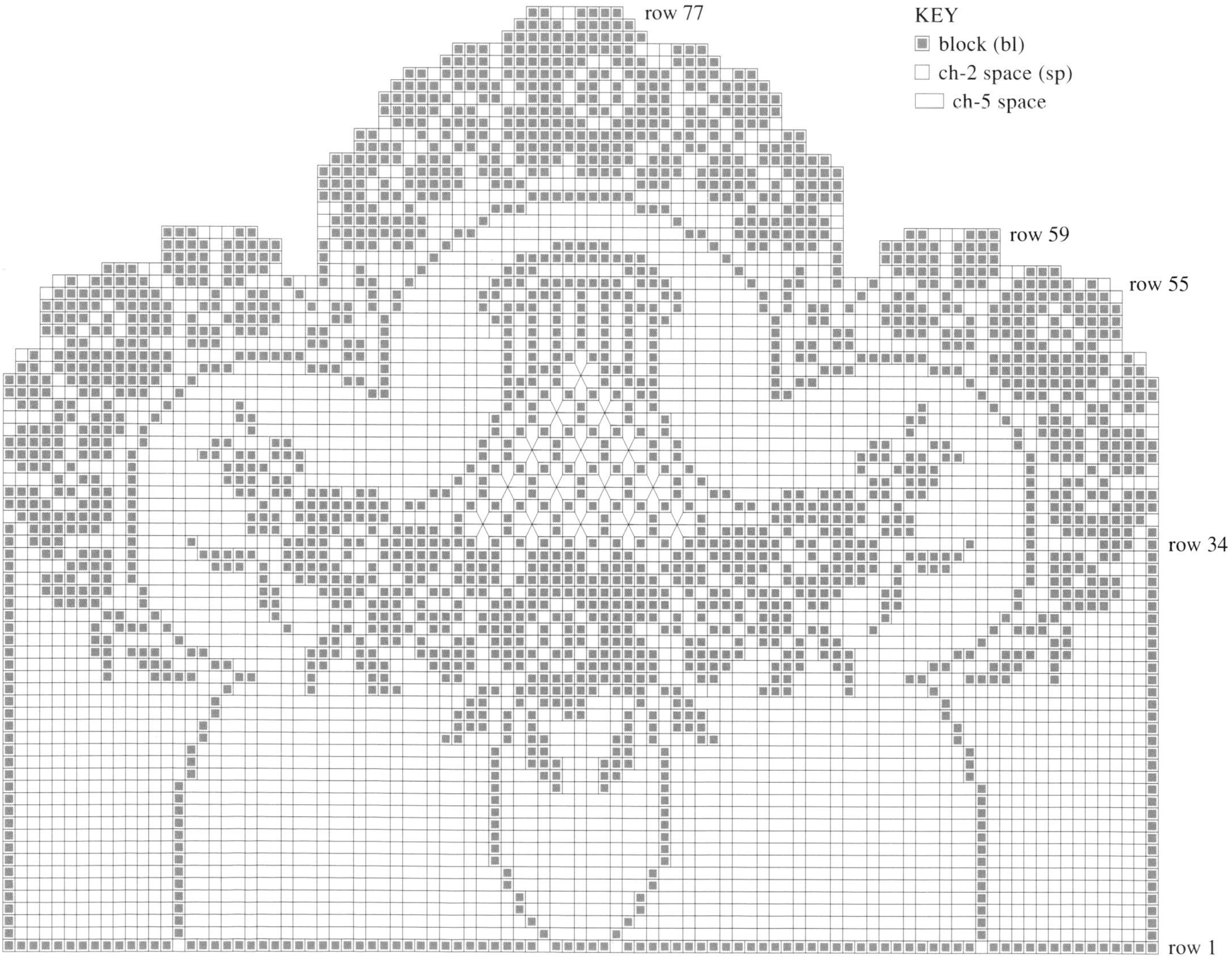

row 77
KEY
block (bl)
ch-2 space (sp)
ch-5 space
row 59
row 55
row 34
row 1

CROCHETED ANTIMACASSAR

dc, 2 dc in ch-2 sp, dc in next 4 dc; ch 5, sk 2 dc, dc in next 4 dc, ch 2, dc in next dc; ch 5, sk 2 dc, dc in next 4 dc, ch 2, sk 2 dc, dc in next 4 dc, ch 5, sk 2 dc, dc in next dc, 2 dc in ch-2 sp, dc in next dc, ch 2, dc in next 4 dc, ch 5, sk 2 dc, dc in next dc, 2 dc in ch-2 sp, ch 2, dc in next dc, 2 dc in ch-2 sp, dc in next dc, ch 5, sk 2 dc, dc in next 4 dc, 2 dc in next ch-2 sp; dc in next 19 dc; ch 2, dc in next dc, 2 dc in next ch-2 sp, dc in next 4 dc; ch 2, dc in next 13 dc, (ch 2, dc in next dc) twice; ch 2, sk 2 dc, dc in next dc; ch 5, sk 5 dc, dc in next dc, (ch 2, sk 2 dc, dc in next dc) twice; 2 dc in ch-2 sp, dc in next dc; ch 2, dc in next dc, ch 5, dc in next dc, ch 2, dc in next 4 dc; ch 2, dc in next dc; (ch 2, sk 2 dc, dc in next dc) 3 times; ch 2, dc in next 7 dc, 2 dc in next ch-2 sp, dc in next dc; ch 2, dc in next 3 dc, dc in top of the turning ch; ch 3, turn.

Row 35: Sk first dc, dc in next 3 dc, ch 2, dc in next 10 dc; (2 dc in next ch-2 sp, dc in next dc) 3 times; (ch 2, dc in next dc) twice; dc in next 3 dc; ch 2, dc in next dc, ch 5, dc in next dc, ch 2, dc in next dc; ch 5, sk 3 dc, dc in next dc, ch 2, dc in next dc, ch 5, dc in next dc; (2 dc in ch-2 sp, dc in next dc) 3 times; (ch 2, sk 2 dc, dc in next dc) twice, dc in next 6 dc; 2 dc in ch-2 sp, dc in next dc; (ch 2, sk 2 dc, dc in next dc) twice; 2 dc in ch-2 sp, dc in next dc; ch 2, sk 2 dc, dc in next 13 dc; ch 2, sk 2 dc, dc in next 4 dc; (ch 9, sk next 6 dc, dc in next dc, 2 dc in next ch-2 sp, dc in next dc) 4 times; ch 9, sk next 6 dc, dc in next 4 dc, ch 2, sk 2 dc, dc in next 13 dc, ch 2, sk 2 dc, dc in next dc; 2 dc in next ch-2 sp, dc in next dc; (ch 2, sk 2 dc, dc in next dc) twice; 2 dc in next ch-2 sp, dc in next 7 dc; (ch 2, sk 2 dc, dc in next dc) twice; (2 dc in next ch-2 sp, dc in next dc) 3 times; ch 5, dc in next dc, ch 2, dc in next dc; ch 5, sk next 3 dc, dc in next dc, ch 2, dc in next dc; ch 5, dc in next dc, ch 2, dc in next 4 dc; (ch 2, dc in next dc) twice; (2 dc in next ch-2 sp, dc in next dc) 3 times; dc in next 9 dc, ch 2, dc in next 3 dc, dc in top of turning ch; ch 5, turn.

Row 36: Sk 2 dc, dc in next dc, 2 dc in next ch-2 sp; dc in next 19 dc, 2 dc in next ch-2 sp, dc in next dc; ch 2, dc in next 4 dc, (ch 2, dc in next dc, ch 5, dc in next dc) 3 times; (ch 2, sk 2 dc, dc in next dc) 3 times, ch 2, dc in next dc, 2 dc in next ch-2 sp, dc in next 10 dc, (2 dc in next ch-2 sp, dc in next dc) twice; dc in next 3 dc, 2 dc in next ch-2 sp, dc in next dc; (ch 2, sk 2 dc, dc in next dc) 4 times; ch 2, dc in next 4 dc, (ch 6, sc around the two ch lps below, ch 6, dc in next 4 dc) 5 times; ch 2, dc in next dc, (ch 2, sk 2 dc, dc in next dc) 4 times; 2 dc in next ch-2 sp, dc in next 4 dc, (2 dc in next ch-2 sp, dc in next dc) twice; dc in next 9 dc; 2 dc in next ch-2 sp, dc in next dc; ch 2, dc in next 10 dc; (ch 5, dc in next dc, ch 2, dc in next dc) 3 times; dc in next 3 dc, ch 2, dc in next dc, 2 dc in next ch-2 sp, dc in next 19 dc; 2 dc in next ch-2 sp, dc in next dc, ch 2, dc in top of turning ch; ch 3, turn.

Rows 37–54: Cont to work from chart. As bls dec at beg of rows, *do not* work ch to turn; simply turn work, sl st over to starting point, then ch 3 (or ch 5 for a sp), and complete the beg bl (or sp).

Rows 56–67: Work first scallop over 15 sts following chart; fasten off at end of Row 59. Join thread and work second scallop over center 43 sts following chart. Fasten off at end of Row 67.

Join thread and work last scallop over rem 15 sts following chart. Fasten off at end of Row 59. Block and press finished piece.

CROCHETED TEA COZY

Shown on page 52.
Tea cozy measures 15x8½ inches.

MATERIALS

DMC Cordonnet Special crochet cotton, Size 50 (286-yard ball): 3 balls of white
Size 14 steel crochet hook
Tissue paper for the pattern
¼ yard *each* of quilt batting, solid color backing, and lining fabric
¼ yard of print fabric for the ruffle
1¼ yards of ⅛-inch-wide cording
1¼ yards of 1½-inch-wide bias tape (or fabric to cover cording)

Abbreviations: See page 99.
Gauge: 7 sp = 1 inch; 7 rows = 1 inch.

INSTRUCTIONS

Note: The tea cozy is worked following the chart on page 62. This piece is worked using the filet crochet technique. For additional information on working filet crochet patterns, refer to page 157.

CROCHETED COZY (make two): Beg along the bottom edge, ch 320.

Row 1: Dc in eighth ch from hook, * ch 2, sk 2 ch, dc in next ch; rep from * across row—105 sp made; ch 3, turn.

Row 2: Work 2 dc in first ch-2 sp, dc in next dc; * 2 dc in ch-2 sp, dc in dc; rep from * across row; ch 5, turn.

Rows 3–70: Work from thc chart on page 62. As bls dec at beg of rows, *do not* work ch to turn; simply turn work, sl st over to starting point, then ch 5, and complete the beg sp.

Fasten off at end of Row 70.

BOTTOM EDGING: *Row 1:* At the bottom of each half of the tea cozy, work sc in each dc, and 2 sc in each ch 2-sp; ch 1, turn.

Row 2: Sc in first sc, * ch 3, sk 2 sc, sc in next sc, rep from * to end; fasten off. Block both pieces.

FINISHING: Trace 1 inch beyond the outside of the tea cozy shape on tissue paper; cut out the tissue pattern.

Cover the cording with fabric or bias tape to make piping that fits around all sides of the cozy.

Cut one 3x44-inch strip of print fabric for the ruffle. Fold the strip with right sides together; sew across both narrow ends and turn right side out. Machine-stitch two rows of gathering thread along the length of the strip ¼ and ½ inch from the raw edges; gather the ruffle to fit the curved side of the cozy.

Using the tissue pattern, cut out two shapes each from the backing, lining, and batting fabrics. Baste the batting shapes to the wrong sides of each lining piece.

With right sides together and raw edges even, machine-stitch the piping

continued

around all edges of just one of the lining shapes using ½-inch seams. Pin, then baste the ruffle atop the piping along the curved edge of the same piece.

With right sides facing, sew the two lining pieces together, leaving the bottom edge open. Take care not to catch the ruffle in the seam. Trim the batting seam to ⅛ inch. Turn under and press ¼ inch along the bottom edges.

With right sides facing, sew the two backing pieces together, leaving the bottom edge open.

With wrong sides facing, slip the backing piece over the lining piece. Turn back the edges of the bottom of the lining piece and blindstitch the lining to the backing. Turn the cozy right side out. Tack the lining to the inside top.

Sew each crocheted tea cozy piece to the sides of the fabric tea cozy.

CROCHETED TEA COZY

KEY
■ Block (bl)
□ Space (sp)

CROCHETED TEAPOT DOILY

Shown on page 53.
Doily measures 7¾ inches square.

MATERIALS

DMC Cebelia crochet cotton, Size 40 (249-yard ball): 1 ball of white
Size 13 steel crochet hook

Abbreviations: See page 99.
Gauge: 6 sp = 1 inch; 7 rows = 1 inch.

INSTRUCTIONS

Note: This doily is made by working the center square and one side of the edging first. The remaining three sides of the edging then are worked separately onto the square.

Ch 120.

Row 1: Dc in fourth ch from hook and in next 92 chs; ch 2, sk 2 ch, dc in next ch; ch 5, sk 5 ch, dc in next ch; ch 3, sk 2 ch; sc in next ch, ch 3, sk 2 ch, dc in next ch; ch 2, sk 2 ch, dc in last 7 ch; ch 3, turn.

Row 2: Sk first dc, dc in next 3 dc; ch 3, sk 2 dc, sc in next dc, ch 3, dc in next dc, ch 5, dc in next dc, ch 3, sc in ch-5 lp, ch 3, dc in next dc; ch 2, dc in next 4 dc; (ch 2, sk 2 dc, dc in next dc) 29 times; dc in last 3 dc; ch 3, turn.

Rows 3–31: Work from the chart, *right.*

To inc one bl at ends of odd-numbered rows: *** Yo hook, draw up lp in base of last dc made, yo, draw through 1 lp on hook—base ch for next dc;** (yo, draw through 2 lps on hook) twice; working in base ch, rep from * 3 times more; ch 3, turn.

To dec one bl at beg of even-numbered rows: Do not ch 3 to turn at end of previous row; turn and sl st across 4 dc; ch 3 (counts as first dc of first bl), and cont to work from chart.

Row 32: Sl st across 4 dc, ch 3, sk next dc, dc in next 3 dc; 2 dc in next ch-2 sp, dc in next dc; 2 dc in ch-3 sp of lacet, dc in sc of lacet, 2 dc in ch-3 sp of lacet; dc in next dc, 5 dc in ch-5 sp, dc in next dc; ch 2, dc in next dc; ch 3, turn.

Rows 33–38: Cont to work from chart until the corner is complete; fasten off.

SECOND SIDE OF EDGING: Join the thread into the top of the dc on Row 31 (the red dot on the chart) and work the shaded rows 39–76, working these stitches perpendicular to the existing work. Row 39 is worked into the sides of the stitches of rows 32–38. When Row 76 is completed, fasten off. Whipstitch the side of the edging to the side of the square.

Rep the shaded portion of the chart for the remaining two sides of the doily. Whipstitch beg and ending rows of the last corner and the first side of the crocheted edging together.

TEATIME CROSS-STITCH

Shown on page 53.
Finished size of stitchery is 4⅔x6¾ inches on 14-count Aida cloth. Design is 65x95 stitches.

MATERIALS

10x12-inch piece of 14-count ivory Aida cloth
One skein *each* of DMC embroidery floss in colors listed on the color key
Size 24 or 26 tapestry needle
White paper tape

INSTRUCTIONS

Work from the chart on page 64.

Tape the raw edges of the fabric before beginning to stitch to prevent the threads from raveling.

Separate the floss and use two strands to work cross-stitches over one square of Aida cloth. A stitch diagram on page 69 illustrates how to work this stitch.

Measure 3½ inches up and 5 inches in from the bottom left corner of the fabric. Begin stitching the plate of cookies here.

continued

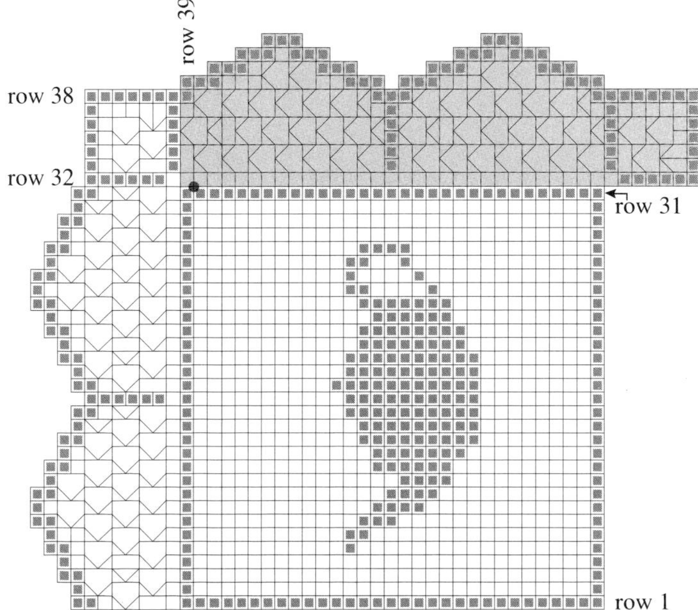

KEY
☐ Space (sp)
▣ Block (bl)
Ch-5 Loop
Lacet st

CROCHETED TEAPOT DOILY

TEATIME CROSS-STITCH

DMC

000 white
208 lavender - vy dk
209 lavender - dk
347 salmon - dk
353 peach flesh
415 pearl gray - lt
435 brown - vy lt
437 tan - lt
522 seafoam green - med
524 seafoam green - vy lt
743 yellow - med
744 yellow - lt
754 peach flesh - lt
792 cornflower blue - dk
793 cornflower blue - med
948 peach flesh - vy lt
950 rose brown - lt
962 dusty pink - med
987 forest green - dk
989 forest green - med
3326 rose - med lt
3328 salmon - med dk
3371 black brown

Backstitch:

3371 girl's eyes
3371 all other backstitching

Straight stitch:

3326 & 962 (1 strand each)—ribbon on girl's dress
3328 & 347 (1 strand each)—ribbon in doll's hair
437 & 433 (1 strand each)—girl and doll's hair

Lazy daisy stitch:

3326 & 962 (1 strand each)—bow on girl's dress
3328 & 347 (1 strand each)—bow in doll's hair
white & 415 (1 strand each)—daisies

Wrapped stitch:

437 & 433 (1 strand each)—girl's hair

French knot:

743 daisy centers
3326 & 962 (1 strand each)—little pink flowers
000 girl's collar, cuff & buttons on dress (2X)
3371 girl's eyes (2X)

Decorative stitches

When the foundation cross-stitching is complete, work the following decorative stitches for added dimension. Illustrative diagrams for these stitches can be found on pages 69 and 79.

BACKSTITCHES: For the pupils of the girl's eyes, work short backstitches using three strands of No. 3371.

For all outlining, work backstitches using one strand of No. 3371.

STRAIGHT STITCHES: For the ribbons of the bow on the neck of the girl's dress, work straight stitches using one strand of No. 3326 and one strand of No. 962 held together.

For the ribbons of the bow in the doll's hair, work straight stitches using one strand of No. 3328 and one strand of No. 347 held together.

For the girl's bangs and the doll's braids and bangs, work straight stitches over the cross-stitches using one strand of No. 437 and one strand of No. 433 held together.

LAZY DAISY STITCHES: For the bow on the girl's dress, work lazy daisy stitches using one strand of No. 3326 and one strand of No. 962 held together.

For the bow in the doll's hair, work lazy daisy stitches using one strand No. 3328 and one of No. 347 held together.

For the daisy flowers, work lazy daisy stitches using one strand of white and one strand of No. 415 held together.

WRAPPED STITCHES: *Note:* To make wrapped stitches, first work long straight stitches and then wrap them loosely with the same thread.

For the girl's ringlets, work wrapped stitches using one strand of No. 437 and one strand of No. 433 held together.

FRENCH KNOTS: For the lace on the girl's collar and cuffs and for buttons on the girl's pinafore, work French knots using two strands of white.

For the daisy flower centers, work French knots using two strands of No. 743.

For the wildflowers, work French knots using one strand of No. 3326 and one strand of No. 962 held together.

When stitching is complete, remove tape; press stitchery on the wrong side, using a damp cloth and warm iron. Frame as desired.

Robins and Roses Tablecloth

Shown on pages 54 and 55.
Border edging measures approximately 4½ inches across. Triangle insertion measures approximately 14 inches along the baseline (Row 1) of the triangle.

MATERIALS

DMC Cordonnet Special crochet cotton, Size 50 (286-yard ball): 15 balls of white (1 ball makes approximately 19 inches of border lace)
Size 14 steel crochet hook
50-inch square of linen fabric for cloth
White sewing thread
Sewing needle

Abbreviations: See page 99.
Gauge: 19 dc = 1 inch; 8 rows = 1 inch.

INSTRUCTIONS

Note: This piece is worked using the filet crochet technique (see page 157 for more information).

For the triangle insertion

Beg along the base leg of the triangle, ch 275.

Row 1: Dc in eighth ch from hook; * ch 2, sk 2 ch, dc in next ch; rep from * across; ch 4, turn.

Row 2: Sk first dc, dc in next dc; (2 dc in ch-2 sp, dc in next dc) 88 times; ch 2, sk 2 ch of turning ch, dc in next ch; ch 5, turn.

Row 3: Sk first dc, dc in next 4 dc; (ch 2, sk 2 dc, dc in next dc) 80 times; dc in next 6 dc; (ch 2, sk 2 dc, dc in next dc) twice; dc in next 6 dc; sk 2 dc, trc in last dc; ch 4, turn.

Rows 4–90: Work from the Triangle Insertion chart on page 66, ending the odd-numbered rows with trc in last dc, ch 4, and turn. The trc and the turning ch-4 make a straight edge that easily can be sewn to the fabric. To begin all even-numbered rows, sk 2 dc, dc in next dc.

Read all even-numbered rows from left to right and all odd-numbered rows from right to left. Follow the chart across the page to complete each row. Fasten off at end of Row 90. In the same manner, make three more triangle insertions.

For the border edging

Ch 90.

Row 1: Dc in fourth ch from hook, dc in next 2 ch; (ch 2, sk 2 ch, dc in next ch) 14 times; dc in next 6 ch; ch 2, sk 2 ch, dc in next 10 ch; ch 2, sk 2 ch, dc in next 10 ch; (ch 2, sk 2 ch, dc in next ch) 3 times; dc in next 3 ch; ch 6, turn.

Row 2: **Dc in fourth ch from hook and in next 2 ch—1 bl inc at beg of even-numbered row made;** dc in 3 dc; (ch 2, dc in next dc) twice; 2 dc in ch-2 sp, dc in next 4 dc; ch 2, sk 2 dc, dc in next 4 dc; 2 dc in ch-2 sp, dc in next dc; (ch 2, sk 2 dc, dc in next dc) 3 times; 2 dc in ch-2 sp, dc in next 7 dc; 2 dc in next ch-2 sp, dc in next dc; (ch 2, sk 2 ch, dc in next dc) 8 times; 2 dc in next ch-2 sp, dc in next dc; (ch 2, dc in next dc) 4 times; dc in next 2 dc and in top of turning ch; ch 3, turn.

continued

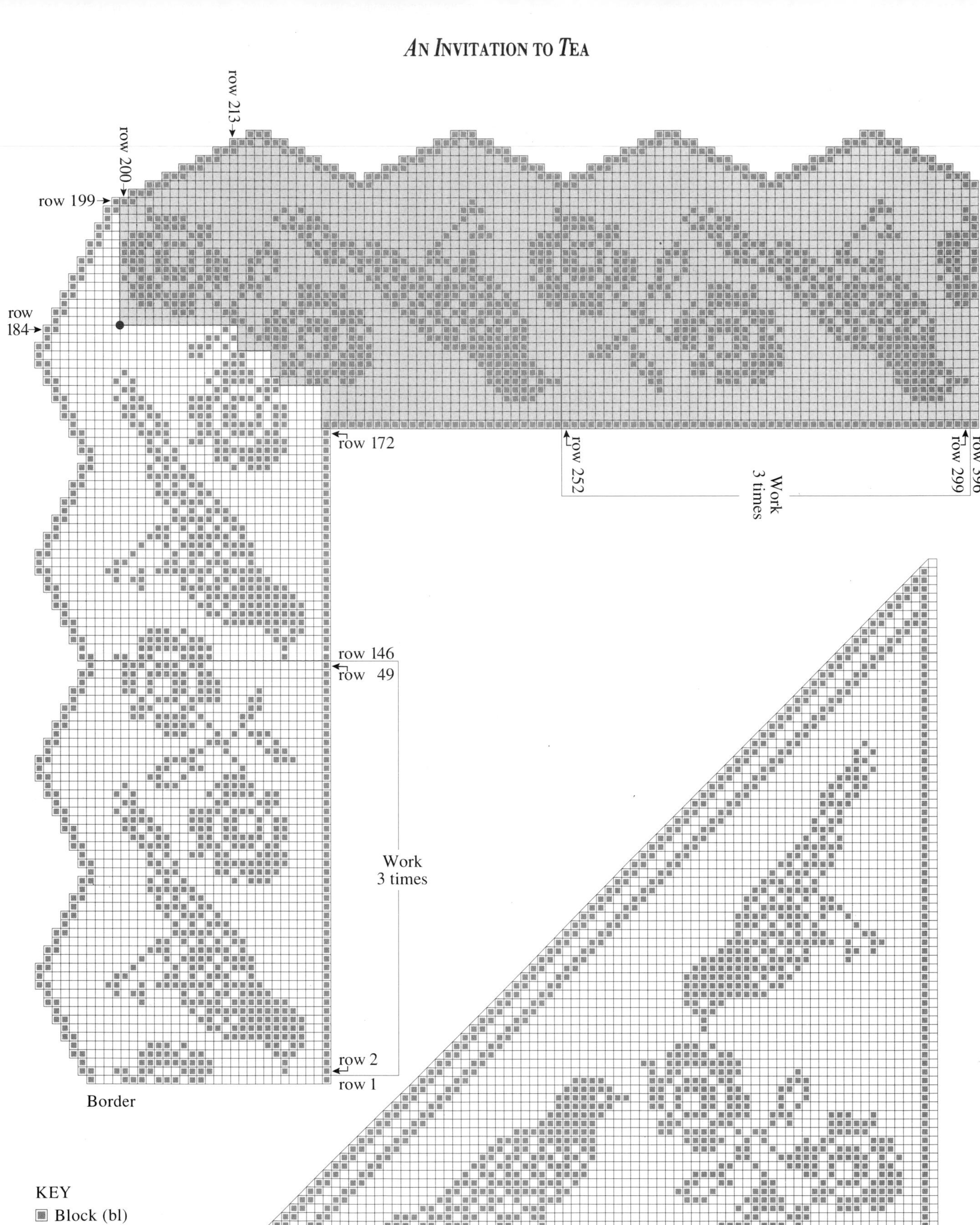

ROBINS AND ROSES TABLECLOTH

Triangle insertion

Rows 3–49: Work from the Robins and Roses Border chart, *opposite.*

Rows 50–145: Work rows 2–49 two times more—145 rows completed.

Rows 146–172: Work from chart to complete side and to establish pat to beg corner.

Rows 173–199 (mitered corner): Cont to work from chart; do not work beyond the right side of the red line. Work short rows to establish half of corner design; fasten off at end of Row 199.

Row 200: Join thread at red dot on chart (Row 185); work across sides of rows 185–199; ch 6, turn.

Rows 201–213: Work following chart; join into tops of dcs on Row 184 of mitered corner. At end of Row 213, sl st across three rows.

Rows 214–251: Cont to work from the chart, completing the mitered corner and start of second side of edging.

Rows 252–395: Work rows 252–299 three times.

Row 396: Work following the chart.

Rep rows 2–396 to work the complete side, the next corner, and the start of the next side. Work as established to complete the next two sides and corners; fasten off. Whipstitch the first and last rows together.

CLOTH ASSEMBLY: Wash and press the fabric and crochet pieces before assembly. Lay the border edging atop the cloth and baste in place, keeping the edges of the fabric straight and even on all sides; sew the border edging to the fabric. Trim the fabric along the edges, leaving ½ inch for the hem. Turn under ¼ inch twice; press and hand-sew the hem in place.

Evenly space the triangle motifs on the center portions of the cloth so the adjacent points of the triangles meet (diagonal sides of triangles form the center square); baste, then sew triangles in place. Cut fabric away from behind the triangle insertions, leaving ½ inch for the hem. Turn under ¼ inch twice; press and hand-sew hems in place.

CROCHET AND RICKRACK COASTERS

Shown on page 57.
Coasters measure 5½ inches in diameter from point to point.

MATERIALS

J. & P. Coats Knit-Cro-Sheen (225-yard ball): 1 ball *each* of mid-rose (No. 46A) and lilac (No. 36)
Coats Medium Rickrack: dark rose (No. 32B) and lilac (No. 91)
Size 8 steel crochet hook
Large, sharp, pointed needle for piercing rickrack

Abbreviations: See page 99.

INSTRUCTIONS

Using mid-rose or lilac thread, ch 6, sl st in beg ch to form ring.

Rnd 1: Ch 3, work 17 dc in ring; join with sl st in top of beg ch-3—18 dc.

Rnd 2: Ch 4, (dc in next dc, ch 1) 17 times; join with sl st in the third ch of the beg ch-4.

Rnd 3: Ch 3, (yo and draw up lp in first ch-1 sp, yo and draw through 2 lps on hook) twice, yo and draw through all lps on hook, ch 2; *** (yo and draw up a lp in next ch-1 sp, yo and draw through 2 lps on hook) 3 times, yo and draw through all lps on hook—dc-cluster made;** ch 2, rep from * 16 times more; join with sl st to top of beg ch-3.

Rnd 4: Sl st over to first ch-2 sp; ch 8, dc in same sp, ch 2, (dc in next ch-2 sp, ch 2) twice; * in next ch-2 sp work dc, ch 5, and dc; ch 2; (dc in ch-2 sp, ch 2) twice, rep from * 4 times; join with sl st to third ch of beg ch-8.

Rnd 5: Ch 3, in first ch-5 sp work 2 dc, ch 2, and 3 dc; ch 2, sc in next ch-2 sp, ch 6, sk next ch-2 sp, sc in next ch-2 sp, ch 2; * in next ch-5 sp work 3 dc, ch 2, and 3 dc; ch 2, sc in next ch-2 sp, ch 6, sk next ch-2 sp, sc in next ch-2 sp, ch 2; rep from * 4 times; join with sl st to top of beg ch-3.

Rnd 6: Sl st over to first ch-2 sp, ch 3, in same sp work 2 dc, ch 2, and 3 dc; ch 2, sc in next ch-2 sp, ch 5; in ch-6 sp work sc, ch 3, and sc; ch 5, sc in next ch-2 sp, ch 2; * in next ch-2 sp work 3 dc, ch 2, and 3 dc; ch 2, sc in next ch-2 sp, ch 5; in next ch-6 sp work sc, ch 3, and sc; ch 5, sc in next ch-2 sp, ch 2; rep from * 4 times; join with sl st to top of beg ch-3.

Note: Cut two pieces of matching color rickrack, one with 35 points along one edge and the other with 41 points along one edge. Prepare the rickrack by piercing each point of the 35-point-long rickrack and the points on one side of the 41-point-long rickrack with the sharp needle to make it easier to insert the crochet hook.

Rnd 7: Sl st over to the first ch-2 sp, ch 3, in same sp work 2 dc, ch 1, sc in third and fourth points of 35-point-long rickrack, ch 1, 3 dc in same sp, ch 2, sc in next rickrack point, ch 2; in next ch-5 sp work sc, ch 3, and sc; ch 2, sc in next rickrack point, ch 2; in next ch-5 sp work sc, ch 3, and sc; ch 2, sc in next rickrack point, ch 2, sk next ch-2 sp, * in next ch-2 sp work 3 dc, ch 1, insert hook through next 2 rickrack points and work sc, ch 1, 3 dc; ch 2, sc in next rickrack point, ch 2; in next ch-5 sp work sc, ch 3, and sc; ch 2, sc in next rickrack point, ch 2, in next ch-5 sp work sc, ch 3, and sc; ch 2, sc in next rickrack point, ch 2, sk next ch-2 sp, rep from * 4 times; join with sl st to top of beg ch-3; fasten off thread.

Rnd 8: Working along the top unworked edge of the first row of rickrack and second row of the rickrack piece (41-point-long), ch 1, insert the hook through the rickrack point opposite the first point worked and the third and fourth points of the 41-point rickrack piece, work sc, ch 5, (insert the hook through the next point of each piece of rickrack and work sc, ch 5) 4 times; * insert the hook through the next point of the first row of rickrack, and through the next 2 points of the second row of rickrack, work sc, ch 5, (insert hook through next point of each piece

continued

of rickrack and work sc, ch 5) 4 times; rep from * 4 times; join to beg ch-1; fasten off thread.

Fold the excess beginning and ending rickrack to the wrong side and tack in place; tack them together at the fold for the beginning points.

RICKRACK TABLECLOTH

Shown on page 56.
Tablecloth measures 54x72 inches.

MATERIALS

J. & P. Coats Best Big Ball 6-cord crochet cotton, Size 20 (300-yard ball): 9 balls of white
43 packages of medium 5-yard-long white rickrack
Size 10 steel crochet hook
Sewing needle; white sewing thread
Crewel needle
Large, sharp, pointed needle for piercing rickrack

Abbreviations: See page 99.

INSTRUCTIONS

Note: Prepare the rickrack by piercing each point of the rickrack with the sharp needle to make it easier to insert the crochet hook.

When sewing the rickrack together to form circles, do not sew to the outer point. To finish the raw ends of the rickrack, turn under the raw ends and sew.

Leave a 2-inch tail of crochet cotton to sew to the wrong side of the rickrack with the crewel needle.

To work sc through rickrack, insert the hook through the point of the rickrack, draw up a lp, yo and draw thread through 2 lps on hook. When working ch-5 bet the points of the rickrack, take care that the rickrack lies flat.

SMALL RICKRACK CIRCLES: Cut 30-point-long pieces of rickrack. Fold both ends of the rickrack back in the center of the second point from the end. Sew the two half points together so there are 28 complete points on the outside edge of the rickrack circle when it is joined to the crocheted squares.

LARGE RICKRACK CIRCLES: Cut 38-point-long pieces of rickrack. Fold both ends of the rickrack back in the center of the second point from the end. Sew the two half points together so there are 36 complete points on the outside edge of the rickrack circle.

First Square

Ch 5; join with sl st to form ring.

Rnd 1: Sc in ring, (ch 3, sc in ring, ch 5, sc in ring) 3 times; ch 3, sc in ring, ch 3, dc in beg sc.

Rnd 2: Sc in lp just made, * ch 5, in ch-3 lp work (yo and draw up a lp, yo and draw through 2 lps on hook) 5 times, yo and draw through 6 lps on hook; ch 5, sc in ch-5 lp **; ch 5, sc in same ch-5 lp—corner made; rep from * around; end last rep at **; ch 3, dc in first sc.

Rnd 3: Sc in lp just made, * ch 5, sc in next ch-5 lp, ch 3, sc in next ch-5 lp, ch 5, sc in next ch-5 lp **, ch 5, sc in same ch-5 lp, rep from * around, end last rep at **; ch 3, dc in sc.

Rnd 4: Sc in lp just made, * ch 5, sc in next ch-5 lp, 6 dc in ch-3 lp, sc in next ch-5-lp, ch 5, sc in next ch-5 lp **, ch 5, sc in same ch-5 lp, rep from *, end last rep at **; ch 3, dc in sc.

Rnd 5: Sc in lp just made, * ch 5, sc in next ch-5 lp, dc in dc, (ch 1, dc in next dc) 5 times, sc in ch-5 lp, ch 5, sc in next ch-5 lp, ** ch 5, sc in same ch-5 lp, rep from *, end last rep at **; ch 3, dc in sc.

Rnd 6: Hold the small rickrack circle in back of the work with the right sides of the rickrack and the square facing. Sc in lp just made, * ch 3, sc through second point of the rickrack from the seam, ch 3, sc in next ch-5 lp, ch 3, sc through next point, ch 3, sk next ch-1 sp, sc in next ch-1 sp, ch 2, sc through next point, ch 2, sk next ch-1 sp, sc in next ch-1 sp, ch 3, sc through next point, ch 3, sc in ch-5 lp, ch 3, sc through next point, ch 3, sc in next ch-5 lp, ch 4, **draw up a lp through each of the next two rickrack points, yo and draw through 3 lps on hook—corner made,** ch 4, sc in same ch-5 lp, rep from *, end last rep draw up a lp through each of the next 2 points, yo and draw up a lp in first sc, yo and draw through 2 lps on hook, yo and draw through 4 lps on hook, ch 6; **turn.**

Note: In Rnd 7, work in the outside points of the small rickrack circle and in the inside points of the large rickrack circle. The ch-6 from Rnd 6 carries the thread to Rnd 7 instead of fastening off. Insert the hook through the seam fold of the corner point of the small rickrack circle; hold the large rickrack circle in back of the work with the right sides of the rickrack and the square facing.

Rnd 7: Beg in the eighth point from the seam, **draw up a lp through each of next 3 rickrack points, yo and draw through 5 lps on hook—double corner point made,** * ch 5, draw up a lp through the next point of both the small and large rickrack circles, yo and draw through 3 lps on hook, rep from * to corner point, draw up a lp through corner point, draw up a lp through each of the next 3 points of large rickrack circle, yo and draw through 5 lps on hook, rep from * around; end with sl st in first double corner; fasten off.

Second (Joining) Square

Work as for the First Square through Rnd 7; *do not fasten off.*

Hold the squares tog, right sides facing, with the square to be joined in back of the work. Make sure that the seamed points are not joined in the same corner. Ch 6, draw up a lp through second point of double corner, draw up a lp through adjoining point of other square, yo and draw through 3 lps on hook, * ch 5, draw up a lp through the next point of the Second Square and next point of the First Square, yo and draw through 3 lps on hook, rep from *, ending at first point of next double corner; fasten off.

Rep Second Square 10 times more, until there are a total of 12 squares joined into a strip. Make 16 strips.

Push the folds of the corners to the wrong side of the work.

FINISHING: With the right sides of two strips facing each other, join the thread into the second corner point of the two end squares (large rickrack circle) of both strips, (ch 5, draw up a lp through the next adjoining point of each strip, yo and draw through 3 lps on hook) 8 times, dtr (yo hook 3 times) in joining bet two squares to right (mark this joining), ch 5, sl st in joining of two squares to left, ch 5, join next two points of next two squares of strip, dtr in marked joining; cont joining consecutive squares in the same manner until two strips are completely joined; fasten off.

Join another strip to the previous strips until all 16 strips are joined.

EDGING: Holding the rickrack in back of the work, with the wrong side of the tablecloth facing, attach thread in the second corner point of any corner of the tablecloth. Ch 1, draw up a lp, draw up a lp through sixth point from end of rickrack, yo and draw through 3 lps on hook, * ch 5, join next 2 points. Cont joining rickrack along one side of the tablecloth to the next corner of the tablecloth; (ch 5, draw up a lp through the next corner point, draw up a lp through each of the next 2 points of rickrack, yo and draw through 3 lps on hook) twice. Rep from *; end ch 5, sl st in first corner join.

Note: Add rickrack by seaming pieces together as in the rickrack circles.

Join two more rows of rickrack around the cloth, working a corner point over each corner point.

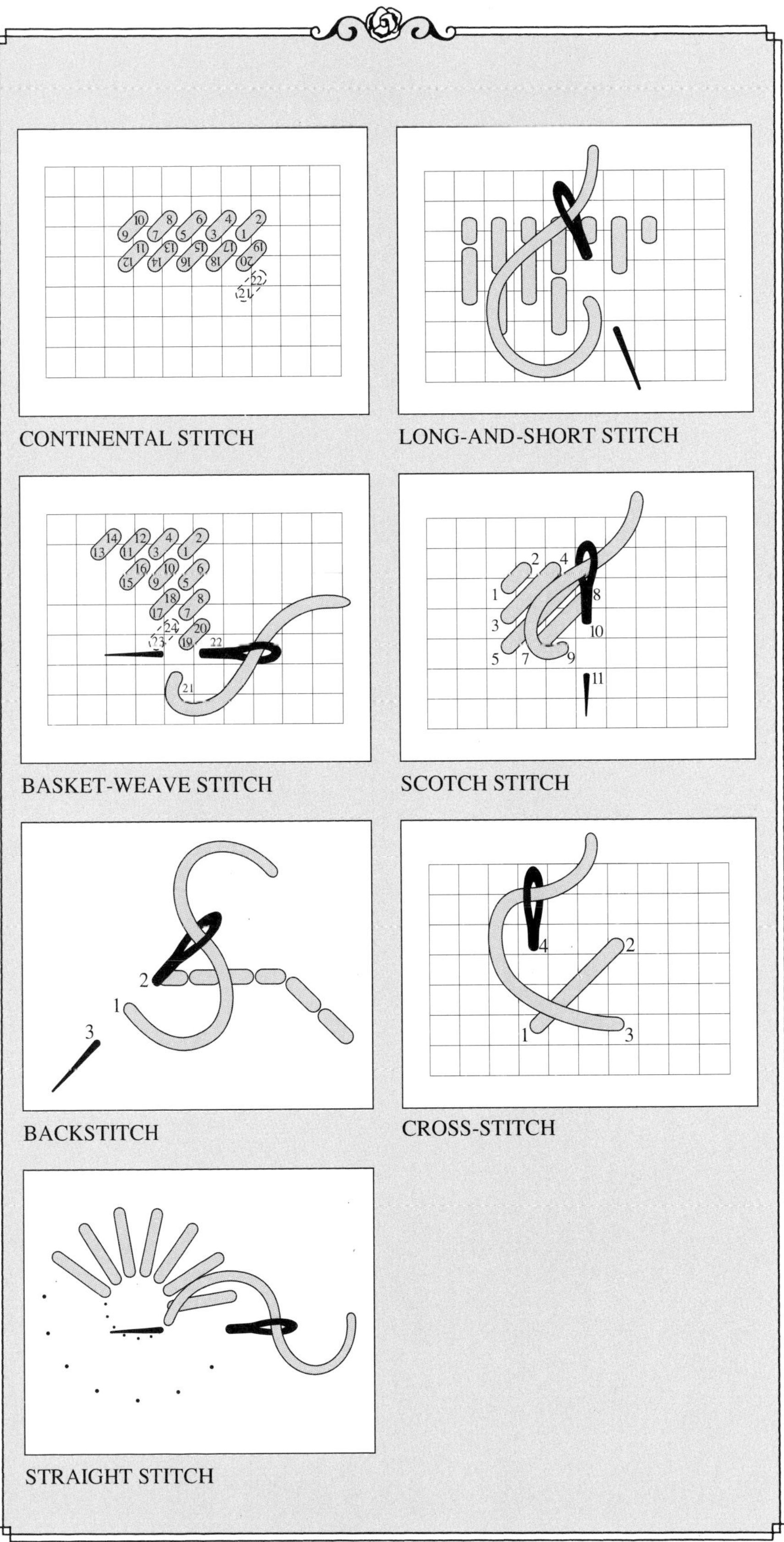

Parlor Arts

According to Mary Gay Humphreys, a social arbiter of the day, "The parlor . . . should convey a sense of elegance, good taste, recognition of the polite arts, and of graceful social amenities." It was the parlor where turn-of-the-century families gathered for evenings of conversation, edification, and amusement. Family members would read aloud to each other, play a card game, or stage an impromptu musicale. And here, too, the mistress of the house displayed her proudest accomplishments in the needle arts.

o provide the requisite touches of elegance and good taste, Victorians stitched up a storm of doilies and tidies, coverlets and cushions. Every chair sported an antimacassar, some of which were lacy confections of filet crochet like the flower and vine pattern on page 71. Tables were bedecked with doilies or draped with a crocheted cloth like the intricately patterned picot wheel design, *opposite.* Quaint mementos, decorative bric-a-brac, and family photographs clustered on every surface. Favorite pictures often were framed with handcrafted mats, which served to illustrate milady's mastery of yet another form of fancywork. The delicate morning-glory design cross-stitched on perforated paper, *opposite,* is a charming example of such a mat. Instructions begin on page 82.

Among the most intriguing and American needlework fads of the late 19th century was the passion for crazy quilting. First introduced in the late 1870s, richly patterned coverlets, stitched from random scraps of fabric and lavished with embroidery, were an immediate and widespread sensation, and crazy quilting remained a popular pastime for decades. Many were pieced from fancy bits of silk, satin, brocades, and ribbons, like the velvet-bound beauty on page 71. Others were fashioned from humbler materials—cottons and wools—but the piecing was just as "crazy" and the embroidery just as lavish. The coverlet pictured *below*—a crazy patchwork version of a friendship quilt—is one example. Here, each plain patch is embellished with a name, initials, or pictures reminiscent of loved ones and special events—like the 400th anniversary of Christopher Columbus' journey to the Americas (the patch to the left of center). For information on embellishing and making your own crazy quilt, turn to pages 78–81.

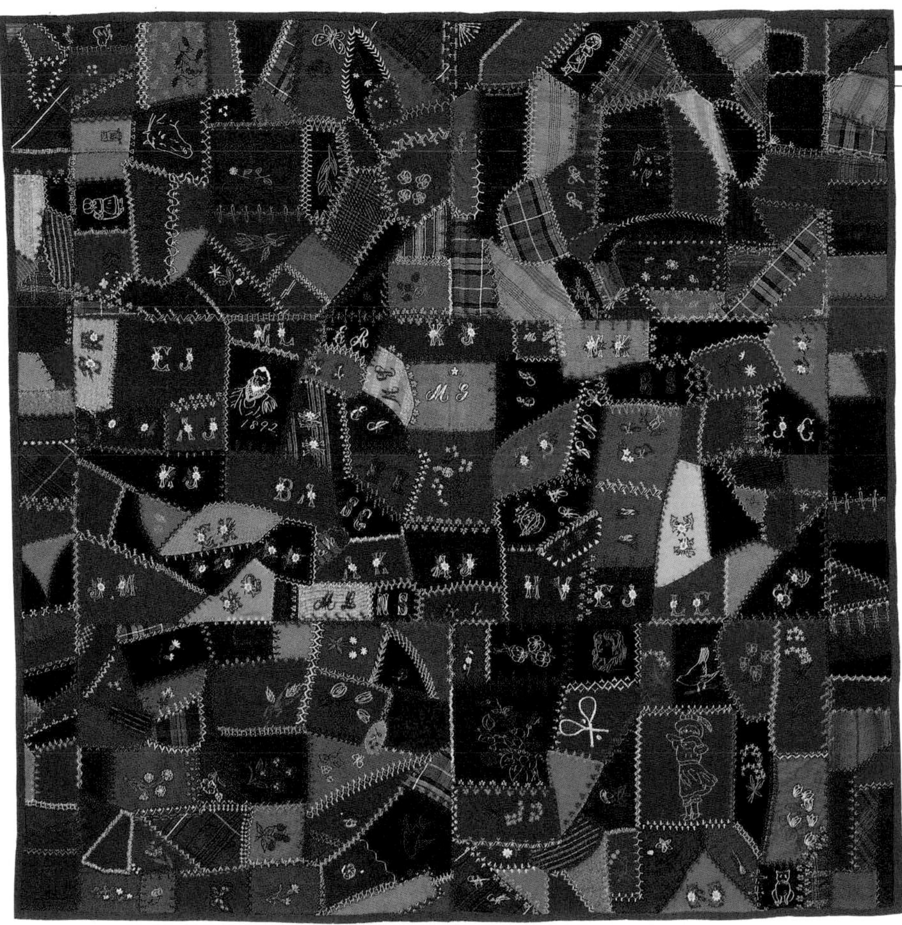

Stitchery mottoes are another fancywork fad that blossomed in the 1870s. Biblical quotations, familiar homilies, and sentimental sayings were among the favored motifs, but Home Sweet Home was the most popular motto of all to stitch.

In 1878, at the height of the fashion, an influential decorating manual of the day observed that these embellishments had become so popular, a tasteful home could not be considered finished without at least one framed motto.

Early designs were stitched in silk or wool thread over punched paper designs. Preprinted patterns either could be purchased by mail order or copied from fashionable publications such as *Peterson's Magazine.* Innovative stitchers later adapted similar designs for needlepoint or fabric embroidery.

Pictured *below* and *opposite* are cross-stitch versions of two Victorian favorites, declarations of hospitality that are as heartwarming today as they were a century ago.

Both designs are stitched in cotton floss on even-weave Aida cloth, but either easily could be translated into needlepoint or paper embroidery. (As an example, note that one corner of the morning-glory border on the Home Sweet Home sampler, *below,* is used to charming effect for the perforated paper picture mat on page 72.)

Rich jewel tones typical of the late Victorian era dominate these designs, but either would be equally handsome worked in a more subdued palette; select colors to complement your own decor. Instructions and patterns for the stitched mottoes pictured here are on pages 84–87.

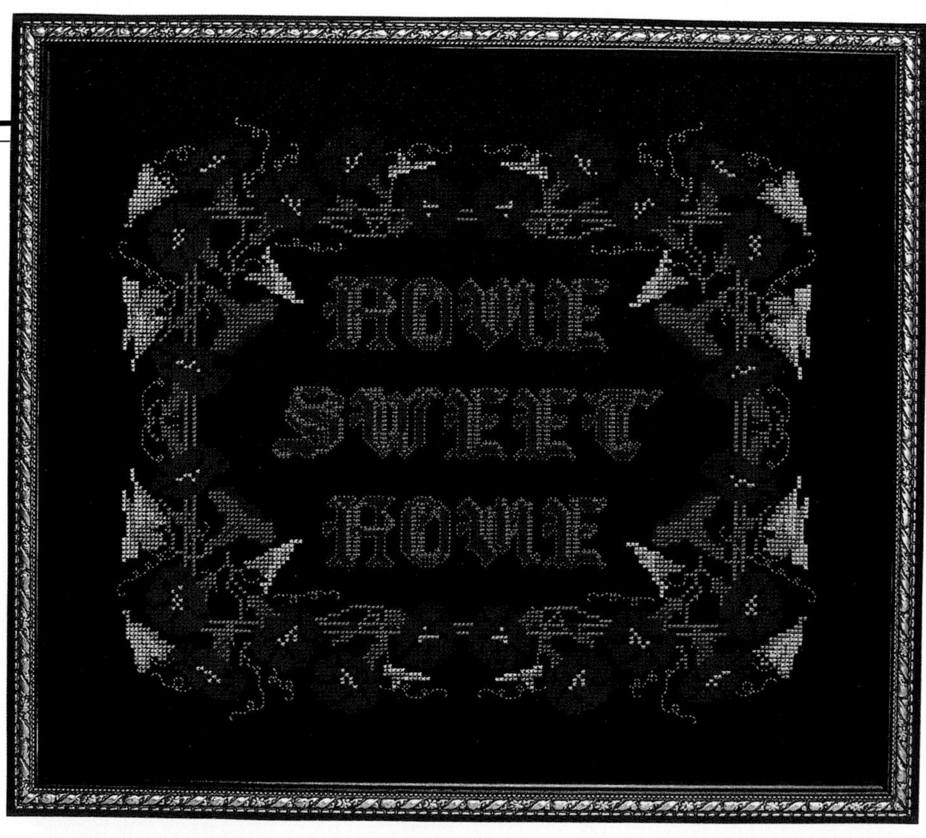

Welcome

THE HEART
REVEALED

Perhaps the most popular and enduring of all Victorian needle arts was Berlin work, named for the city where the first grid-printed patterns were produced in the early 1800s. Made of cross-stitches on canvas, this fashionable forerunner of today's needlepoint once was praised as the most elegant of all feminine accomplishments.

By mid-century, the well-dressed parlor—indeed, every room in the house—was apt to be filled to overflowing with lambrequins, bellpulls, footstools, pictures, and pillows stitched up in this simple, yet wonderfully versatile, technique. By 1840, more than 14,000 different designs were in print, many of an astonishing complexity and sophistication.

Early designs were worked in silk, but wool soon became the thread of choice, and later in the century beads often were mixed in among the cross-stitches. As new stitches were developed or adapted from other needlework techniques, the modern-day art of needlepoint came into its own.

A bouquet of tulips bound by a blue-checked bow graces the pillow *opposite,* and the lavish bowl of fruit on the pillow *below* springs from the black background. This pair of pillows are needlepoint adaptations of traditional Berlin-work motifs.

Crochet a wonderfully textured afghan like the one shown, *opposite,* from soft, fluffy, strawberry-color yarn to go with either of the needlepoint pillows.

Instructions for the needlepoint pillows and the crocheted afghan begin on page 88.

EMBELLISHMENTS FOR CRAZY QUILTING

It is the profusion of varied fabrics and personalized decorative detail that makes antique crazy quilts interesting to examine and new crazy quilts so much fun to make.

Today's fabric stores stock a myriad of lush fabrics, delectable laces, novelty buttons, and colorful ribbons that offer great possibilities for crazy quilting.

Selecting fabrics

Because crazy quilts rarely are used and washed in the same manner as other quilts, any fabric can be used—even ones considered too fragile or impractical for traditional quilts.

For elegance, experiment with velvet, velveteen, moiré, satin, and silk. For a more informal look, use cotton, wool, and thin-wale corduroy. The remnant table at any fabric store is a wonderful hunting ground for small pieces of exotic fabrics suitable for crazy quilting.

Scraps of ribbon, clothing, handkerchiefs, neckties, upholstery, and leftover fabrics are fun to use, especially if they have sentimental value.

Mix textures, patterns, and solids

Use different fabric textures and patterns to achieve the integrated mix that makes a crazy quilt so delightful.

A solid fabric without nap displays embroidery to its best advantage, but a quilt made with just solids requires a lot of embellishment to be interesting—add random pieces of brocade or paisley print to balance the solids. In the same way, napped fabrics, such as velvet, will add interesting texture when mixed with other fabrics.

Embroidery

Embroidery is to crazy quilting as frosting is to a cake. The stitches *opposite* and others can be used to cover seam lines or embellish a narrow fabric strip or ribbon. Victorian crazy quilts are rich tapestries of embroidered animals, flowers, and Oriental motifs. Outlines of a baby's hands or feet often appear.

Stitch embroidery motifs and pictures onto large fabric pieces that can be trimmed to fit into the patchwork, or onto a pieced block before the quilt is assembled.

Any drawing or photograph you can trace can become an embroidery motif.

Spiders and webs

Victorian crazy quilts frequently feature an embroidered spider and a web. According to European folklore, spiders in needlework are a symbol of good fortune.

A web is easy to stitch. The spokes and concentric rings of the web are couched in place as shown, *opposite*. Use metallic threads to make a web shimmer. A web is most effective when it is stitched in a light-color thread on a dark background.

Use beads for the spider's body; make lazy daisy or straight stitches for the legs.

Other embellishments

Once the quilt is completely filled, add trims such as lace, ribbon, and appliqués. Small doilies and lacy handkerchiefs add interest.

Cover seam lines and appliqués with embroidery, then add beads and buttons as desired. Clusters of buttons create interesting shapes. Novelty buttons, such as flowers, stars, and animals, add a touch of whimsy.

BASIC EMBROIDERY STITCHES

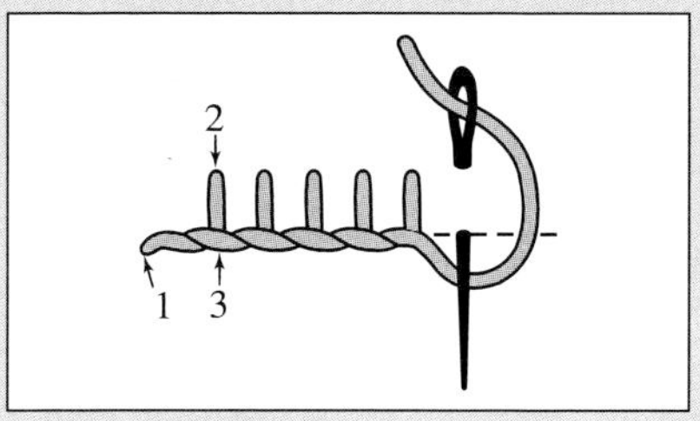

BUTTONHOLE STITCH

CHAIN STITCH

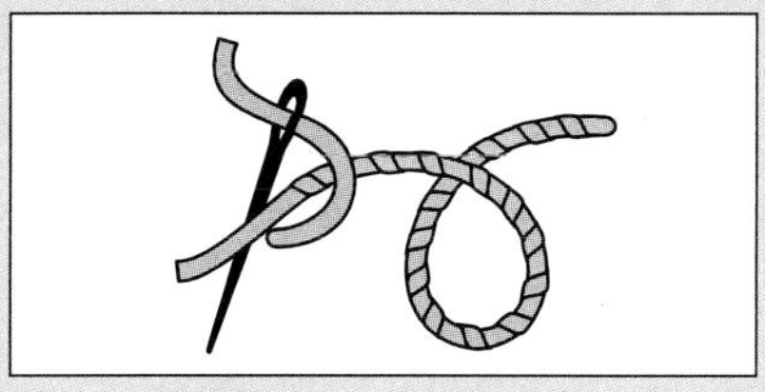

COUCHING STITCH

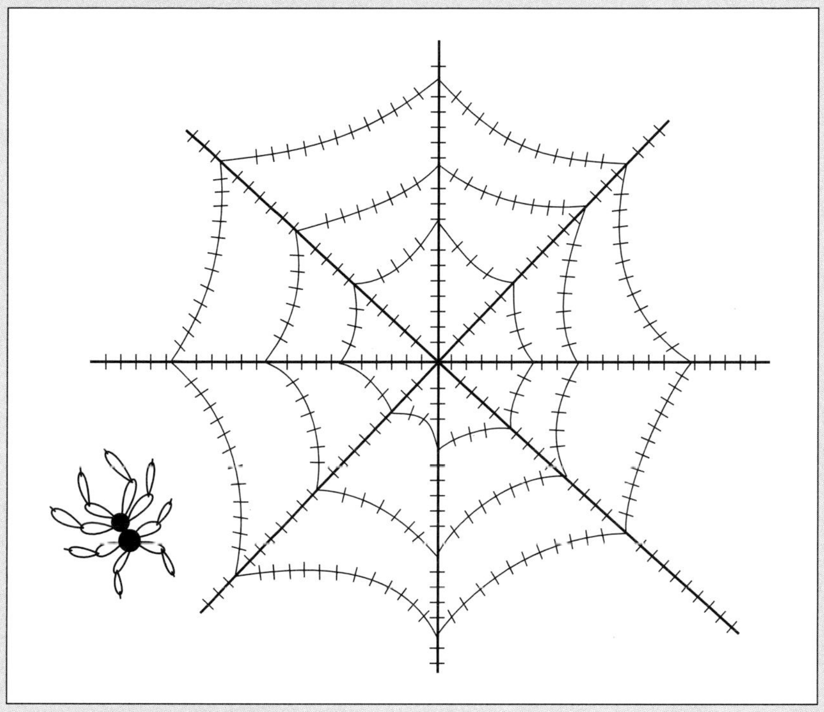

SPIDER WEB AND SPIDER

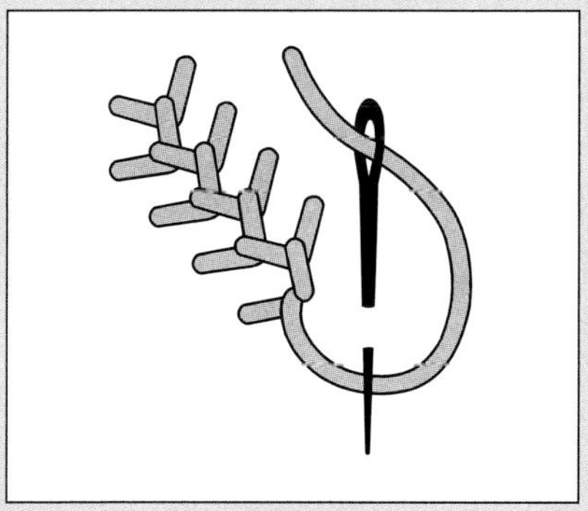

FEATHER STITCH

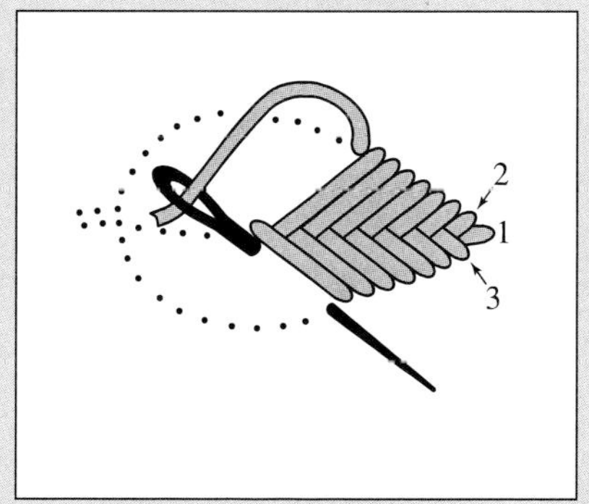

FISHBONE STITCH

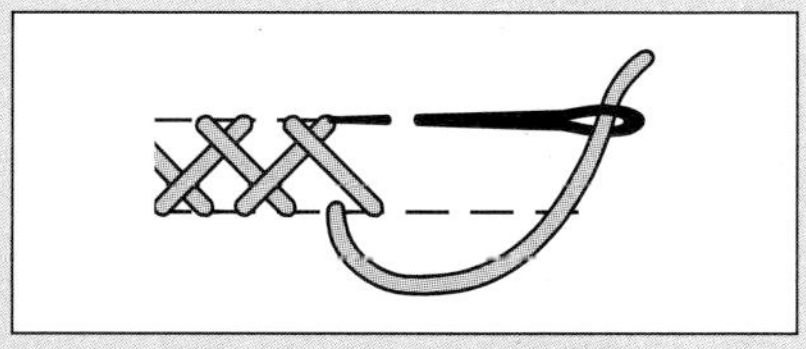

HERRINGBONE STITCH

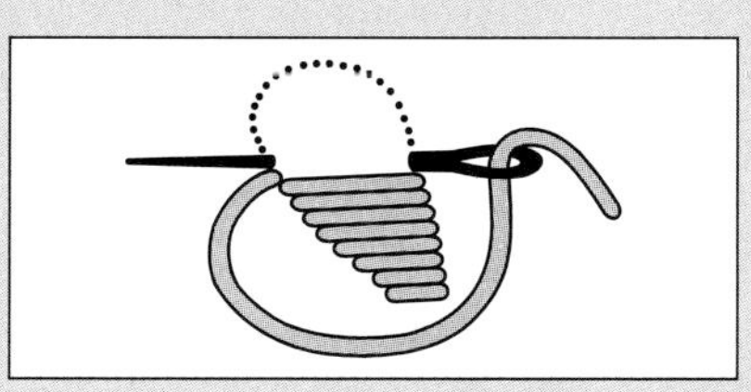

SATIN STITCH

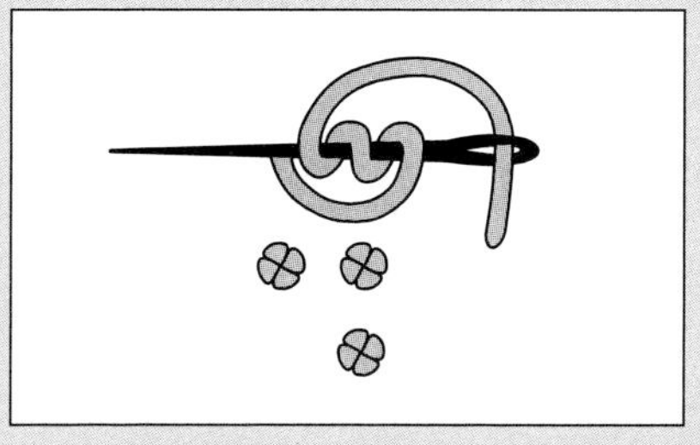

FRENCH KNOT

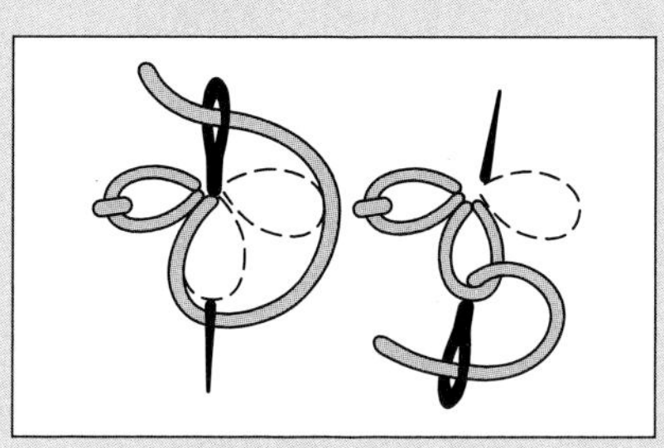

LAZY DAISY STITCH

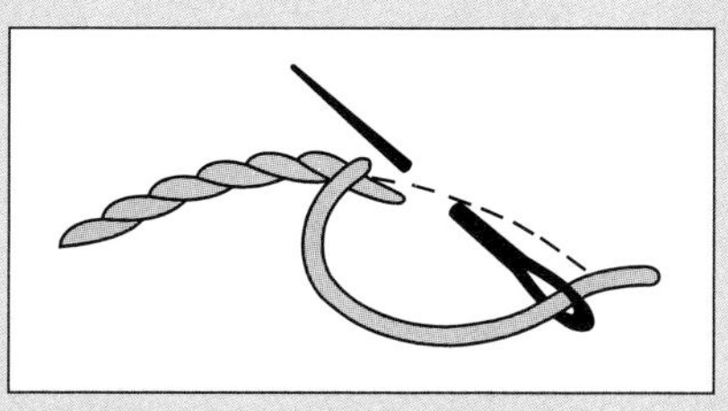

OUTLINE (or STEM) STITCH

CRAZY-QUILTING TECHNIQUES

The charm of crazy quilting is that there is no set pattern, thus no two quilts are the same. A crazy quilt grows as it is worked—too much planning rarely produces the satisfactory results achieved by spontaneity.

Working on a foundation

A base fabric serves as a foundation for a crazy quilt. Crazy quilting is done by embellishing the foundation with fabrics, embroidery, and trims. For a large quilt, it is practical to make small units that are then joined.

To make a crazy-quilted garment, begin with foundation pieces that are slightly larger than the actual pattern piece; once the foundation pieces are covered with crazy quilting, cut them to the size and shape of the patterns.

Victorian construction techniques

Victorian crazy quilters nearly always appliquéd the fabric pieces onto the foundation in a random fashion. In some cases, a large piece was basted onto the foundation and then smaller pieces were stitched on or around it.

In some quilts, construction units remain defined in the finished work. In others, pieces at the edges of adjacent blocks were appliquéd over each other to obscure the joining line.

Modern construction techniques

Crazy quilts can be stitched by machine. Two techniques are described here. Steps 1a–d, *right,* describe the Fan Method; steps 2a–c, *opposite, top,* explain the Center Method. A combination of techniques is shown in steps 3, 4, and 5, *opposite, bottom.*

When the crazy-quilted piece is completely assembled, layer it atop backing fabric and bind the edges (few crazy quilts have batting between the layers). Tying the top and backing fabric together is optional.

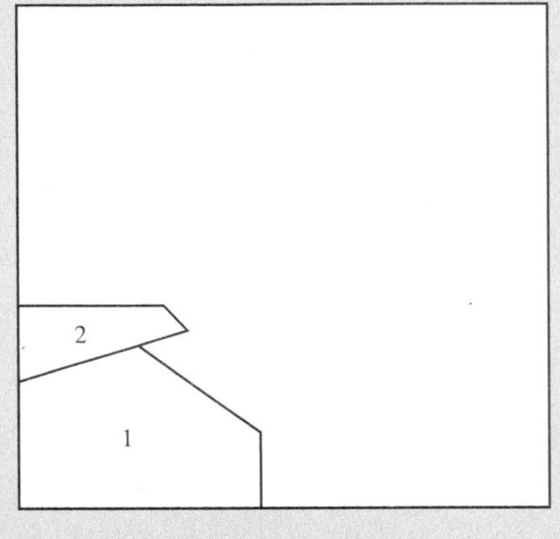

1a. With the Fan Method, you start in a corner and build outward, fanning from one side of the foundation to the other. Begin by placing Piece 1 flush with one corner of the foundation. This piece should have four or five sides as shown *above.* Place Piece 2 on top of Piece 1 with right sides together; machine-stitch through the pieces and the foundation. Flip the second piece right side up and press.

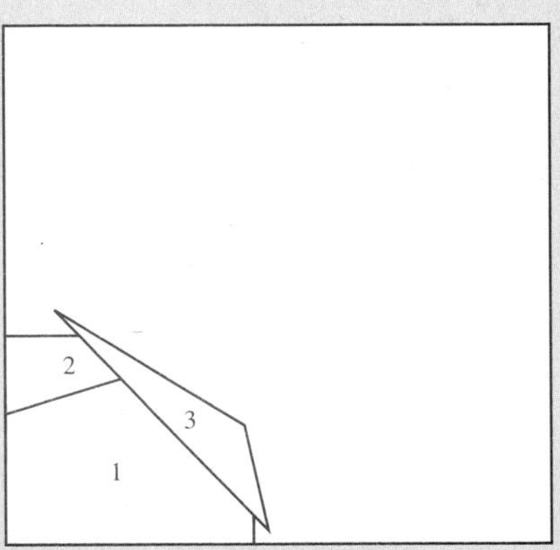

1b. Align Piece 3 with the second side of the corner piece, making sure it extends over both of the previously sewn pieces. Stitch it down in the same manner as before. Trim any excess fabric from the seam allowance, then flip Piece 3 right side up and press it flat.

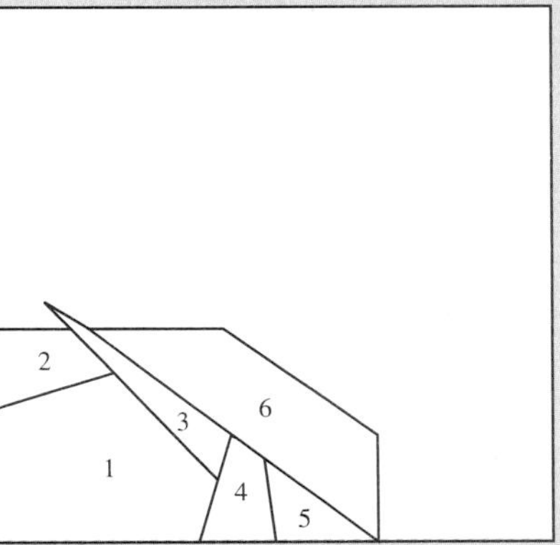

1c. Cover the third side of the corner piece with Piece 4 in the same manner—sew it down, flip it over, and press it flat. When all the sides of Piece 1 are stitched, start working back in the opposite direction to lay down the next level as indicated by pieces 5 and 6, *above.*

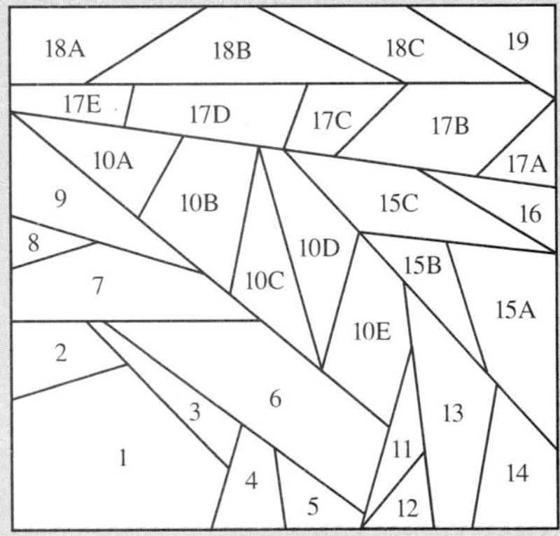

1d. Fan back and forth from right to left, then left to right, adding pieces until the foundation is filled. If you encounter an awkward angle, it's easiest to appliqué the edges in place. To fill in a long edge, piece a separate unit that can be stitched in place as one piece (see pieces 10, 15, 17, and 18, *above*). Trim each seam allowance and press each piece flat before adding another.

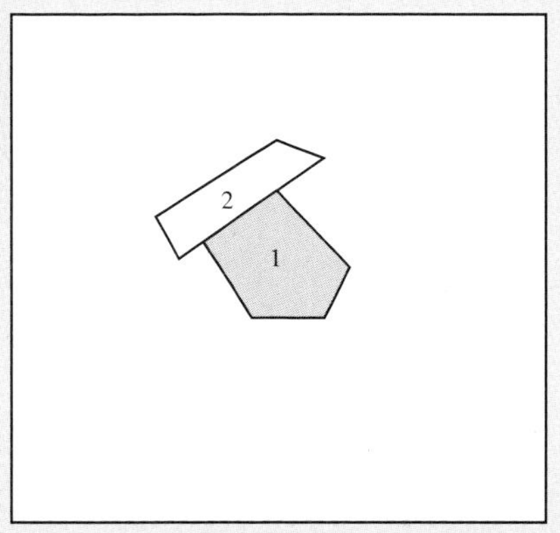

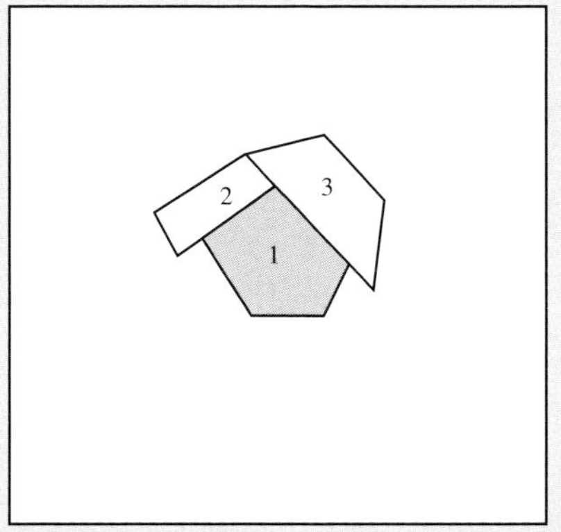

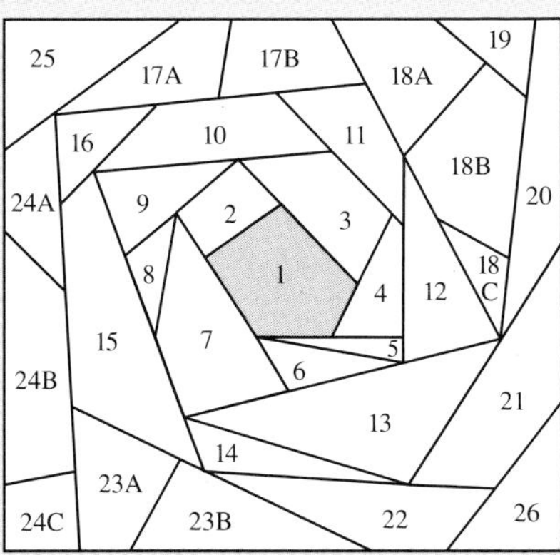

2a. Begin the Center Method by placing Piece 1 at the approximate center of the foundation. If this is a dark fabric, it will appear to recede, bringing attention to the center; a light fabric will have the opposite effect. Piece 1 should have five or six sides. With right sides together, sew the next fabric piece onto any side of Piece 1 using a standard ¼-inch seam allowance. Flip Piece 2 right side up, then press it flat.

2b. Stitch Piece 3 onto the next side of the center piece, making sure it completely covers the edges of pieces 1 and 2 as shown *above*. Trim excess fabric from the seam allowance, flip Piece 3 right side up, then press. The work can go clockwise or counterclockwise, but maintain the same direction throughout construction of the block.

2c. Continue adding fabric pieces in this manner, working outward from the center. To fill in a long edge, piece a separate unit that can be sewn in place as one piece (see pieces 17, 18, 23, and 24, *above*). Once the foundation is filled, trim all pieces even with the edges of the foundation. If you are working with separate blocks, stitch embroidery designs on each block as desired before joining them.

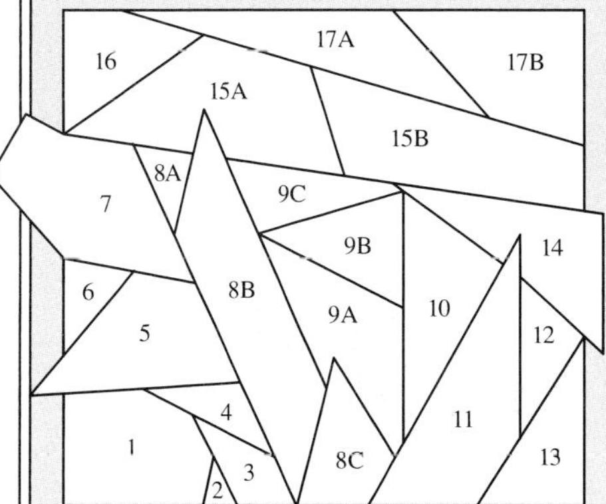

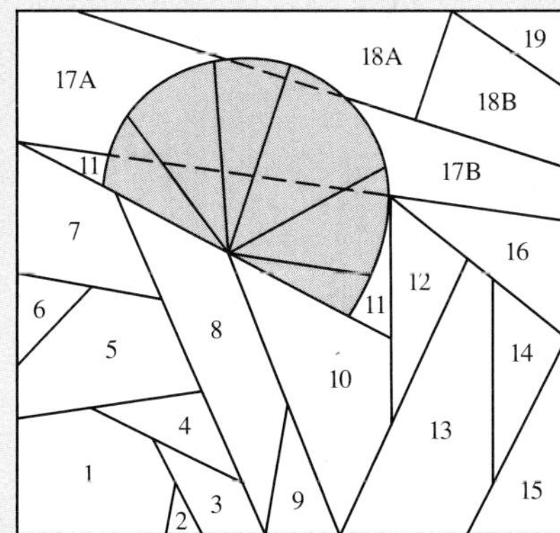

3. Combine techniques for added interest. As you sew, leave some points and angles unstitched so they can be appliquéd over an adjacent piece later (see pieces 8B, 8C, and 11, *above*). Overlapping pieces break up long seam lines. Leave some pieces at the block edges untrimmed (see pieces 5, 7, and 14, *above*) so they can be appliquéd onto the next block to cover the seam.

4. Appliqués cover seam lines and trouble spots, and their varied shapes add charm to a crazy quilt. Hearts, crescent moons, bows, and flowers are some appliqué motifs that work nicely in crazy quilting. When the piecing is complete, hand-stitch appliqués over the seams to interrupt straight lines.

5. Pieced fans frequently are seen in antique crazy quilts. A fan can be appliquéd onto the crazy quilt piecing or stitched into a seam as shown *above*. The curved edge is left loose as you add more pieces; then it is appliquéd over the completed patchwork. This is an excellent way to introduce curves and shapes that break up long, straight seam lines.

FLOWER AND VINE ANTIMACASSAR

Shown on page 71.
Antimacassar measures 18x12 inches.

MATERIALS

Clark's Big Ball crochet cotton, Size 20 (300-yard ball): 2 balls of ecru
Size 10 steel crochet hook

Abbreviations: See page 99.
Gauge: 5 sp = 1 inch; 5 rows = 1 inch.

INSTRUCTIONS

Note: To make the antimacassar, follow the chart *below* and work from the top of the design (the straight edge) toward the bottom. This piece is worked using the filet crochet technique. Refer to page 157 for more information.

Beg along the top edge, ch 255.

Row 1: Dc in fourth ch from hook, and in next 251 chs; ch 3, turn.

Row 2: Sk first dc, dc in 3 dc, * ch 2, sk 2 dc, dc in next dc; rep from * across row—82 sp made; dc in last 2 dc and in top of turning ch-3; ch 3, turn.

Rows 3–68: Work following the chart, *below.* Fasten off at the end of Row 68.

As bls dec at the beg of rows, do not work ch to turn; simply turn work, sl st over to starting point, then ch 3, and complete the beg bl.

Block and press the finished piece.

PICOT WHEEL-MOTIF TABLECLOTH

Shown on page 72.
Cloth measures approximately 66x90 inches.

MATERIALS

Clark's Big Ball 3-cord crochet cotton, Size 20 (400-yard ball): 26 balls of cream (No. 42)
Size 11 steel crochet hook

Abbreviations: See page 99.
Gauge: One motif measures approximately 3½ inches in diameter.

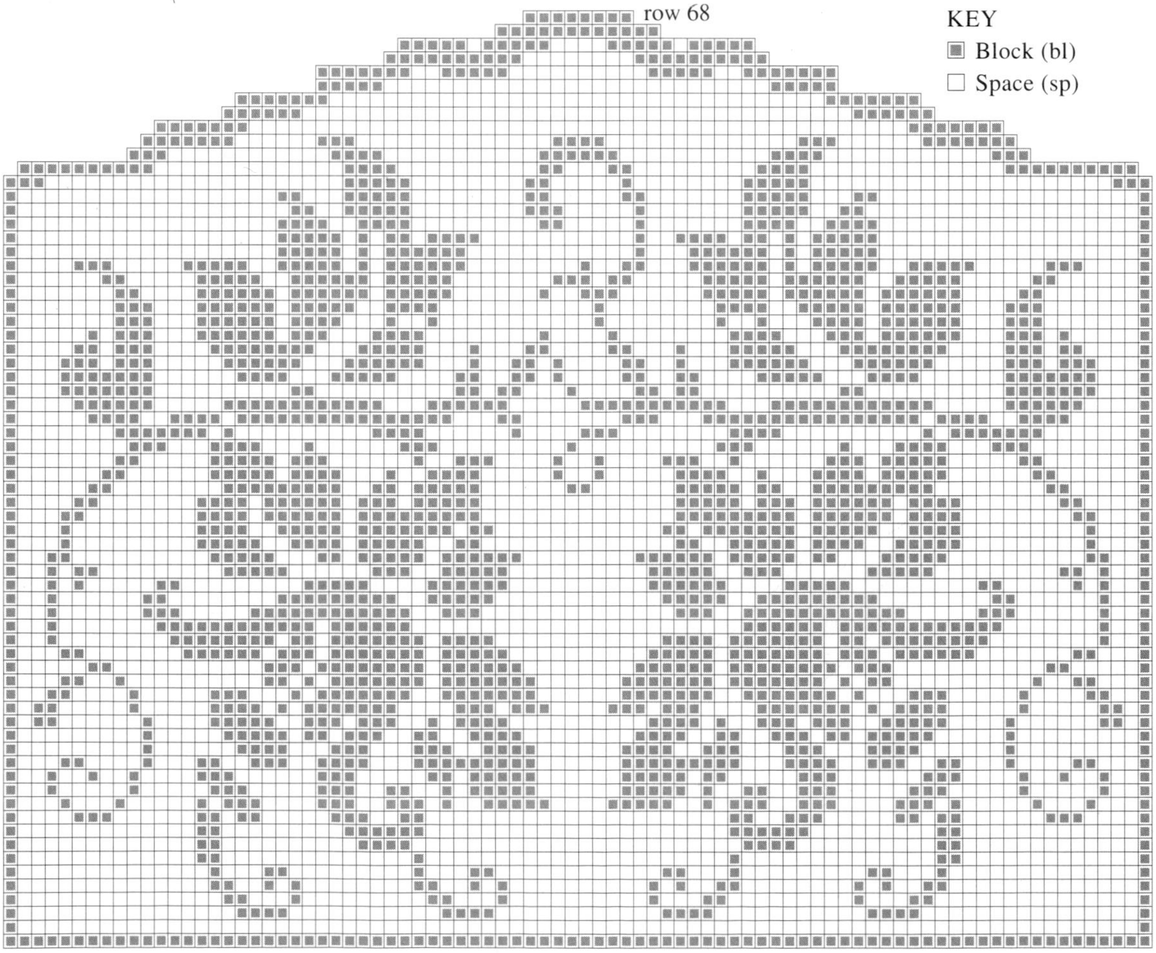

row 68

KEY
■ Block (bl)
□ Space (sp)

row 1

FLOWER AND VINE ANTIMACASSAR

INSTRUCTIONS

Note: This cloth consists of 561 motifs. There are 22 rows; the even-numbered rows consist of 26 motifs, and the odd-numbered rows consist of 25 motifs.

First Motif

Ch 6, join with sl st to form ring.

Note: The spokes in the center of the wheel are made from quintuple treble crochets (qt-trc). To make a qt-trc, yo hook 6 times, draw up lp in ring, (yo, draw through 2 lps on hook) 7 times.

Rnd 1: Ch 9 to count as 1 qt-trc and ch-1; (qt-trc, ch 1) 23 times in ring; join with sl st in eighth ch of beg ch-9.

Rnd 2: Sl st into next ch-1 sp, ch 3, 2 dc in same sp; * ch 1, 3 dc in next ch-1 sp; rep from * around; end ch 1, join with sl st in top of beg ch-3.

Rnd 3: Ch 1, sc in same st as join; (ch 5, sk 3 dc, sc in next sp) 24 times; join last ch-5 to beg sc.

Rnd 4: Sl st to third ch of ch-5, ch 3, in same ch work dc, ch 1, and 2 dc; * **in third ch of next ch-5 work 2 dc, ch 1, and 2 dc—shell made;** rep from * around; join with sl st in top of beg ch-3—24 shells.

Rnd 5: * Ch 3, dc in ch-1 sp of shell, **(ch 3, sl st in top of dc—picot made)** 3 times, ch 3, sc bet shells; rep from * around; end sc bet last 2 shells; fasten off.

Second Motif

Work as for First Motif through Rnd 4.

Rnd 5 (joining rnd): * Ch 3, dc in ch-1 sp of shell, picot in top of same dc, ch 1, sc in center picot of corresponding point of First Motif, sl st in top of same dc of Second Motif and picot in top of same dc; ch 3, sc bet shells; rep from * 3 times more (4 points joined), then complete as for Rnd 5 of First Motif.

Rep the Second Motif, joining a total of 25 motifs for the first row of the cloth.

For the first motif of the second row, rep the Second Motif, joining it into the four picots in the side of the first motif of the first row. Make another motif, joining it into four picots of the last motif worked, then into four picots in the first motif of the first row and into four picots of the second motif in the first row. Cont joining each motif in the same manner until 26 motifs are joined.

Note: The picots you join into will be opposite the motif you are working on. Eventually, all 12 picots are joined into all of the rows except the first and last row of the cloth.

CROSS-STITCHING WITH BEADS

Cross-stitching with beads is similar to traditional cross-stitch on fabric except you consider bead color rather than floss color and work only the first half of the stitch.

Materials needed

For the projects in this book we used 28-count linen for stitching with beads. Use a floss color that matches the fabric you are using.

Glass beads for cross-stitching are available from needlework stores.

A No. 11 quilting needle is narrow enough to go through the holes in the beads, yet the eye is large enough that a strand of floss will fit through it.

Stitching

To begin stitching, hold the thread in back of the fabric and bring the needle up in the lower left corner of the thread intersection. Run the needle through a bead and back through the fabric from front to back, crossing two threads diagonally and ending in the upper right corner.

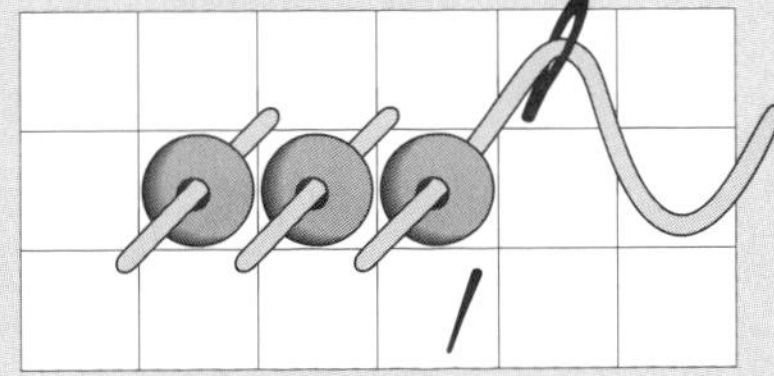

MORNING-GLORY PICTURE MAT

Shown on page 72.
The mat opening measures approximately 4¾x6¼ inches.

MATERIALS

10x12-inch pieces of tan perforated paper and tan paper
One skein *each* of DMC embroidery floss in the colors listed on the color key
Size 24 or 26 tapestry needle
Crafts knife to cut opening

INSTRUCTIONS

Use the chart for the sampler on pages 84 and 85. The chart is given in two sections. The shaded row of stitches on page 85 is repeated from page 84 and is used only as a guide in moving from one pattern section to the other. Do not rework this row of stitches.

Separate floss and use three strands to work cross-stitches over one square of perforated paper.

Measure 2⅜ inches up from the bottom and 2¼ inches in from the left side of the perforated paper; stitch the left side of the double border lines with No. 725. Stitch the morning-glory design as indicated by the blue line at the top left corner of the chart above the border lines just stitched. Stitch the border lines about 1 inch beyond the flower at the far right.

Stitch the border lines across the bottom for 4¼ inches. Turn the chart sideways and work the two flowers and the bud that are below the dashed line on page 85. Continue the double border lines up the right side for about 5 inches or until they come to the border lines stitched at the top. Use two strands of No. 700 and backstitch the tendrils. Backstitch the flowers with No. 333.

Cut out the center of the mat leaving two squares of paper beyond the stitches.

Cut a mat from tan paper of the same dimensions and shape to go behind the perforated paper mat so the photo doesn't show through the holes.

HOME SWEET HOME SAMPLER

Shown on page 74.
Finished size of stitchery is 11¾x10 inches on 14-count Aida cloth.
Design is 163x140 stitches.

MATERIALS

18x24-inch piece of 14-count black Aida cloth
DMC embroidery floss in the colors listed on the color key; number of skeins required appears in parentheses
Size 24 or 26 tapestry needle
White paper tape

INSTRUCTIONS

The *top half* of the chart is in two sections, *right* and *opposite.* The shaded row of stitches on page 85 is repeated from page 84 and is used only as a guide when moving from one page to the other. Do not rework this row of stitches.

Tape the raw edges of the fabric to prevent threads from raveling. Separate floss and use three strands to work cross-stitches over one square of Aida cloth. Refer to page 69 for a diagram of this stitch.

Measure 9 inches up from the bottom and 6½ inches in from the left side of the fabric. Begin stitching the bottom left side of the top half of the border here.

Once you complete the chart as shown, turn the chart upside down to complete the bottom border. The areas shaded gray below the halfway point are for placement only. When the border stitches are complete, stitch the saying.

Use two strands of No. 3607 to backstitch the outline of all letters. Backstitch the vine tendrils with No. 580. Backstitch the flowers with No. 915. Refer to page 69 for a diagram of this stitch.

When stitching is complete, remove the tape and press the back of the fabric with a damp cloth and a warm iron. Frame as desired.

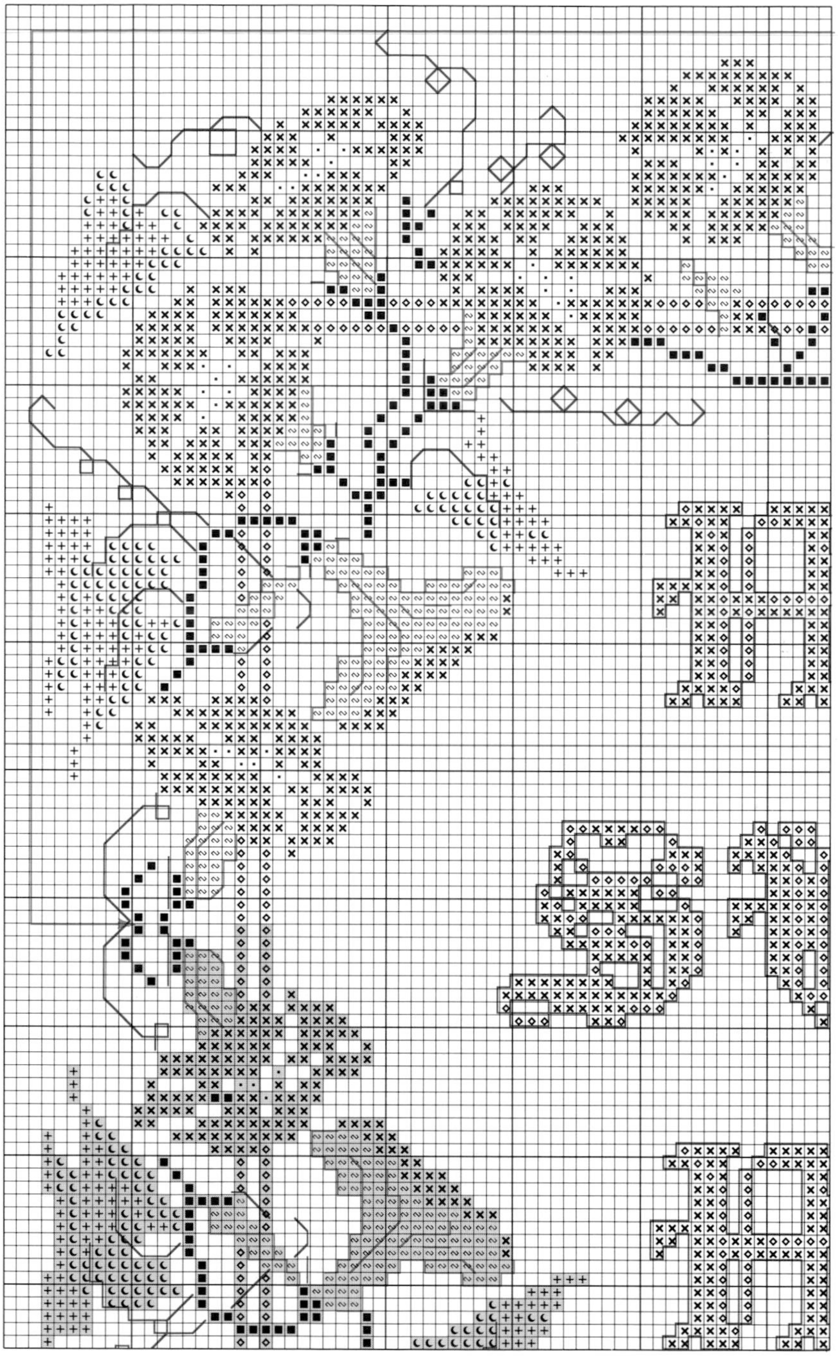

HOME SWEET HOME SAMPLER AND MORNING-GLORY PICTURE MAT

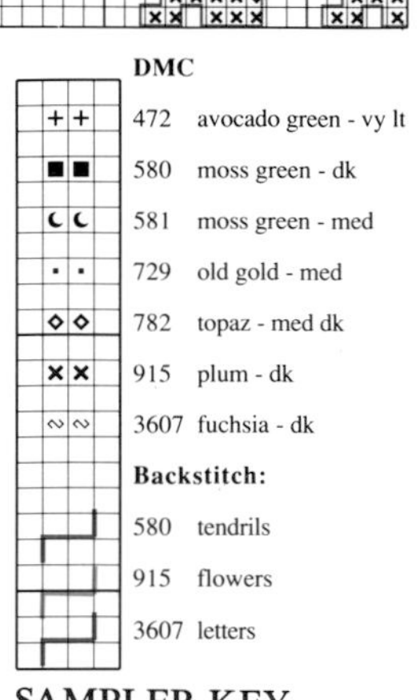

SAMPLER KEY

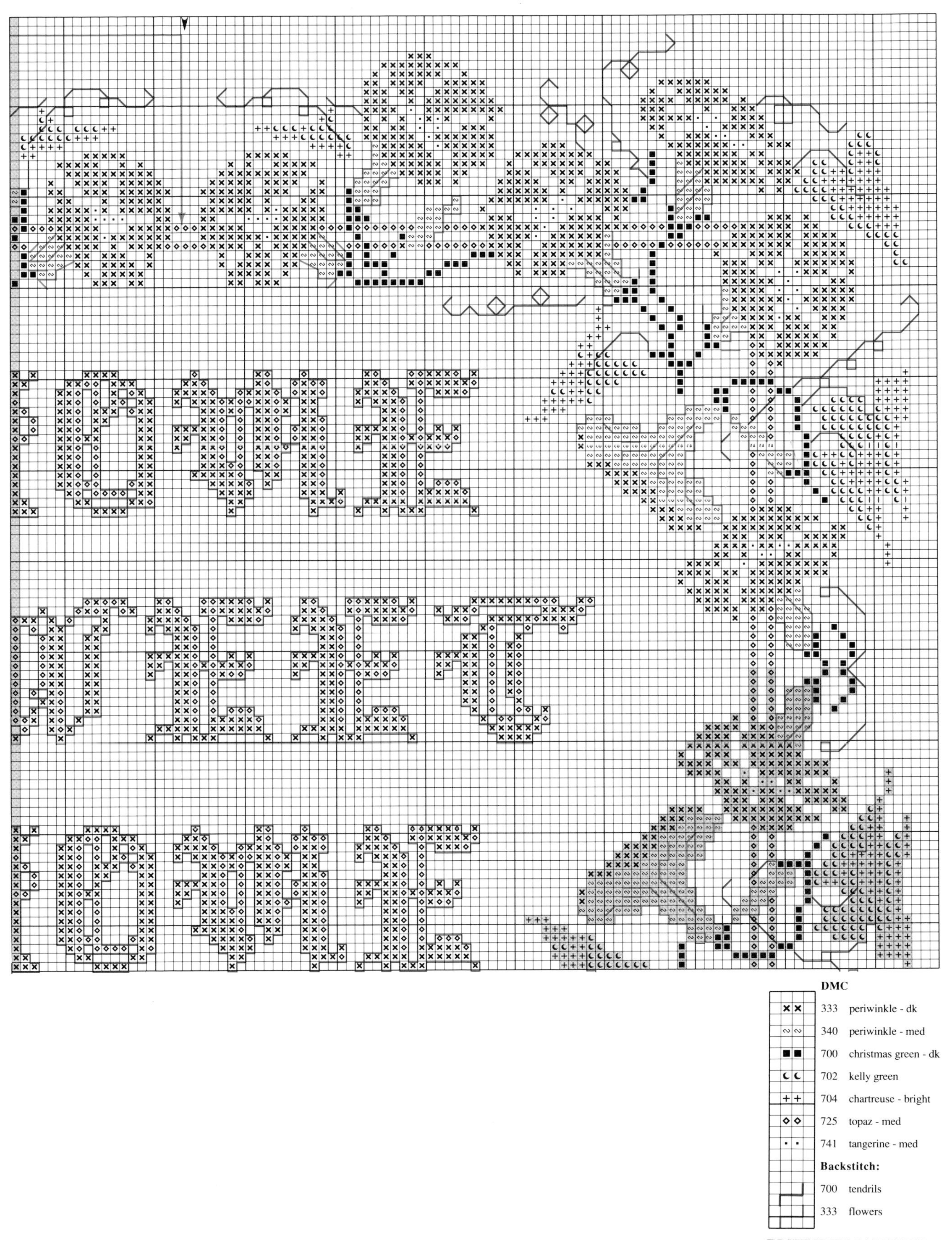
DMC
333 periwinkle - dk
340 periwinkle - med
700 christmas green - dk
702 kelly green
704 chartreuse - bright
725 topaz - med
741 tangerine - med
Backstitch:
700 tendrils
333 flowers
PICTURE MAT KEY

FLORAL WELCOME SAMPLER

Shown on page 75.
Finished size of stitchery is 13⅝x8 inches on 14-count Aida cloth.
Design is 193x111 stitches.

MATERIALS

18x24-inch piece of 14-count Aida cloth—we used Tuscan Tan by Charles Craft

DMC embroidery floss in the colors listed on the color key; number of skeins required appears in parentheses

Size 24 or 26 tapestry needle

White paper tape

INSTRUCTIONS

The chart is given in two sections, *right* and *opposite.* The shaded row of stitches on page 87 is repeated from page 86 and is used only as a guide in moving from one page to the other. Do not rework this row of stitches.

Tape the raw edges of the fabric to prevent threads from raveling. Separate the floss and use three strands to work cross-stitches over one square of Aida cloth. Refer to page 69 for a diagram that illustrates how to work this stitch.

Measure 7½ inches up and 7 inches in from the bottom left corner of the fabric. Begin stitching the bottom of the W there. Finish stitching the word, then stitch the border.

Use three strands of No. 3689 to make French knots in the flowers at the top of the W. Refer to page 79 for a diagram that illustrates how to work this stitch.

When stitching is complete, remove the tape and press the back of the fabric with a damp cloth and a warm iron. Frame as desired.

FLORAL WELCOME SAMPLER

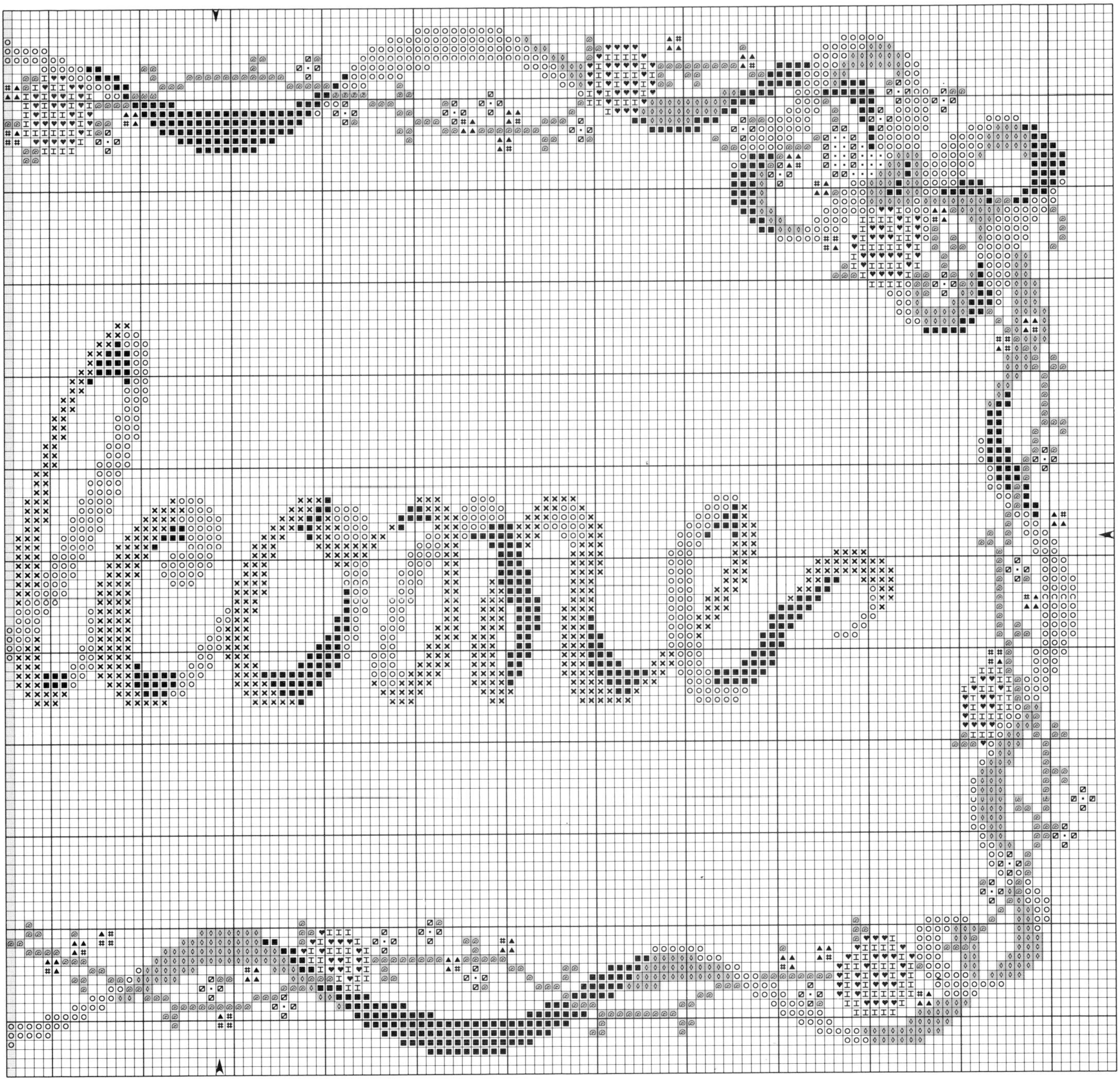

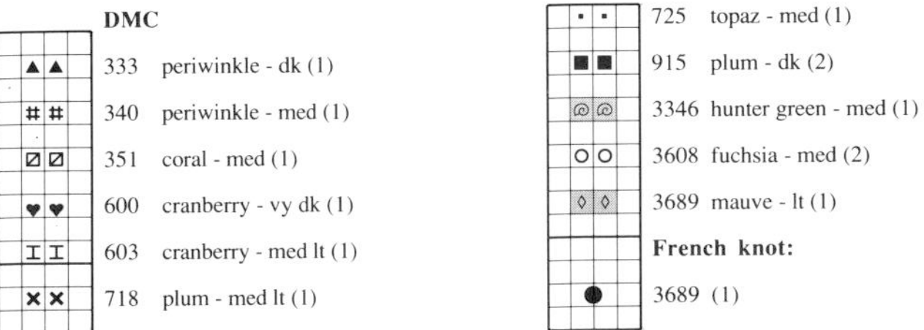

DMC	
333	periwinkle - dk (1)
340	periwinkle - med (1)
351	coral - med (1)
600	cranberry - vy dk (1)
603	cranberry - med lt (1)
718	plum - med lt (1)
725	topaz - med (1)
915	plum - dk (2)
3346	hunter green - med (1)
3608	fuchsia - med (2)
3689	mauve - lt (1)

French knot:

3689	(1)

FRUIT COMPOTE PILLOW

NEEDLEPOINT FRUIT COMPOTE PILLOW

Shown on page 77.
Design makes a 12x16-inch pillow top.

MATERIALS

18x22-inch piece of 10-count needlepoint canvas
Paternayan 3-strand yarn in the colors listed on the color key; number of yards are listed in parentheses
Tapestry needle
White paper tape

INSTRUCTIONS

Work from the chart, *opposite.*

Tape the raw edges of the canvas to prevent yarns from catching and the canvas from raveling as you work.

Using three strands of yarn, work the design in continental or basket-weave stitch over one mesh of canvas. Refer to page 69 for diagrams that illustrate how to work these stitches.

Measure 8 inches from the left side of the canvas and 4½ inches from the bottom. Begin stitching the foot of the compote dish there.

Fill in the background in basket-weave stitch with black yarn to complete a piece that measures 12x16 inches.

Block the finished needlepoint; refer to page 14 for tips. Finish the stitched design as a pillow or as desired.

PATERNAYAN

970 red (14 yards)
942 pink red (8 yards)
804 peach (14 yards)
800 rust orange (14 yards)
770 yellow orange (5 yards)
853 orange (9 yards)
261 white (38 yards)
312 lavender (10 yards)
313 light lavender (7 yards)

STRAWBERRY LACE CROCHETED AFGHAN

Shown on page 76.
Afghan measures approximately 49x60 inches.

MATERIALS

Brunswick Windmist yarn (135-yard skein): 24 skeins of cherry (No. 2857)
Size J crochet hook

Abbreviations: See page 99.
Gauge: Each panel = 16⅓ inches wide.

INSTRUCTIONS

PANEL (make 3): *Note:* The ch-2 turning at the end of each row is *not* counted as hdc.

Ch 60.

Foundation row: Hdc in third ch from hook, dc in next ch, sk ch; ch 1, in next ch work hdc, ch 1, and hdc; sk 2 ch, **insert hook in next ch, (yo, pull up lp) 3 times, yo and draw through all all lps on hook—puff st made,** puff st in same ch; sk ch, dc in next ch; sk ch, (in next ch work sc and 2 dc, sk 2 ch) 5 times; dc in next ch, sk 3 ch, ch 1, in next ch work (dc, ch 1) 5 times; sk 3 ch, dc in next ch; sk ch, (in next ch, work sc and 2 dc, sk 2 ch) 5 times; dc in next ch, sk ch, ch 1, in next ch work hdc, ch 1, and hdc; sk 2 ch, work 2 puff sts in next ch; sk ch, dc in next ch, hdc in last ch; ch 2, turn.

Note: To work a front post dc in the next row, yo, insert the hook from the front, around the back to the front of the post of the dc; then complete the dc stitch. You will not work in the top lps of the dc, but around the post.

Row 1 (right side): Hdc in hdc, **dc around post of next dc from the front—front post (FP) dc made;** ch 1, in ch-1 bet puff sts work hdc, ch 1, and hdc; work 2 puff sts in ch-1 sp bet hdcs; FP around next dc, (in next sc, work sc and 2 dc) 5 times; work FP around next dc, ch 2; (sc in ch-1 sp, ch 3) 3 times, sc in ch-1 sp, ch 2; FP around next dc, (in next sc, work sc and 2 dc) 5 times; FP around next dc, ch 1, in ch-1 sp bet puff sts work hdc, ch 1, and hdc; work 2 puff sts in ch-1 sp bet hdcs; FP around next dc, hdc in hdc; ch 2, turn.

Note: To work a back post dc in the next row, yo, insert the hook from the back, around the front to the back of the post of the dc; then complete the dc stitch. You will not work in the top lps of the dc, but around the post.

Row 2 (wrong side): Hdc in hdc, **dc around post of next dc from the back—back post (BP) dc made;** ch 1, in ch-1 sp bet puff sts, work hdc, ch 1, and hdc; in ch-1 sp bet hdcs, work 2 puff sts; BP around FP, (in next sc, work sc and 2 dc) 5 times; BP around FP, (ch 3, sc in ch-3 sp) 3 times, ch 3; BP around FP, (in next sc, work sc and 2 dc) 5 times; BP around FP, ch 1, in ch-1 sp bet puff sts work hdc, ch 1, and hdc; in ch-1 sp bet hdcs, work 2 puff sts; BP around FP, hdc in hdc; ch 2, turn.

Row 3: Hdc in hdc, FP around BP, ch 1, in ch-1 sp bet puff sts work hdc, ch 1, and hdc, in ch-1 sp bet hdcs work 2 puff sts; FP around BP, (in next sc, work sc and 2 dc) 5 times; FP around BP, sk ch-3, (ch 3, sc in next ch-3 sp) 2 times, ch 3; FP around BP, (in next sc, work sc and 2 dc) 5 times; FP around BP, ch 1, in ch-1 sp bet puff sts work hdc, ch 1, and hdc; work 2 puff sts in ch-1 sp bet hdcs; FP around BP, hdc in hdc; ch 2, turn.

Row 4: Hdc in hdc, BP around FP, ch 1, in ch-1 sp bet puff sts work hdc, ch 1, and hdc; in ch-1 sp bet hdcs work 2 puff sts; BP around FP, (in next sc, work sc and 2 dc) 5 times; BP around FP, sk ch-3, in next ch-3 sp work (ch 1, dc) 5 times, ch 1; BP around FP, (in next sc, work sc and

continued

2 dc) 5 times; BP around FP, ch 1, in ch-1 sp bet puff sts work hdc, ch 1, and hdc; in ch-1 sp bet hdcs work 2 puff sts; BP around FP, hdc in hdc; ch 2, turn. Rep rows 1–4 32 times or until desired length. Fasten off.

ASSEMBLY: With wrong sides of two panels together, attach yarn at bottom of hdcs. * Sc through matching hdcs, ch 2, and sc in next matching hdcs; rep from * along two panels, making adjustments to make work lie flat; end with sc in last two matching hdcs. Fasten off. Rep with remaining panel.

With right side of afghan facing you, attach yarn at the bottom corner of the left long edge. * Working along the length of the afghan, sc in hdc, ch 2; rep from * along the edge, making any adjustment so work will lie flat; end with sc in last hdc, sl st in end. Fasten off. Rep this edging on the opposite edge of the afghan, working from top to bottom.

With right side facing you, sc across the top and bottom ends, taking care to make work lie flat.

FRINGE: Cut yarn into 24-inch strands. With four strands held together and the right side of the afghan facing you, fold strands in half. Using the crochet hook, pull the strands through the first sc on the end; pull yarn ends through the loop just formed. Continue to add fringe in every fourth sc across each end. To alternate the fringe knots, take four strands from adjoining tassels and knot them 1½ inches from the afghan edge. Repeat for the other end. Trim the fringe ends even.

	PATERNAYAN
△△	613 light green (6 yards)
@@	612 medium green (14 yards)
★★	620 shamrock green (7 yards)
⊠⊠	611 green (7 yards)
▮▮	610 dark green (12 yards)
○○	845 light peach (4 yards)
ЖЖ	846 peach (6 yards)
☾☾	844 dark peach (8 yards)
++	944 light pink (3 yards)
◆◆	943 pink (7 yards)
♥♥	942 dark pink (7 yards)
✳✳	814 yellow orange (1 yards)
■■	220 black (1 yard)
##	332 lavender (2 yards)
⋈⋈	331 purple (5 yards)
••	546 light blue (4 yards)
∾∾	544 medium blue (4 yards)
II	543 blue (4 yards)
▲▲	541 royal blue (4 yards)
✥✥	542 light royal blue (6 yards)
	Background:
	262 cream (160 yards)

Needlepoint Tulip Bouquet Pillow

Shown on page 76.
Design makes a 14-inch-square pillow.

MATERIALS

18-inch-square piece of 10-count needlepoint canvas
Paternayan 3-strand yarn in the colors on the color key; number of yards is listed in parentheses
Tapestry needle; white paper tape

INSTRUCTIONS

The chart is in two sections, *right* and *opposite.* The shaded row of stitches on page 91 is repeated from page 90 and is used only as a guide in moving from one page to the other. Do not rework this row of stitches.

Tape the raw edges of the canvas to prevent yarns from catching.

Using three strands of yarn, work the design first in continental or basket-weave stitch over one mesh of canvas. Measure 3 inches from the left side of the canvas and 2¾ inches up from the bottom. Begin stitching the base of the flower stems there. Work the checks in the bow in Scotch stitch using three strands of yarn. Refer to page 69 for diagrams that illustrate how to work these stitches.

Fill in the background in basket-weave stitch with off-white yarn to complete a 14-inch square.

Block the finished needlepoint; refer to page 14 for tips. Finish as desired.

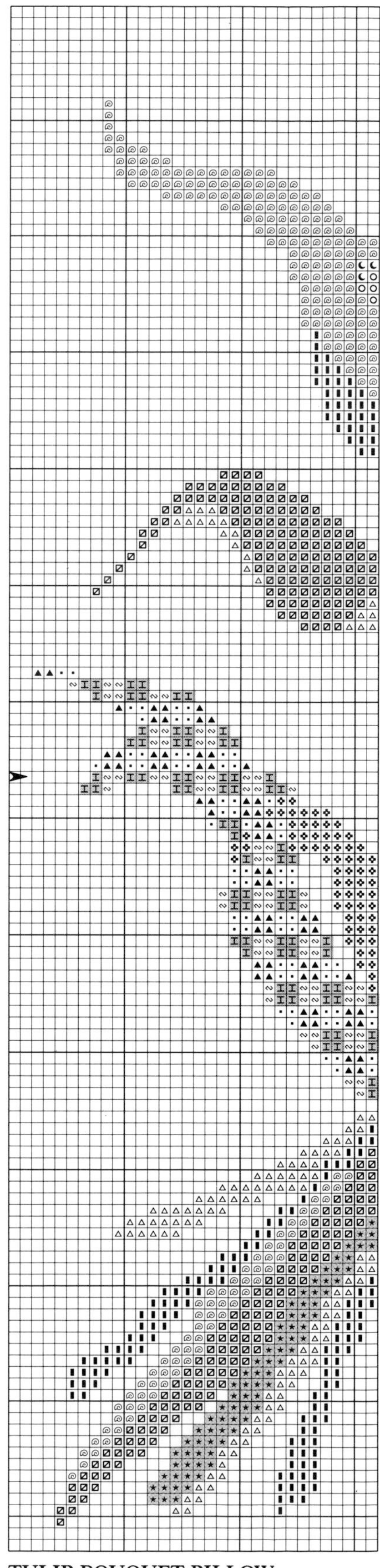

TULIP BOUQUET PILLOW

Gentleman's Domain

Whether it be an oak-paneled den in a sumptuous mansion or a chair by the fire in a simple cottage, every Victorian gentleman claimed one corner of the house as his very own, his sanctum sanctorum. Here he sought refuge from the hustle and bustle of the workaday world, taking a moment to peruse his paper, smoke his pipe, and contemplate the day's events in comfort and tranquillity.

Bowlsby hits stride
in new Iowa position
Tiger in training

Furnishings for a gentleman's private retreat were designed to impart a sense of ease and repose. Fine leather upholstery, polished wood, and richly patterned carpets in subdued tones offered a handsome backdrop for decorative accents in more exuberant shades. Indeed the very latest colors for gentlemen's appointments, as described in the fashionable *Delineator* magazine of October 1894, included such intriguing hues as "Delgado (deep dregs-of-wine), Volnay (a new marine), Lunel (geranium), Ameroes (shade of sky) . . . and Isolde (new gold)"—a palette that inspired the crocheted afghan-stitch afghan and needlepoint pillow pictured on page 93. Cozy coverlets like this jewel-tone beauty and the lovely knitted blue throw, *opposite,* are just the thing to keep a gentleman snug as he settles down for a short read or a long Sunday nap.

Other accessories with traditional masculine motifs include a cheery chicken-pattern pillow worked in filet crochet, *above,* and the striking stag's head needlepoint stool, *opposite.* Footstools were considered especially appropriate gifts to stitch for men in the Victorian era, and patterns were published regularly in magazines of the day. Fashions in designs and coloration changed over the years, of course; needlepoint backgrounds worked in Prussian blue, for example, were commonly seen after the 1870s.

Instructions and patterns for the projects shown on page 93, *opposite,* and *above* are on pages 96–101.

JEWEL-TONE AFGHAN

Shown on page 93.
Afghan measures 51x64 inches.

MATERIALS

Brunswick Pomfret sport yarn (1¾-ounce ball): 26 balls of black (No. 560)
Size F afghan hook or size to obtain gauge cited below
Size D aluminum crochet hook
Paternayan 3-strand yarn in the following colors and quantities of ¼-pound hanks: 3 hanks of yellow (No. 770); 1 hank *each* of fuchsia (No. 352), violet (No. 300), royal blue (No. 541), teal blue (No. 591), and green (No. 682)
Tapestry needle

Abbreviations: See page 99.
Gauge: With Size F afghan hook, 6 sts and 5 rows = 1 inch.

INSTRUCTIONS

In afghan stitch, there are two steps to each row. In these instructions, the steps are referred to as the first half of the row and the second half of the row.

On the first half of the row, you work from right to left into the stitches of the previous row, picking up loops and keeping them all on the afghan hook. On the second half of the row, you work from left to right, removing the loops from the hook. This back and forth stitching creates the afghan-stitch pattern.

Narrow panel (make 2)

With black yarn and afghan hook, ch 63.

Row 1 (first half): Insert hook in the top lp of second ch from hook, yo (wrap the yarn around the hook), draw the yarn through the ch and leave the lp on the hook—2 lps on the hook; * insert the hook in the top lp of the *next* ch, yo, draw the yarn through the ch and leave the lp on the hook; rep from the * across the row—63 lps on hook.

Row 1 (second half): Working from left to right, yo, draw the yarn through the *first* lp on the hook. * Yo, draw the yarn through 2 lps on hook; rep from * across the row until 1 lp rem on hook. The last lp is the first st of the next row. The upright bars formed in the completed row are the foundation for working pat sts in subsequent rows.

Row 2 (first half): Sk the first upright bar; * insert the hook behind the *front* lp of the next upright bar, yo, draw the yarn through the bar and leave the lp on the hook; rep from * across the row until 62 lps on hook; draw up lp in next bar and in lp behind last st—63 lps on hook.

Row 2 (second half): Rep the second half of Row 1.

Rows 3–302: Rep Row 2 (first and second halves).

Last row (bind-off row): Sk the first upright bar, * **insert hook in front of the next bar, yo, draw the yarn through the bar and through the lp on the hook—sl st made and 1 lp on hook;** rep from the * across the row; fasten off.

Wide panel (make 1)

Ch 103. Work afghan stitch as for the narrow panels; bind off after Row 302.

CROSS-STITCHING THE PANELS: Following the color key for the chart, *opposite,* use two strands of Paternayan yarn and a tapestry needle to cross-stitch the geometric pattern on the three panels.

Skip the first edge stitch on the left side and the first row on the bottom of the panels.

Begin cross-stitching the narrow panels with Row 1 of the chart from A to B one time, then A to C one time. Work rows 1 through 40 of the chart seven times and rows 1 through 20 one time more.

Begin cross-stitching the wide panel with Row 1 of the chart from C to B one time, then A to B two times. Work rows 1 through 40 of the chart seven times and rows 1 through 20 one time more.

Shell strip (make two)

With black yarn and Size D crochet hook, ch 24.

Row 1: Sc in second ch from hook and in each ch to end; ch 3, turn.

Row 2: Sk first sc, dc in next sc; * ch 5, sk 4 sc, in next sc work **2 dc, ch 1, 2 dc—shell made;** rep from *, ending ch 5, dc in last 2 sc; ch 3, turn.

Row 3: Sk first dc, dc in next dc, * ch 5, shell in ch-1 sp of next shell; rep from *, ending ch 5, dc in last dc, dc in top of turning ch; ch 3, turn.

Row 4: Sk first dc, dc in next dc, * ch 2, sc in third ch of ch-5 of Row 2 working over the ch-5 of Row 3, ch 2, shell in next shell; rep from *, ending dc in last dc, dc in top of turning ch; ch 3, turn.

Row 5: Sk first dc, dc in next dc, * ch 5, shell in next shell; rep from *, dc in last dc, dc in top of turning ch; ch 3, turn.

Rep rows 3–5 for pat until the strip measures the same length as the afghan-stitch panels.

Sew a shell strip to each side of the wide afghan-stitch panel and sew the narrow afghan-stitch panels to the outside of both shell strips.

BORDER: *Rnd 1:* Beg at any corner, sc in each st around; end sl st to first sc.

Rnd 2: Ch 3, dc in next 2 sc, * ch 5, sk 4 sc, in next sc work a shell; rep from * to 3 sc from corner, work **dc in 3 sc, ch 3, ** and dc in next 3 sc—corner made;** rep from * along each side then work the corner; end last rep at **, sl st in top of beg ch-3.

Rnd 3: Ch 3, dc in next 2 dc, * ch 5, shell in ch-1 sp of next shell; rep from * to corner; dc in 3 dc, ch 4, ** dc in next 3 dc—corner; rep from * along each side then work the corner; end last rep at **, sl st in top of beg ch-3.

Rnd 4: Ch 3, dc in next 2 dc, * ch 2, sc in third ch of ch-5 of Row 2 working over the ch-5 of Row 3, ch 2, shell in next shell; rep from * to corner; dc in next 3 dc, ch 5, ** dc in next 3 dc—corner; rep from * along each side then work the corner; end last rep at **, sl st in top of beg ch-3; fasten off.

Lightly block finished afghan.

JEWEL-TONE PILLOW

Shown on page 93.
Pillow front measures approximately 14 inches square.

MATERIALS

18-inch-square piece of 10-count needlepoint canvas
Paternayan 3-strand yarn in colors and number of yards listed in parentheses on the color key
Tapestry needle; white paper tape
Fiberfill; 1 yard of fabric to make backing and ruffled wide piping and 60 inches of wide cotton cording for piping to make pillow as shown (optional)

INSTRUCTIONS

Bind the raw edges of the canvas with tape to prevent catching the yarn or raveling the canvas.

Follow the chart for the design, *below*. Use three strands of yarn to work the design in continental or basket-weave stitch and three strands to work the black background in basket-weave stitch. See page 69 for stitch diagrams.

Note: To make a larger or smaller pillow, work more or fewer repeats from the chart. Use the same half of the pattern you began with to end your design.

Begin stitching the design 2 inches from the top and 2 inches from the left side of the canvas. Begin stitching the first half of the design at the arrow (Row 20) on the chart. Work from Row 20 to Row 1 and from A to B. Repeat from A to B 2½ times more across the top of the canvas (end at C).

Stitch the second half of the chart directly below Row 1 on the canvas. Begin at the left side of Row 40. Work from Row 40 to Row 21 and from A to B on the chart. Repeat from A to B 2½ times more (end at C).

Alternate the first and second halves of the chart until there are three of each half; complete the stitching by working 20 more rows of the first half of the chart.

Fill in the background with black yarn. To make the pillow assembly easier, work an extra row of black continental stitches around the design.

FINISHING: Refer to the blocking tips on page 14; block the needlepoint to shape.

Assemble the stitched piece into a pillow as shown or as desired.

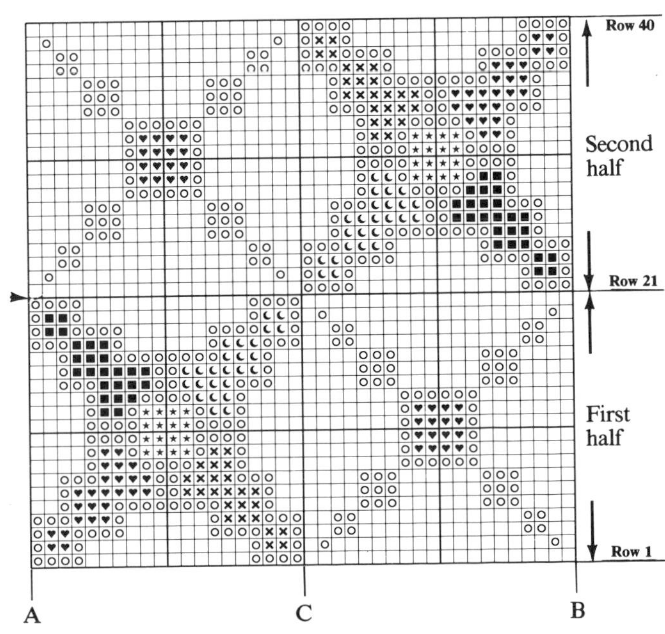

JEWEL-TONE AFGHAN AND PILLOW

PATERNAYAN		
♥♥	352	fuchsia (20 yards)
☾☾	300	violet (12 yards)
■■	541	royal bue (12 yards)
××	591	teal blue (12 yards)
★★	682	green (7 yards)
○○	770	yellow (70 yards)
	Background:	
	220	black (140 yards)

FILET CROCHET CHICKENS

Shown on page 95.
The finished size of the crocheted rectangle is approximately 16x12 inches.

MATERIALS

Clark's Big Ball crochet cotton, Size 30 (350-yard ball): 2 balls of ecru
Size 13 steel crochet hook
17x13-inch piece of solid color fabric for pillow front; ¾ yard of print fabric for wide ruffled piping and pillow backing; 2 yards of 1-inch-wide cording; sewing thread; sewing needle; fiberfill (optional)

Abbreviations: See page 99.
Gauge: 6 sp = 1 inch; 7 rows = 1 inch.

INSTRUCTIONS

Ch 264.

Row 1: Dc in fourth ch from hook and in each ch across—262 dc, counting turning ch as dc; ch 3, turn.

Row 2: Sk first dc, dc in next 3 dc; * ch 2, sk 2 dc, dc in next dc; rep from * across until 4 sts remain—85 sp; dc in next 3 dc and in top of turning ch; ch 3, turn.

Row 3: (Refer to the chart on page 98.) Sk first dc, dc in next 3 dc, ch 2, dc in next dc, (2 dc in next ch-2 sp, dc in next dc) 3 times; * (ch 2, dc in next dc) twice; (2 dc in next ch-2 sp, dc in next dc) twice; rep from * 8 times more; (ch 2, dc in next dc) twice; 2 dc in next ch-2 sp, dc in next dc; ** (ch 2, dc in next dc) twice; (2 dc in next ch-2 sp, dc in next dc) twice, rep

continued

FILET CROCHET CHICKENS
KEY ■ Block (bl) □ Space (sp)

from ** 8 times more; (ch 2, dc in next dc) twice; (2 dc in next ch-2 sp, dc in next dc) 3 times; ch 2, dc in next 3 dc, dc in top of turning ch; ch 3, turn.

Rows 4–87: Keeping to pat as established on the chart, *opposite,* work all even-numbered rows from left to right and all odd-numbered rows from right to left; fasten off at end of Row 87.

FINISHING: Wash and steam-press crocheted rectangle to shape.

Make pillow as desired. Tack the crocheted rectangle to the front of the completed pillow with plain fabric behind it.

TEXTURED BLUE KNIT AFGHAN

Shown on page 94.
Afghan measures approximately 48x60 inches.

MATERIALS

Coats & Clark Red Heart Classic yarn (3½-ounce skein): 13 skeins of blue gray (No. 807)

28-inch-long Size 6 and Size 8 circular knitting needles or size to obtain gauge

Abbreviations: See *right.*

Gauge: In pattern stitch 4½ sts = 1 inch.

INSTRUCTIONS

Using Size 6 circular needles, cast on 215 sts.

Row 1: K 5, p 205, k 5.

Row 2: K across.

Row 3: K 4, * yo, k 2 tog, k 2; rep from * across row to last 3 sts; yo, k 2 tog, k 1.

Row 4: K across.

Change to Size 8 needles.

Row 5: K 5, p 205, k 5.

Row 6: K across.

Row 7 (right side): K 7, * k 1, yo, k 8, sl 1, k 2 tog, psso, k 8, yo; rep from * across row to last 8 sts; k 8.

Row 8 and all even-numbered rows unless specified: K 5, p to last 5 sts, k 5.

Row 9: K 7, * k 2, yo, k 7, sl 1, k 2 tog, psso, k 7, yo, k 1; rep from * across row to last 8 sts; k 8.

Row 11: K 7, k 2 tog, * yo, k 1, yo, k 6, sl 1, k 2 tog, psso, k 6, yo, k 1, yo, sl 1, k 2 tog, psso; rep from * across row to last 9 sts; yo, ssk, k 7.

Row 13: K 7, * k 4, yo, k 5, sl 1, k 2 tog, psso, k 5, yo, k 3; rep from * across row to last 8 sts; k 8.

Row 15: K 7, * k 1, yo, sl 1, k 2 tog, psso, yo, k 1, yo, k 4, sl 1, k 2 tog, psso, k 4, yo, k 1, yo, sl 1, k 2 tog, psso, yo; rep from * across row to last 8 sts; k 8.

Row 17: K 7, * k 6, yo, k 3, sl 1, k 2 tog, psso, k 3, yo, k 5; rep from * across row to last 8 sts; k 8.

Row 19: K 7, k 2 tog, * yo, k 1, yo, sl 1, k 2 tog, psso, yo, k 1, yo, k 2, sl 1, k 2 tog, psso, k 2, (yo, k 1, yo, sl 1, k 2 tog, psso) twice; rep from * across row to last 9 sts; yo, ssk, k 7.

Row 21: K 7, * k 8, yo, k 1, sl 1, k 2 tog, psso, k 1, yo, k 7; rep from * across row to last 8 sts; k 8.

Row 23: K 7, * (k 1, yo, sl 1, k 2 tog, psso, yo) 5 times; rep from * across row to last 8 sts; k 8.

Row 24: K across.

Rep rows 5–24 until afghan measures approximately 59 inches; end with a Row 24. Change to Size 6 needles and work rows 1–5. Bind off all sts.

Block lightly.

KNITTING AND CROCHETING ABBREVIATIONS

beg	begin(ning)
bet	between
bl(s)	block(s)
CC	contrasting color
ch(s)	chain(s)
cl	cluster
cont	continue
dc	double crochet
dec	decrease
dtr	double treble crochet
grp	group
hdc	half-double crochet
inc	increase
k	knit
LH	left hand
lp(s)	loop(s)
MC	main color
p	purl
pat	pattern
pc	popcorn
psso	pass sl st over
rem	remaining
rep	repeat
RH	right hand
rnd	round
sc	single crochet
sk	skip
sl	slip
sl st	slip stitch
sp	space(s)
ssk	slip, slip, knit
st(s)	stitch(es)
st st	stockinette stitch
tbl	through back loop
tog	together
trc	treble crochet
ttr	triple treble crochet
yo	yarn over
*	repeat from * as indicated
**	repeat from ** as indicated or end last repeat at ** as indicated
( )	repeat between ( ) as indicated
[ ]	repeat between [ ] as indicated

STAG'S HEAD FOOTSTOOL COVER

Shown on page 94.
The center design area measures 10x12 inches. Our needlepoint cover measures 20 inches square.

MATERIALS

26-inch-square piece of 10-count canvas (or the amount needed for your project)
Paternayan 3-strand yarn in the colors and number of yards listed in parentheses on the color key
White paper tape
Tapestry needle
Needlepoint frame (optional)

INSTRUCTIONS

Bind the raw edges of the canvas with tape to prevent yarn from catching on it and the canvas from raveling. If desired, use a needlepoint frame for ease in working on a project of this size.

The chart for the stag's head is given in two sections, *right* and *opposite.* The shaded row of stitches on page 101 is repeated from page 100 and is used only as a guide in moving from one pattern section to the other. Do not rework this row of stitches.

Use three strands of yarn to work the design and background in continental or basket-weave stitch. Use two strands of yarn to cross-stitch the background dots over one canvas thread. See page 69 for diagrams of all three stitches.

Locate the center of the canvas and the center of the chart; begin stitching here. After the design area is stitched, work the background area to the size of your cushion top or pillow form. Add a few extra rows of blue to the background for seam allowance. After the blue background is completed, cross-stitch the tan dots.

Refer to page 14 for tips for blocking needlepoint; block the finished piece. Use it as upholstery for a footstool or assemble it into another project as desired.

PATERNAYAN

Symbol	No.	Color
⧄	465	lt. beige (5 yards)
≈	464	beige (3 yards)
▲	463	dk. beige (2 yards)
▪ (shaded)	444	tan (2 yards)
✚	571	navy blue (1 yard)
▬	441	brown (8 yards)
Ж	440	dk. brown (10 yards)
●	220	black (1 yard)
◇	612	lt. green (6 yards)
⋈	611	green (8 yards)
■	690	dk. green (10 yards)
✣	903	med. rose (10 yards)
♥	902	rose (7 yards)
Λ	901	dk. rose (5 yards)
○	443	lt. brown (90 yards)
Background:		
(blank)	501	blue gray (400 yards)

STAG'S HEAD FOOTSTOOL COVER

A Romantic Retreat

Lighter, airier, and more simply furnished than other rooms in the Victorian household, milady's bedchamber was the center of her private world, a room for every season and purpose. Here she primped and prepared for her daily role as wife and mother. It also was here that she withdrew for a moment of repose, to collect her thoughts, pamper herself, and dream her own special dreams.

Perhaps the most personal piece of furniture in a woman's boudoir was her vanity table. Stocked with combs and brushes, powders and perfumes, and all the exotic accoutrements of madam's toilette, it also was furnished with enchanting needlework trifles—often called bedroom elegancies—like those pictured on page 103.

Among milady's treasures are a dainty potpourri jar with a beaded lid and a heart-shape whimsy, stitched from velvet and trimmed with buttons, to hold her supply of hatpins. All are displayed on a lacy, star-shape, crocheted doily.

Although the bedchamber generally was considered off-limits to all but family members, it was nonetheless a showcase for some of the household's finest needlework. A handsome Arrowhead Star quilt, *opposite,* adds the finishing touch to a bed bedecked in lace. The hand-tucked top sheet boasts a double row of insertion lace and a deep, scalloped border, all worked in fine filet crochet. Completing the ensemble is a sumptuous pair of filet crochet pillow shams with a star flower pattern and scalloped edging.

Nestled in one corner of the bedchamber, a cozy settee, *below,* offers the perfect setting for a cup of tea, a quiet read, or a bit of needlework before bedtime. Comfortable complements like the redwork embroidered pillow with the crocheted bird border and the textured afghan knitted in squares of pink yarn invite one to settle in, relax, and unwind.

Instructions for the projects shown on page 103, *below,* and *opposite* are on pages 110–121.

In Victorian times, a woman often changed her personal surroundings to suit the seasons, much as she changed her wardrobe. For example, the simple muslin coverlet, *opposite,* with its lyrical pattern of grapes and vines, would have made a charming summer spread, perhaps replacing the patchwork quilt used during the winter. With alternating panels of plain fabric and filet crochet, the spread easily can be adapted to suit any size bed, and the crocheted designs also might be used for shutter or screen inserts or window panels, if one fancies.

The whimsical crocheted bag, *opposite,* was called a reticule in Great-Grandmother's day, and was once as essential an element of a lady's attire as her paisley shawl or a pair of gloves. Fashion decreed that this pretty but practical little pouch be small enough to dangle gracefully from wrist or waist, yet large enough to hold a lady's necessaries: handkerchief, fan, card case, and smelling salts. Our modern-day version is just the right size, stitched of glittery rainbow-color ombré yarn and finished with a flourish of tassels.

Sachets, *right,* are another dainty legacy from Great-Grandmother's day, when sweetly scented linens were considered the hallmark of a well-kept home. Many Victorian women took pride in composing their own recipes for potpourri, but these little pockets—patterned after antique cookie-cutter shapes—are filled with a store-bought mixture. We stitched them from fine mesh lace (to allow the scent to circulate freely), and trimmed the edges with a dash of braid, ribbons, and antique buttons.

Instructions for these projects begin on page 121.

Floral motifs were a perennial Victorian favorite, particularly for milady's chamber. And if one cared to believe the traditional "Language of Flowers"—a charming 18th-century conceit, which held that every blossom had its own special significance—then the flower pattern chosen conveyed an important message.

For example, the pretty pansy (also called heartsease) symbolized "thinking of you"—a most appropriate sentiment to encircle the portrait of a beloved friend or family member, as it does on the picture mat *below.* The original design might have been stitched in silks a century ago, but wool crewel yarn is used here to work the pattern in satin, long-and-short, and outline stitches.

Stylized forget-me-nots, worked in filet crochet for the panels of the small vanity screen *opposite,* were traditional symbols of true love. Needless to say, forget-me-nots were a favorite motif with women of all ages, but were considered particularly appropriate—and lucky—for those on the verge of marriage. This screen creates a lovely backdrop for showing off your favorite antique jewelry pieces or would look equally nice as a window shutter.

Beneath the screen, offering an elegant resting place for a special collection, is an unusual square doily with a triangular crocheted edging worked in a shell and block-and-space pattern that is similar to filet crochet.

Instructions and patterns for these projects begin on page 124.

HEART WHIMSY

Shown on page 103.
Whimsy measures approximately 6¼ inches across at its widest part.

MATERIALS

18-inch square of off-white velour
1 yard of white satin braid
1 yard of white satin cording
Three ½-inch pink ribbon roses
Assorted old buttons and pearl beads
Ecru sewing thread; sewing needle
Polyester fiberfill
6-inch square of mat board
Tracing paper
Nonpermanent fabric marker
Straight pins
Crafts knife
White crafts glue
Hot-glue gun and glue sticks
Fray Check liquid

INSTRUCTIONS

Trace the heart pattern, *below,* onto tracing paper; cut out the pattern.

Fold the fabric with right sides together; align the straight-of-grain arrow on the pattern with the straight grain of the fabric. Draw around the heart pattern. Cut out two hearts adding a ½-inch seam allowance to each.

On the right side of one heart, mark the blue topstitching lines.

On the wrong side of the other heart, mark the red slash lines. Put Fray Check on the marked slash lines. Allow the Fray Check to dry thoroughly. Cut along each slash line, taking care not to cut outside the area covered with the Fray Check.

Place the two heart shapes with right sides together. Machine-stitch the two heart pieces together. Clip the curves and the top center of the heart.

Carefully turn the heart right side out

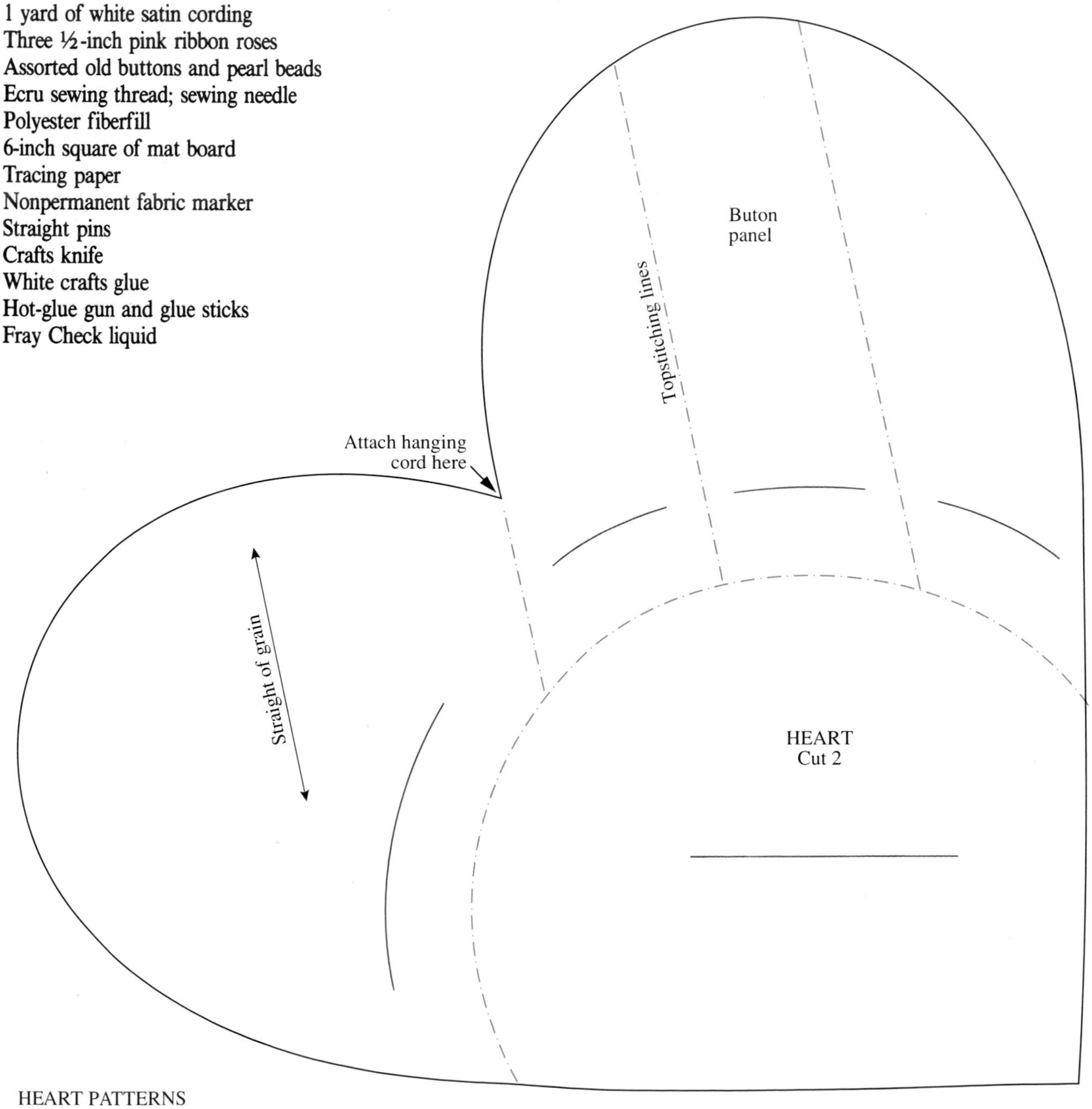

HEART PATTERNS

through one of the slashed openings.

With the marked side up, machine-stitch along blue topstitching lines.

Stuff each divided section firmly through the slashed openings in the back of the heart; hand-sew openings closed.

Trace the heart back pattern, *below,* onto tracing paper; cut out the pattern. Draw around the heart back pattern atop the mat board; cut out the heart back with the crafts knife.

Trace around the heart back pattern atop the velour fabric; add a ½-inch seam allowance when cutting the heart piece from the fabric. Clip the curves up to the pattern line.

Center the heart mat piece on the wrong side of the velour fabric piece. Clip the bottom point from the fabric heart; fold over the clipped edges of the fabric and glue them to the back of the mat board with white crafts glue.

Cut the cord into the following lengths: one 3-inch piece, two 5-inch pieces, and one 9-inch piece. Coat the ends of the cords with Fray Check to keep them from raveling. Using crafts glue, attach the 3-inch piece of cord along the shortest topstitching line. Pin in place at the top and bottom of the stitched line. Allow the glue to dry.

Use crafts glue to attach the two 5-inch pieces of cord along both sides of the button panel in the same manner.

Use crafts glue to attach the 9-inch piece of cord along the curved horizontal stitching line, covering and pinning the cord over all of the vertical cord ends. Allow the glue to dry.

Remove all the pins and turn the heart over. Glue the cord ends to the back of the heart.

With the right side up, glue then pin braid around the outside edge of the heart. Allow glue to dry. Remove all of the pins.

HANGING CORD: Turn the heart wrong side up. Cut a 12-inch piece of cord. Use a generous amount of glue to attach both ends to the center top of the back of the heart. Pin in place and allow the glue to dry. Remove the pins.

Tie an overhand knot in the cord loop close to the heart.

Place hot glue on the raised areas of the back of the fabric heart that will be covered by the heart back; place the heart back on top of the hot glue with the fabric-covered side facing out. Press firmly until the glue dries.

With the right side of the fan facing up, use crafts glue to attach ribbon roses over the horizontal cord on the right side of the center of the heart.

Referring to the photograph on page 103, hot-glue assorted buttons and pearls to fill the middle panel on the right side of the heart.

BEADED POTPOURRI JAR LID

Shown on page 103.
Design measures 2½ inches in diameter.

MATERIALS

6-inch square of 28-count ecru linen
Size 11 quilting needle
Ecru embroidery floss
Size 11 glass beads in the following colors: light lilac, dark lilac, medium blue, light blue, light pink, medium pink, light green, medium green, dark green
2⅝-inch round hunter green jar from Anne Brinkley Designs (see page 158 for the address)

INSTRUCTIONS

Following the chart, *below,* center and work the design using two strands of floss over two threads of the linen.

Work only the first half of every cross-stitch, attaching a bead with each stitch. Refer to the beaded cross-stitch tip on page 83 before beginning the design.

After the beaded design is complete, mount it in the lid of the jar according to the manufacturer's instructions.

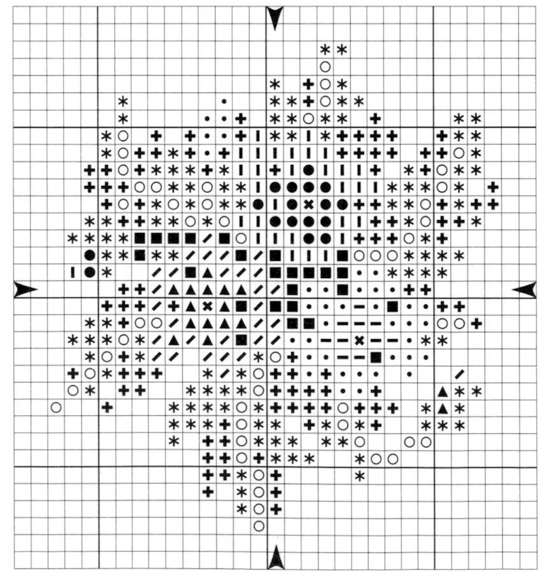

BEADED POTPOURRI JAR LID PATTERN

COLOR KEY
⊡ Light green
⊛ Medium green
⊞ Ivy green
■ Dark green
Ⅰ Light blue
● Blue
⊡ Light pink
⊟ Pink
⧄ Light lilac
▲ Lilac
⊠ Yellow

CROCHETED STAR DOILY

Shown on page 103.
Doily measures 22 inches across from point to opposite point.

MATERIALS

J. & P. Coats Knit-Cro-Sheen mercerized cotton (225-yard ball): 3 balls of cream (No. 42)
Size 7 steel crochet hook

Abbreviations: See page 99.
Gauge: 10 dc = 1 inch.

INSTRUCTIONS

Starting at center, ch 11; sl st in first ch to form ring.

Rnd 1: Ch 5, (3 dc in ring, ch 2) 7 times; 2 dc in ring; join with sl st to third ch of beg ch-5—8 ch-2 sp.

Rnd 2: **Sl st in first ch-2 sp, ch 3, in same sp make dc, ch 2, and 2 dc—starting shell made;** * ch 1, sk 3 dc; **in next sp make 2 dc, ch 2, and 2 dc—shell made;** rep from * around, end with ch 1; join to top of beg ch-3.

Note: In all rnds that follow, work starting shell in first ch-2 sp of starting shell of previous rnd. At end of rnd, join with sl st to top of beg ch-3; then sl st into ch-2 sp of starting shell unless otherwise instructed.

Rnd 3: Starting shell, * ch 1, dc in next ch-1 sp, ch 1; **shell in sp of next shell—shell over shell made;** rep from *; end with ch 1; join.

Rnd 4: Starting shell, * ch 1, dc in next ch-1 sp, dc in *back* lp of next dc, dc in next ch-1 sp, ch 1, ** shell over shell, rep from *; end last rep at **; join.

Rnd 5: Starting shell, * ch 1, dc in next ch-1 sp, dc in *back* lp of next 3 dc, dc in ch-1 sp, ch 1, ** shell over shell, rep from *; end last rep at **; join.

Rnd 6: Starting shell, * ch 1, dc in ch-1 sp, dc in *back* lp of next 2 dc, ch 1, sk dc, dc in *back* lp of next 2 dc, dc in ch-1 sp, ch 1, ** shell over shell, rep from *; end last rep at **; join.

Note: Hereafter, when making a dc directly over another dc, work in the back lp only as established throughout.

Rnd 7: Starting shell, * dc in ch-1 sp, dc in 2 dc, ch 1, dc in ch-1 sp, ch 1, sk dc, dc in 2 dc, dc in sp, ch 1, ** shell over shell, rep from *; end last rep at **; join.

Rnd 8: Starting shell, * ch 1, dc in ch-1 sp, dc in 2 dc; (ch 1, dc in next ch-1 sp) twice; ch 1, sk dc, dc in 2 dc, dc in sp, ch 1, ** shell over shell, rep from *; end last rep at **; join.

Rnd 9: Starting shell, * ch 1, dc in ch-1 sp, dc in 2 dc; (ch 1, dc in next ch-1 sp) 3 times; ch 1, sk dc, dc in 2 dc, dc in next ch-1 sp, ch 1, ** shell over shell, rep from *; end last rep at **; join.

Rnd 10: Starting shell, * ch 1, dc in ch-1 sp, dc in 2 dc; (ch 1, dc in next ch-1 sp) twice; dc in dc; (dc in next ch-1 sp, ch 1) twice; sk dc, dc in 2 dc, dc in ch-1 sp, ch 1, ** shell over shell, rep from *; end last rep at **; join.

Rnd 11: Starting shell, * ch 1, dc in ch-1 sp, dc in 2 dc; (ch 1, dc in next ch-1 sp) twice; dc in 3 dc; (dc in next ch-1 sp, ch 1) twice; sk dc, dc in 2 dc, dc in ch-1 sp, ch 1, ** shell over shell, rep from *; end last rep at **; join.

Rnd 12: Starting shell, * ch 1, dc in ch-1 sp, dc in 2 dc; (ch 1, dc in next ch-1 sp) twice; dc in 2 dc, ch 1, sk dc, dc in 2 dc;

(dc in ch-1 sp, ch 1) twice; sk dc, dc in 2 dc, dc in ch-1 sp, ch 1, ** shell over shell, rep from *; end last rep at **; join.

Rnd 13: Starting shell, * ch 1, dc in ch-1 sp, dc in 2 dc; (ch 1, dc in next ch-1 sp) twice; dc in 2 dc, ch 1, dc in ch-1 sp, ch 1, sk dc, dc in 2 dc; (dc in next ch-1 sp, ch 1) twice; sk dc, dc in 2 dc, dc in ch-1 sp, ch 1, ** shell over shell, rep from *; end last rep at **; join.

Rnd 14: Starting shell, * ch 1, dc in ch-1 sp, dc in 2 dc; (ch 1, dc in next ch-1 sp) twice; dc in 2 dc, ch 1, dc in ch-1 sp, dc in next dc, dc in ch-1 sp, ch 1, sk dc, dc in 2 dc; (dc in next ch-1 sp, ch 1) twice; sk dc, dc in 2 dc, dc in ch-1 sp, ch 1, ** shell over shell, rep from *; end last rep at **; join.

Rnd 15: Starting shell, * ch 1, dc in ch-1 sp, dc in 2 dc; (ch 1, dc in next ch-1 sp) twice; dc in 2 dc, ch 1, dc in next ch-1 sp, dc in 3 dc, dc in ch-1 sp, ch 1, sk dc, dc in next 2 dc, (dc in next ch-1 sp, ch 1) twice; sk dc, dc in next 2 dc, dc in ch-1 sp, ch 1, ** shell over shell; rep from *; end last rep at **; join.

Rnd 16: Starting shell, * ch 1, dc in ch-1 sp, dc in 2 dc; (ch 1, dc in next ch-1 sp) twice; dc in 2 dc, ch 1, dc in next sp, dc in 5 dc, dc in ch-1 sp, ch 1, sk dc, dc in 2 dc, (dc in next ch-1 sp, ch 1) twice; sk dc, dc in 2 dc, dc in ch-1 sp, ch 1, ** shell over shell, rep from *; end last rep at **; join.

Rnd 17: Starting shell, * ch 1, dc in ch-1 sp, dc in 2 dc; (ch 1, dc in next ch-1 sp) twice; dc in 2 dc, ch 1, dc in ch-1 sp, dc in 7 dc, dc in ch-1 sp, ch 1, sk dc, dc in 2 dc, (dc in next ch-1 sp, ch 1) twice; sk dc, dc in 2 dc, dc in ch-1 sp, ch 1, ** shell over shell, rep from *; end last rep at **; join.

Rnd 18: Ch 3, 7 dc in same sp, * ch 3, sc in next ch-1 sp, ch 3, sk dc, dc in 2 dc; (dc in next ch-1 sp, ch 1) twice; sk dc, dc in 2 dc, dc in ch-1 sp, ch 1, sk dc, dc in 7 dc, ch 1, dc in ch-1 sp, dc in 2 dc; (ch 1, dc in next ch-1 sp) twice; dc in 2 dc, ch 3, sc in next ch-1 sp, ch 3, ** 8 dc in ch-2 sp of next shell, rep from *; end last rep at **; join.

Rnd 19: Ch 3, dc in 3 dc, * ch 6, dc in 4 dc, ch 3, sk ch-3 lp, sc in next ch-3 lp, ch 3, sk dc, dc in 2 dc; (dc in next ch-1 sp, ch 1) twice; sk dc, dc in 2 dc, dc in ch-1 sp, ch 1, sk dc, dc in 5 dc, ch 1, dc in ch-1 sp, dc in 2 dc; (ch 1, dc in next ch-1 sp) twice; dc in 2 dc, ch 3, sc in next ch-3 lp, ch 3, ** dc in 4 dc, rep from *; end last rep at **; join.

Rnd 20: Ch 3, dc in 3 dc; * in next ch-6 lp make 4 dc, ch 5, and 4 dc; dc in 4 dc, ch 3, sk ch-3 lp, sc in next ch-3 lp, ch 3, sk dc, dc in 2 dc; (dc in next ch-1 sp, ch 1) twice; sk dc, dc in 2 dc, dc in ch-1 sp, ch 1, sk dc, dc in 3 dc, ch 1, dc in ch-1 sp, dc in 2 dc; (ch 1, dc in next ch-1 sp) twice; dc in 2 dc, ch 3, sc in next ch-3 lp, ch 3, ** dc in 4 dc, rep from *; end last rep at **; join.

Rnd 21: Ch 3, dc in 3 dc, *** ch 4, sl st in third ch from hook, ch 1—picot space (pc sp) made;** in next ch-5 lp make 4 dc, ch 5, and 4 dc; make pc sp, sk 4 dc, dc in 4 dc, ch 3, sk ch-3 lp, sc in next ch-3 lp, ch 3, sk dc, dc in 2 dc; (dc in next sp, ch 1) twice; sk dc, dc in 2 dc, dc in ch-1 sp, ch 1, sk dc, dc in next dc, ch 1, dc in ch-1 sp, dc in 2 dc; (ch 1, dc in next ch-1 sp) twice; dc in 2 dc, ch 3, sc in next ch-3 lp, ch 3, ** dc in 4 dc, rep from *; end last rep at **; join.

Rnd 22: Ch 3, dc in 3 dc, * pc sp, dc in 4 dc, in next ch-5 lp make 4 dc, ch 4, and 4 dc; dc in 4 dc, pc sp, dc in 4 dc, ch 3, sk ch-3 lp, sc in next ch-3 lp, ch 3, sk dc, dc in 2 dc; (dc in ch-1 sp, ch 1) twice; sk dc, dc in 2 dc, dc in ch-1 sp, ch 1, dc in next ch-1 sp, dc in 2 dc; (ch 1, dc in next ch-1 sp) twice; dc in 2 dc, ch 3, sc in next ch-3 lp, ch 3, ** dc in 4 dc, rep from *; end last rep at **; join.

Rnd 23: Ch 3, dc in 3 dc, * pc sp, dc in 4 dc, pc sp; in next ch-4 lp make 4 dc, ch 4, and 4 dc; pc sp, sk 4 dc, dc in 4 dc, pc sp, dc in 4 dc, ch 3, sk ch-3 lp, sc in next ch-3 lp, ch 3, sk dc, dc in 2 dc; (dc in next ch-1 sp, ch 1) twice; sk dc, dc in 2 dc, dc in ch-1 sp, dc in 2 dc; (ch 1, dc in next ch-1 sp) twice; dc in 2 dc, ch 3, sc in next ch-3 lp, ch 3, ** dc in 4 dc, rep from *; end last rep at **; join.

Rnd 24: Ch 3, dc in 3 dc; * (pc sp, dc in 4 dc) twice; in next ch-4 lp make 4 dc, ch 4, and 4 dc; (dc in 4 dc, pc sp) twice; dc in 4 dc, ch 3, sk next ch-3 lp, sc in next ch-3 lp, ch 3, sk dc, dc in 2 dc; (dc in ch-1 sp, ch 1) twice; sk dc, dc in 3 dc; (ch 1, dc in next ch-1 sp) twice; dc in 2 dc, ch 3, sc in next ch-3 lp, ch 3, ** dc in 4 dc, rep from *; end last rep at **; join.

Rnd 25: Ch 3, dc in 3 dc; * (pc sp, dc in 4 dc) twice; pc sp; in next ch-4 lp make 4 dc, ch 4, and 4 dc; pc sp, sk 4 dc; (dc in 4 dc, pc sp) twice; dc in 4 dc, ch 3, sk ch-3 lp, sc in next ch-3 lp, ch 3, sk dc, dc in 2 dc; (dc in next ch-1 sp, ch 1) twice; sk dc, dc in next dc; (ch 1, dc in next ch-1 sp) twice; dc in next 2 dc, ch 3, sc in next ch-3 lp, ch 3, ** dc in 4 dc, rep from *; end last rep at **; join.

Rnd 26: Ch 3, dc in 3 dc; * (pc sp, dc in 4 dc) 3 times; in next ch-4 lp make 4 dc, ch 4, and 4 dc; (dc in 4 dc, pc sp) 3 times; dc in 4 dc, ch 3, sk ch-3 lp, sc in next ch-3 lp, ch 3, sk dc, dc in 2 dc; (dc in ch-1 sp, ch 1) 3 times; dc in ch-1 sp, dc in 2 dc, ch 3, sc in next ch-3 lp, ch 3, ** dc in 4 dc, rep from *; end last rep at **; join.

Rnd 27: Ch 3, dc in 3 dc; * (pc sp, dc in 4 dc) 3 times; pc sp, in next ch-4 lp make 4 dc, ch 4, and 4 dc; pc sp, sk 4 dc; (dc in 4 dc, pc sp) 3 times; dc in 4 dc, ch 3, sk ch-3 lp, sc in next ch-3 lp, ch 3, sk dc, dc in 2 dc; (dc in next ch-1 sp, ch 1) twice; dc in ch-1 sp, dc in 2 dc, ch 3, sc in next ch-3 lp, ch 3, ** dc in 4 dc, rep from *; end last rep at **; join.

Rnd 28: Ch 3, dc in 3 dc; * (pc sp, dc in 4 dc) 4 times; in next ch-4 lp make 4 dc, ch 4, and 4 dc; (dc in 4 dc, pc sp) 4 times; dc in 4 dc, ch 3, sk ch-3 lp, sc in next ch-3 lp, ch 3, sk dc, dc in 2 dc, dc in ch-1 sp, ch 1, sk dc, dc in ch-1 sp, dc in 2 dc, ch 3, sc in next ch-3 lp, ch 3, ** dc in 4 dc, rep from *; end last rep at **; join.

Rnd 29: Ch 3, dc in 3 dc; * (pc sp, dc in 4 dc) 4 times; pc sp, in next ch-4 lp make 4 dc, ch 4, and 4 dc; pc sp, sk 4 dc; (dc in 4 dc, pc sp) 4 times; dc in 4 dc, ch 3, sk ch-3 lp, sc in next ch-3 lp, ch 3, sk dc, dc in 2 dc, dc in ch-1 sp, dc in 2 dc, ch 3, sc in next ch-3 lp, ch 3, ** dc in 4 dc, rep from *; end last rep at **; join.

Rnd 30: Ch 3, dc in 3 dc; * (pc sp, dc in 4 dc) 5 times; in next ch-4 lp make 4 dc, ch 4, and 4 dc; (dc in 4 dc, pc sp) 5 times; dc in 4 dc, ch 3, sk ch-3 lp, sc in next ch-3 lp, ch 3, sk dc, dc in 3 dc, ch 3, sc in next ch-3 lp, ch 3, ** dc in 4 dc, rep from *; end last rep at **; join.

continued

Rnd 31: Ch 3, dc in 3 dc; * (pc sp, dc in 4 dc) 5 times; pc sp; in next ch-4 lp make 4 dc, ch 4, and 4 dc; pc sp, sk 4 dc; (dc in 4 dc, pc sp) 5 times; dc in 4 dc, ch 3, sk ch-3 lp, sc in next ch-3 lp, ch 3, sk dc, hdc in next dc, ch 3, sc in next ch-3 lp, ch 3, ** dc in 4 dc, rep from *; end last rep at **; join.

Rnd 32: Ch 3, dc in 3 dc; * (pc sp, dc in 4 dc) 6 times; in next ch-4 lp make 4 dc, pc sp, and 4 dc; (dc in 4 dc, pc sp) 6 times; dc in 4 dc, ch 3, sk ch-3 lp, sc in next ch-3 lp, pc sp, sc in next ch-3 lp, ch 3, ** dc in 4 dc, rep from *; end last rep at **; join; fasten off.

ARROWHEAD STAR QUILT

Shown on page 105.
The finished quilt measures approximately 70x80 inches, not including the 1-inch-wide ruffle. Each block is 10 inches square.

MATERIALS

5½ yards of pink solid fabric
5 yards of white or muslin fabric
5 yards of backing fabric
72x90-inch precut quilt batting
Template material
Rotary cutter, mat, and acrylic ruler

INSTRUCTIONS

This quilt is made of 56 Arrowhead Star blocks arranged in a straight set of eight horizontal rows with seven blocks in each row. The antique quilt shown is finished with a dainty little ruffle, but you can bind your quilt traditionally if you prefer.

All cutting instructions for the pieces that do not have templates include ¼-inch seam allowances.

Cutting the fabrics

Prepare templates for patterns A, B, and D, *opposite.* Using templates for triangles C and E, *opposite,* is optional, as these can be cut with a ruler and rotary cutter as described in the directions, *right.*

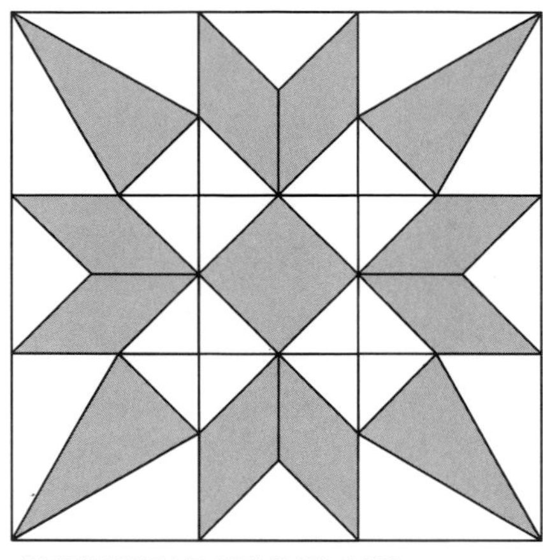

ARROWHEAD STAR BLOCK

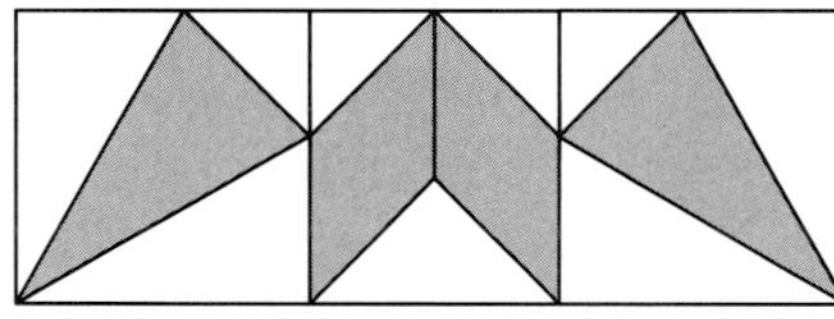

ARROWHEAD STAR BLOCK ASSEMBLY DIAGRAM

Cut all strips on the crosswise grain, using a rotary cutter and mat.

From the white fabric, cut:
❧ Sixteen 4x42-inch strips.
From these strips, cut 224 rectangles, each 3x4 inches. Cut two of Pattern B from each rectangle—a total of 224 of Pattern B and 224 of Pattern B reversed.
❧ Twenty-seven 2⅜x42-inch strips.
Cut these strips into 448 squares, each 2⅜ inches square. Cut each square in half diagonally to obtain 896 C triangles.
❧ Fifty-six 4¼-inch squares.
Cut each square in quarters diagonally to obtain 224 E triangles.

From the pink fabric, cut:
❧ Thirteen 2½x42-inch strips for the ruffle.
❧ Thirteen 4½x42-inch strips.
From these strips, cut 224 of Pattern A.
❧ Thirty-two 2x42-inch strips.
From these strips, cut 448 of Pattern D.
❧ Fifty-six 2⅝-inch squares for the center square of each block (F).

Making the Arrowhead Star block

CENTER UNIT: Sew C triangles onto opposite sides of one F square as shown in Figure 1, *below.* Complete the center unit by adding C triangles to remaining sides of the F square as shown. Press each seam allowance toward the C triangle.

Make 56 center units, one for each block.

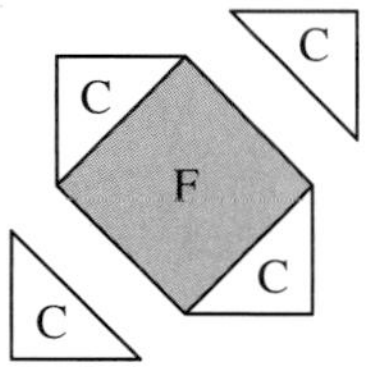

FIGURE 1

CORNER UNIT: Referring to Figure 2, *below,* stitch a C triangle onto the short side of one A piece; press the seam allowance toward the C triangle. Add a B piece and a B reversed piece onto the long sides of the A triangle; press these seam allowances toward the A piece.

Make 224 corner units, four for each block.

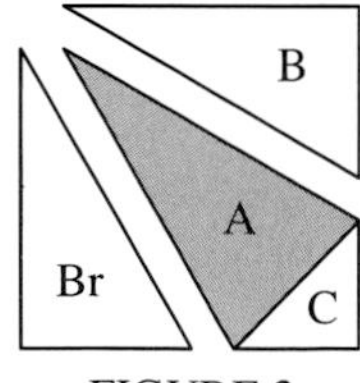

FIGURE 2

SIDE UNIT: Join two D diamonds as shown in Figure 3, *opposite, top,* taking care not to stitch into the seam allowance. Set an E triangle into the V-shaped opening at the top of the D pieces.

Complete the unit by adding a C triangle to the bottom of each D diamond; press the seam allowances toward the triangles. Unlike the other units, the assembled side unit is *not* a square. Make 224 side units, four for each block.

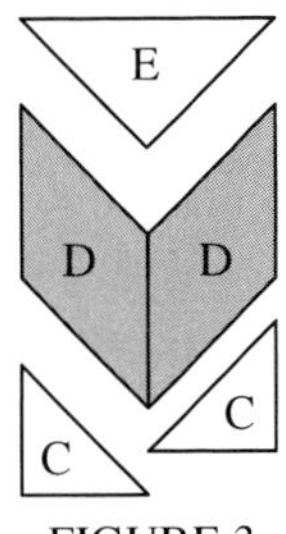

FIGURE 3

JOINING THE UNITS: Refer to the block assembly diagram, *opposite, center,* to join nine units into one Arrowhead Star block. Begin by stitching a corner unit onto the long sides of two side units to make the top and bottom rows; press the seam allowances toward the corner units. Make the center row by sewing a side unit onto opposite sides of one center unit; press the seam allowance toward the center.

Assemble the block by joining the three rows.

Make 56 Arrowhead Star blocks.

Assembling the quilt top

Stitch the blocks together in eight horizontal rows of seven blocks each; press the seam allowances to one side. Join the rows to complete the quilt top.

Adding the ruffle

Sew the 13 ruffle strips end to end to make one continuous piece approximately 540 inches long.

With right sides together, join the ends of the strip to form a large loop.

With wrong sides together, bring raw edges of the ruffle strip together so the strip is 1¼ inches wide. Press the fold.

Machine-stitch a loose gathering stitch through both layers of the ruffle fabric ¼ inch from the raw edge. Stitch a second line of gathering ⅛ inch from the edge. Leave long thread tails to pull gathers.

continued

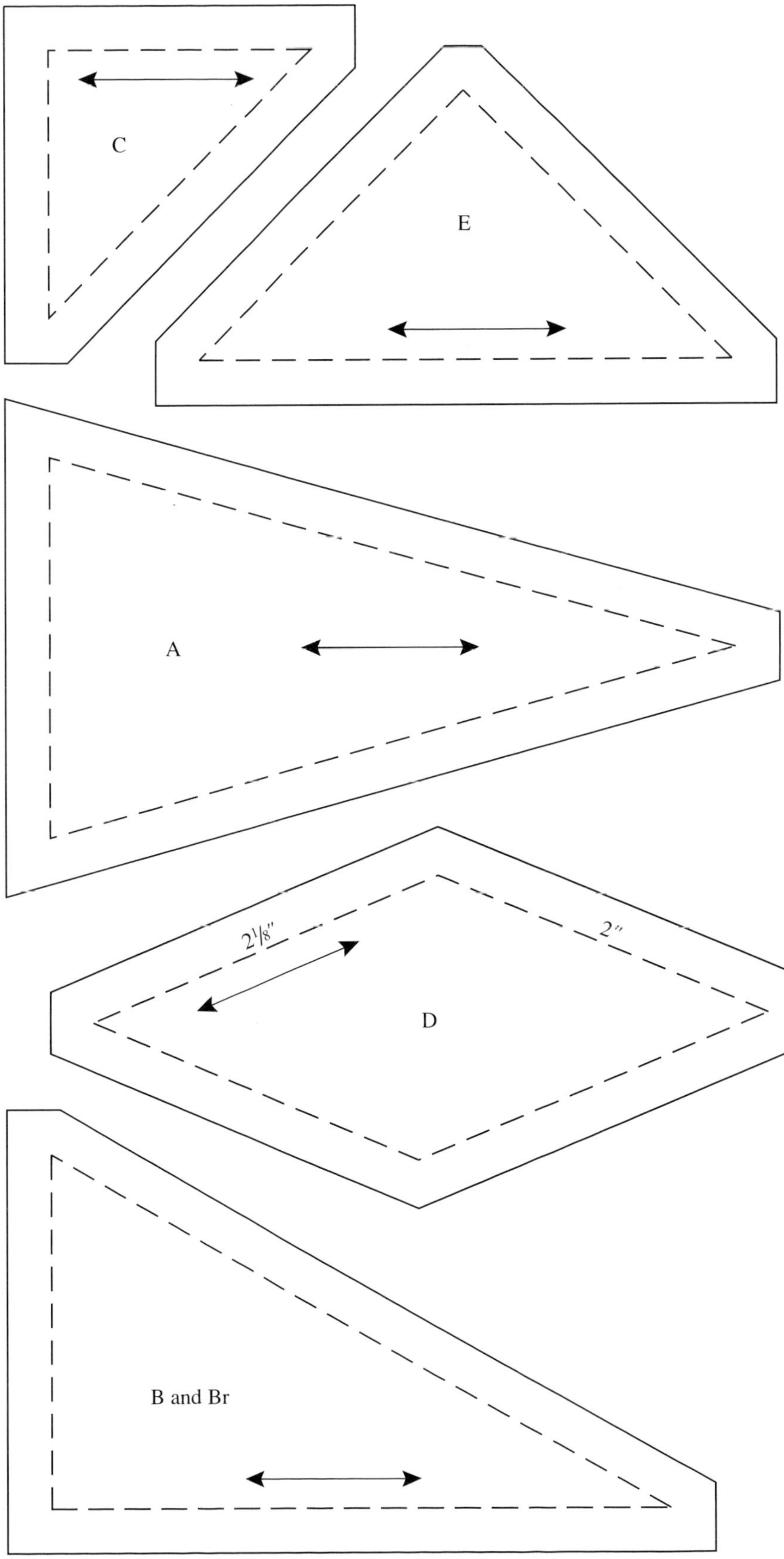

ARROWHEAD STAR QUILT PATTERNS

Fold the ruffle strip into four equal sections; mark each fold with a pin. Gather each section to fit one side of the quilt, using the extra fullness at the top and bottom edges to ease the ruffle around the corner. Pin the raw edge of the ruffle to the right side of the quilt top, spacing the gathers evenly. Machine-baste the ruffle onto the quilt top.

Quilting and finishing

BACKING: Divide the backing fabric into two 2½-yard lengths. Stitch the two panels together side by side; press the seam allowance open.

Sandwich the batting between the backing fabric and the quilt top; baste the three layers together.

QUILTING: Quilt as desired. The antique quilt shown on page 105 has outline quilting inside the seam line of each patchwork piece.

FINISHING: Trim the batting even with the quilt top. Trim the backing, leaving a ¼-inch seam allowance.

Turn in the raw edge of the backing fabric; slip-stitch it in place on the back of the ruffle seam allowance.

REDWORK BIRD PILLOW WITH CROCHETED EDGING

Shown on page 104.
Redwork motif is 15 inches wide and fits a 19x17-inch pillow. Edging is approximately 6 inches wide.

MATERIALS

20x42-inch piece of lightweight cotton fabric for the pillow
Red embroidery floss
Embroidery needle; embroidery hoop
Tracing paper; pencil
Nonpermanent fabric marker
DMC Cebelia crochet cotton, Size 30 (563-yard ball): 1 ball of white
Size 13 steel crochet hook
White sewing thread; sewing needle
Polyester fiberfill

Abbreviations: See page 99.
Gauge: 7 sp = 1 inch; 7 rows = 1 inch.

INSTRUCTIONS

The redwork design

This design is embroidered with one simple stitch—the outline or stem stitch (see stitch diagram, page 79).

The outline stitch is flexible enough to follow any line or curve. The loop of the stitch can be above or below the needle, whichever is more comfortable for you. To create neat lines of stitches, however, work all loops in the same way and in the same direction. For smooth curves, make shorter stitches on curved lines.

TO TRANSFER THE DESIGN: The pattern for the embroidery design is given in two parts, *below*. Trace the pattern on tracing paper, joining it on the dashed line to make one complete pattern. On a hard surface, retrace the drawing to darken the lines.

Join pattern on dotted line

Faith Hope

BIRD PILLOW EMBROIDERY PATTERN

Lay one end of the cotton fabric atop the traced drawing, centering the drawing widthwise on the fabric. Using the nonpermanent fabric marker, trace the design onto the fabric.

WORKING THE DESIGN: Place the fabric in an embroidery hoop. Using two strands of floss, work the design in outline stitches. When all embroidery is completed, remove all markings. Press the wrong side of the fabric. Set aside.

Crocheted bird edging

Beg along narrow edge, with Size 13 crochet hook and crochet thread, ch 63.

Row 1: Dc in fourth ch from hook and in next 2 ch; (ch 2, sk 2 ch, dc in next ch) 14 times; dc in next 3 ch, (ch 2, sk 2 ch, dc in next ch) twice; dc in last 6 ch; ch 3, turn.

Row 2: Sk first dc, dc in 6 dc; ch 2, dc in next dc, 2 dc in next ch-2 sp, dc in next dc, ch 2, sk 2 dc, dc in next dc; 2 dc in next ch-2 sp, dc in next dc; (ch 2, dc in next dc) 3 times; 2 dc in next ch-2 sp, dc in next dc; (ch 2, dc in next dc) 9 times; dc in next 2 dc, dc in top of turning ch; ch 3, turn.

Row 3: Sk first dc, dc in 3 dc, (ch 2, dc in next dc) 8 times; 2 dc in next ch-2 sp, dc in next dc, ch 2, sk 2 dc, dc in next dc, 2 dc in next ch-2 sp, dc in next dc, ch 2, dc in next dc, 2 dc in next ch-2 sp, ch 2, sk 2 dc, dc in next dc, 2 dc in next ch-2 sp, dc in next dc, ch 2, sk 2 dc, dc in next dc, ch 2, dc in next dc, **ch 3, sk 2 dc, sc in next dc, ch 3, sk 2 dc, dc in top of turning ch—lacet st made; (yo hook, draw up lp at base of last dc made; yo, draw through 1 lp on hook—ch-1 made for base for next st; complete st as for dc) 6 times—2 bl inc made at end of row;** ch 3, turn.

continued

row 32
row 1

KEY
☐ Space (sp)
▣ Block (bl)
Ch-5 Loop
Lacet st

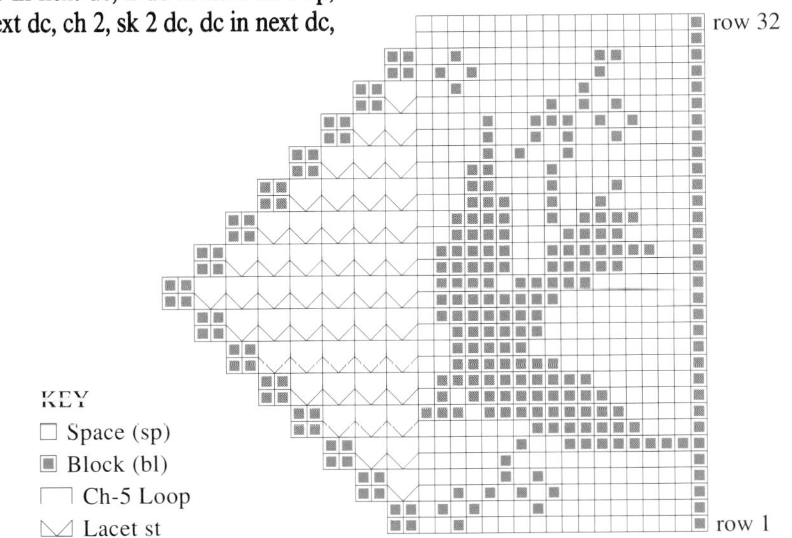

BIRD PILLOW
CROCHETED EDGING
PATTERN

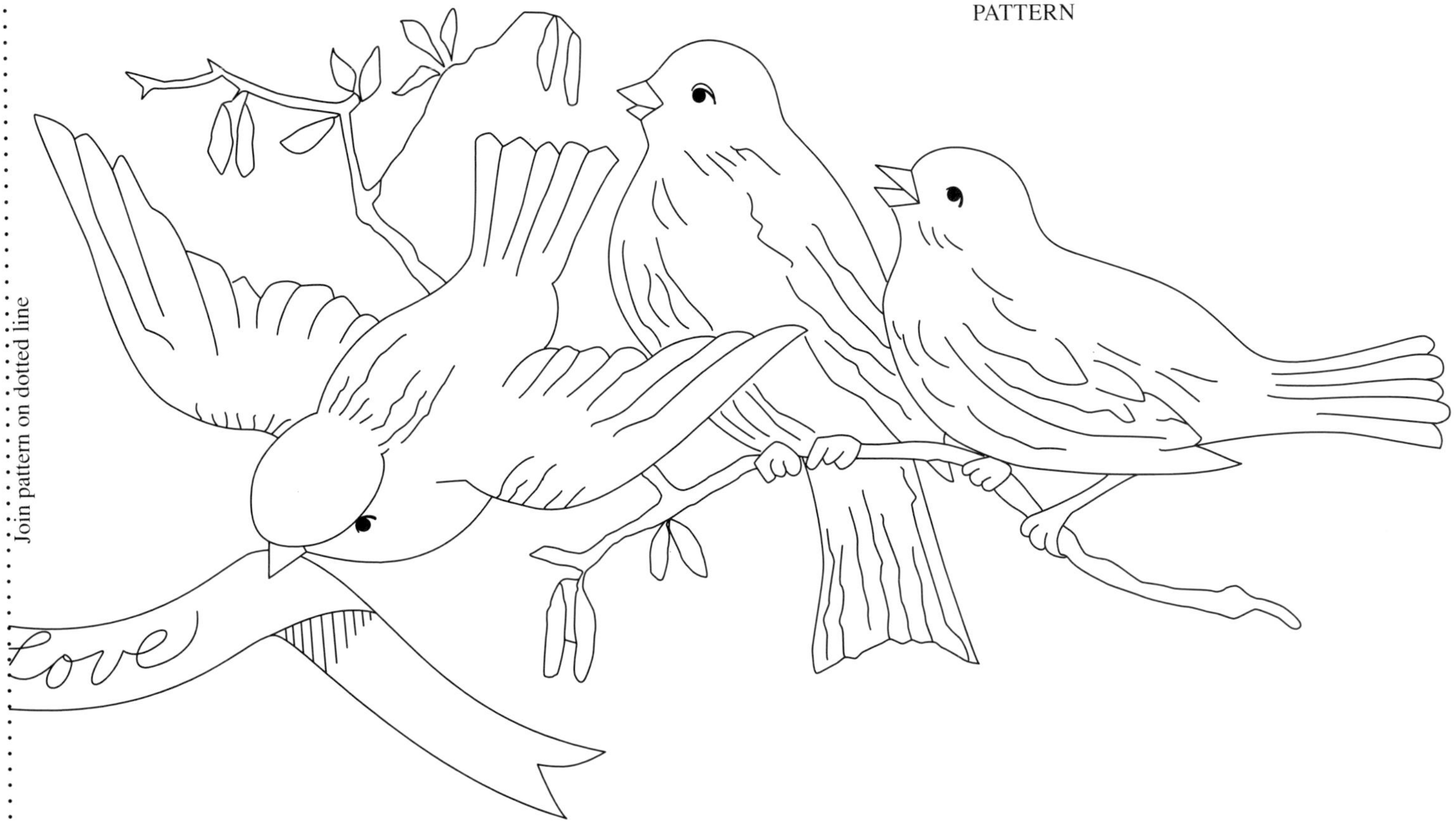

Join pattern on dotted line
love

Row 4: Sk first dc, dc in 6 dc; **ch 5, dc in next dc—ch-5 lp made;** follow the chart on page 117 to complete the row.

Rows 5–32: Refer to the chart and work as established. Rep rows 1–32 for desired length plus 2 or 3 inches to allow for shrinkage. Wash and press edging. Use sewing thread to sew edging to one narrow end of the fabric approximately 3 inches from the bottom of the redwork design. Assemble as desired.

CROCHET-TRIMMED FLAT SHEET

Shown on page 105.
The crocheted insertion measures approximately 3 inches wide. The crocheted edging measures approximately 3½ inches wide.

MATERIALS

Clark's Big Ball crochet cotton, Size 20 (300-yard ball): 1 ball of white makes 45 inches of insertion or 39 inches of edging

One white flat sheet the size to fit your bed; one white twin-size flat sheet for the strips separating the crocheted insertions

Size 13 steel crochet hook

White sewing thread; sewing needle

Abbreviations: See page 99.
Gauge: 15 dc = 1 inch; 5½ rows = 1 inch.

INSTRUCTIONS

Note: This sheet has two crocheted insertions and one piece of edging that are made in strips long enough to fit across the width of the sheet; add about 2 yards for the sides and the mitered corners. The sheet shown on page 105 has fabric strips with ¼-inch tucks sewn into them that separate the crocheted insertions. Our instructions are for plain fabric strips. If you want tucks in your sheet, cut the fabric strips wider to accommodate them.

INSERTION (make 2): Ch 51.

Row 1: Dc in fourth ch from hook and in next 2 ch; * **ch 5, sk 5 ch, dc in next ch—ch-5 lp made;** rep from * across until 3 ch rem; dc in last 3 ch; ch 3, turn.

Row 2: Sk first dc, dc in next 3 dc; **(ch 3, sk 2 ch of ch-5 lp, sc in next ch, ch 3, dc in next dc—lacet st made)** 7 times; dc in last 2 dc and in top of turning ch; ch 3, turn.

Row 3: Sk first dc, dc in next 3 dc; (ch 5, dc in next dc) 7 times; dc in last 2 dc and in top of turning ch; ch 3, turn.

Rows 4–17: Follow the insertion chart, *below right, top,* working from right to left on odd-numbered rows and from left to right on even-numbered rows.

Rep rows 2–17 for the length of the insertion strip required.

EDGING: Refer to the edging chart, *below right, bottom,* and instructions for the Crocheted Pillow Shams, *opposite,* to make the edging for this sheet.

Crochet a length of edging that is long enough to fit across the width of your sheet and then add 2 yards for the sides. This also allows for the corners to be gathered slightly.

FINISHING: Cut the twin-size flat sheet lengthwise into four 3-inch-wide fabric strips. Sew two strips together end to end for one long strip; repeat for a second long strip. Turn under a ¼-inch hem twice on both long edges of each strip; press and set aside.

Note: The insertions and fabric strips are sewn to the wrong side of the sheet. When the sheet is placed on the bed, the top edge of the sheet is folded over and the right sides of the insertions and strips will be facing up.

Referring to the assembly diagram, *below left,* center and pin one of the insertions to the top of the wrong side of the flat sheet. Miter the insertion approximately 10 inches from the sides of the sheet for the corners. Position the remaining sides of the strip 24 inches down each side of the sheet. Sew the mitered corner in place. Machine-stitch the insertion to the sheet on the inside edge only. Trim away the areas of the sheet indicated in gray on the diagram, leaving ½ inch of sheet fabric to hem. Turn under the hem ¼ inch twice and hand-sew to the sheet.

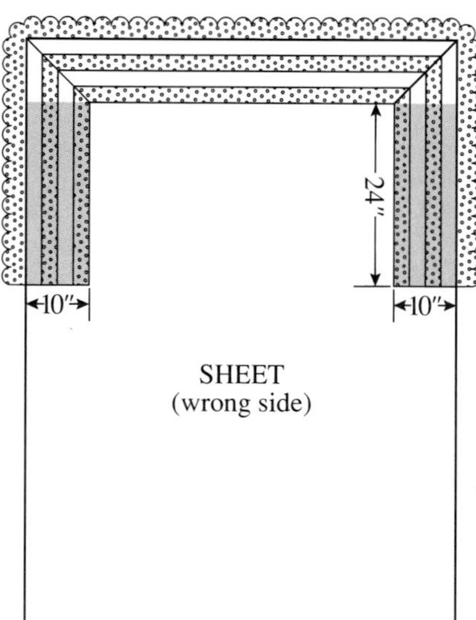

CROCHET-TRIMMED FLAT SHEET ASSEMBLY DIAGRAM

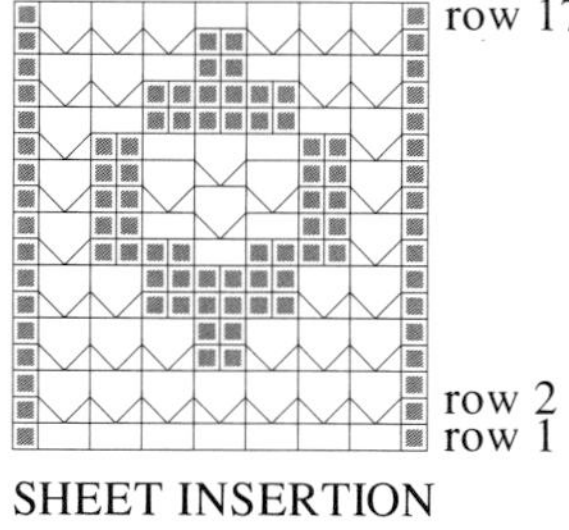

SHEET INSERTION PATTERN

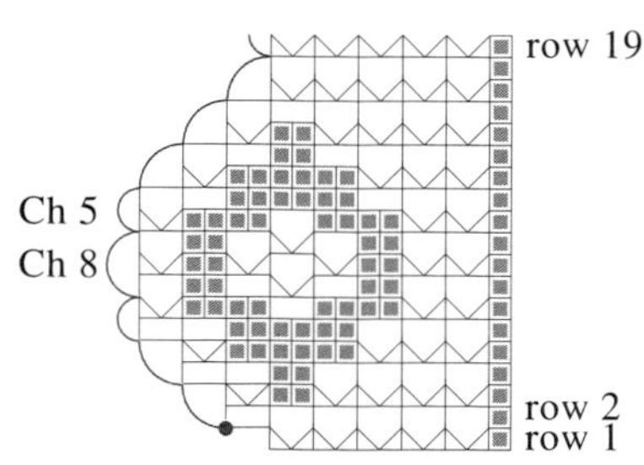

SHEET AND PILLOW SHAM EDGING PATTERN

Center and pin a fabric strip to the top edge of the insertion; miter and sew the corners and pin the sides. Machine-stitch the fabric strip to the insertion. Center, pin, and sew the second insertion and the second fabric strip in the same manner. Machine-stitch the edging to the second fabric strip, gathering the edging in the corners instead of mitering them.

Trim the excess crocheted insertions, fabric strips, and edging to ½ inch. Turn under ¼ inch twice and sew the hemmed ends to the 10-inch edge of the sheet.

To finish the hemmed edge, cut two 2½x10½-inch strips from the remaining sheet fabric. Turn under ¼ inch on all four sides of each strip and press. Fold the strips in half with the wrong sides together to make a 1x10-inch strip; press. Machine-stitch each strip to the wrong side of the sheet below the insertion and fabric strips.

CROCHETED PILLOW SHAMS

Shown on page 105.
Pillow shams measure approximately 27¼x20 inches excluding the edging.

MATERIALS

For one pillow sham

Clark's Big Ball crochet cotton, Size 20 (300-yard ball): 7 balls of white
¾ yard of white cotton fabric
Four ½-inch-diameter white buttons
Size 13 steel crochet hook
White sewing thread; sewing needle

Abbreviations: See page 99.
Gauge: 15 dc = 1 inch; 5½ rows = 1 inch.

INSTRUCTIONS

PILLOW TOP: Ch 315.

Row 1: Dc in fourth ch from hook and in next 2 ch; * **ch 5, sk 5 ch, dc in next ch—ch-5 lp made;** rep from * across until 3 ch rem; dc in last 3 ch; ch 3, turn.

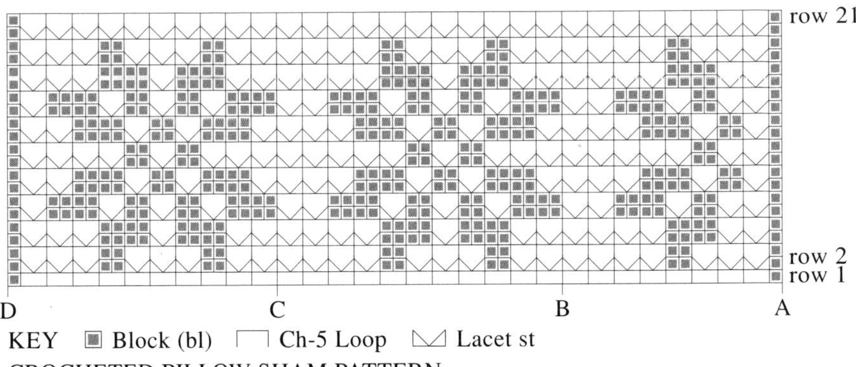

KEY ■ Block (bl) ⌐¬ Ch-5 Loop ⋁ Lacet st
CROCHETED PILLOW SHAM PATTERN

Row 2: Sk first dc, dc in next 3 dc; (**ch 3, sk 2 ch of ch-5 lp, sc in next ch, ch 3, dc in next dc—lacet st made**) 3 times; * 5 dc in next ch-5 lp, dc in next dc; (work lacet st) 3 times; 5 dc in next ch-5 lp, dc in next dc; (work lacet st) 6 times; rep from * 3 times more; 5 dc in next ch-5 lp, dc in next dc; (work lacet st) 3 times; dc in last 2 dc and in top of turning ch; ch 3, turn.

Row 3: Sk first dc, dc in next 3 dc; (ch 5, dc in next dc) 3 times; dc in next 5 dc; * (ch 5, dc in next dc) 6 times; dc in next 5 dc; (ch 5, dc in next dc) 3 times, dc in next 5 dc; rep from * 3 times more; (ch 5, dc in next dc) 3 times; dc in last 2 dc and in top of turning ch; ch 3, turn.

Rows 4–21: Follow the chart, *above;* on odd-numbered rows, work from A–C one time, B–C two times, and C–D one time. On even-numbered rows, work from D–B one time, C–B two times, and B–A one time.

Rep rows 2–21 seven times; fasten off.

EDGING: Ch 36.

Row 1: Dc in fourth ch from hook and in next 2 ch, (ch 3, sk 2 ch, sc in next ch, ch 3, sk 2 ch, dc in next ch) 4 times; ch 3, sk 2 ch, sc in next ch, ch 3, dc in last ch; ch 13, turn.

Row 2: Dc in next dc, (ch 5, dc in next dc) 5 times; dc in next 2 dc and in top of turning ch; ch 3, turn.

Row 3: Sk first dc, dc in next 2 dc; (work lacet st) 4 times; 5 dc in next ch-5 lp, dc in next dc; ch 3, sk 2 ch, sc in next ch, ch 3, sk 2 ch, dc in next ch; ch 13, turn.

Rows 4–19: Follow the edging chart, *opposite,* working from right to left on odd-numbered rows and from left to right on even-numbered rows. The red lines on the chart are the first rnd of the border on the edging. Do not work the border at this time.

Rep rows 2–19 until the edging fits around the crocheted pillow top plus 12 more inches to allow for gathering the edging in the four corners; fasten off. Sew the first and last rows of the edging together. Sew the edging to the outside edges of the pillow top.

For the border: Join thread in the sixth ch of ch-13 at the end of Row 2.

Rnd 1: Following the red lines on the edging chart, ch 5, sc in sixth ch of ch-13 at end of Row 4; ch 5, sc in sixth ch of ch-13 at the end of Row 6; cont to work the ch lps following the chart until you have worked completely around the pillow top and edging. Note the ch-8 lp at the tip of each scallop. Sl st in beg ch on Row 2.

Rnd 2: Ch 3, in same ch-5 lp work 5 dc, hdc, and sc, ch 1; * (in next ch-5 lp work 6 dc, hdc, and sc, ch 1) three times; in next ch-8 lp work 9 dc, hdc, and sc, ch 1; (in next ch-5 lp work 6 dc, hdc, and sc, ch 1) four times; rep from * around edging; sl st to join; fasten off.

FINISHING: Cut a rectangle of white fabric measuring 29x21 inches for the pillow back. Turn under ¼ inch on all four edges and press. Turn one narrow end under 1 inch for the buttonhole placket; press and machine-stitch placket in place.

continued

Cut a 2½x21-inch strip of white fabric for the button placket. Turn under ¼ inch on all four sides and press. With wrong sides together, fold the strip in half lengthwise; press. Machine-stitch along the length of the strip next to the two folded edges.

With right sides together, place the button placket atop the buttonhole placket. Machine-stitch across the 1-inch ends of both plackets taking a ¼-inch seam; turn right side out.

Center the wrong side of the pillow back against the wrong side of the pillow top. Machine-stitch the button placket to the pillow top, sewing along the length of the edge that is next to the pillow top. The stitches should go through the 4-dc edge of the edging attached to the pillow top. Machine-stitch the pillow back to the pillow top, sewing along the three sides of the pillow back. The stitches should go through the 4-dc edge of the edging attached to the pillow top.

Make four ½-inch buttonholes evenly spaced along the 1-inch hemmed edge of the pillow back. Mark the positions for four buttons behind the buttonholes on the button placket. Sew on the buttons.

PINK PATCHWORK KNITTED AFGHAN

Shown on page 104.
Afghan measures approximately 47x62 inches.

MATERIALS

Unger Utopia (100-gram skein): 12 skeins of rose (No. 293)
Size 8 knitting needles or size to obtain gauge cited below
28-inch-long Size 6 circular knitting needles; tapestry needle

Abbreviations: See page 99.
Gauge: In st st, 18 sts = 4 inches; one square = 7½ inches square.

INSTRUCTIONS

SQUARE (make 48): With Size 8 needles, cast on 2 sts.

Row 1 (right side): Yo, k 2.
Row 2 (wrong side): Yo, k 1, p 1, k 1.
Row 3: Yo, (k 1, yo) 2 times; k 2.
Row 4: Yo, k 2, p 3, k 2.
Row 5: Yo, k 1, p 1, k 1, (yo, k 1) 2 times, p 3.
Row 6: Yo, k 3, p 5, k 3.
Row 7: Yo, k 1, p 2, k 2, yo, k 1, yo, k 2, p 4—15 sts.
Row 8: Yo, k 4, p 7, k 4.
Row 9: Yo, k 1, p 3, k 3, yo, k 1, yo, k 3, p 5—19 sts.
Row 10: Yo, k 5, p 9, k 5.
Row 11: Yo, k 1, p 4, k 4, yo, k 1, yo, k 4, p 6—23 sts.
Row 12: Yo, k 6, p 11, k 6.
Row 13: Yo, k 1, p 5, k 5, yo, k 1, yo, k 5, p 7—27 sts.
Row 14: Yo, k 7, p 13, k 7.
Row 15: Yo, k 1, p 6, ssk, k 9, k 2 tog, p 8—27 sts.
Row 16: Yo, k on k, p on p across row.
Row 17: Yo, k 1, p 7, ssk, k 7, k 2 tog, p 9—27 sts.
Row 18: Rep Row 16.
Row 19: Yo, k 1, p 8, ssk, k 5, k 2 tog, p 10—27 sts.
Row 20: Rep Row 16.
Row 21: Yo, k 1, p 9, ssk, k 3, k 2 tog, p 11—27 sts.
Row 22: Rep Row 16.
Row 23: Yo, k 1, p 10, ssk, k 1, k 2 tog, p 12—27 sts.
Row 24: Rep Row 16.
Row 25: Yo, k 1, p 11, sl 1, k 2 tog, psso, p 13.
Row 26: Yo, k across.
Row 27: Yo, k 1, p across.
Row 28: Rep Row 26.
Row 29: Rep Row 27.
Rows 30 and 31: Rep Row 26.
Row 32: Rep Row 27.
Rows 33 and 34: Rep Row 26.
Row 35: Yo, k 2, * p 3, k 1; rep from * across until 2 sts rem; end k 2.
Row 36: Yo, k 2, * in next st, work (p 1, yo, p 1), ** k 3; rep from *; end last rep at **; k 2—56 sts.
Row 37: Yo, k 1, p 1, * k 3, p 3; rep from * across—57 sts.
Row 38: Yo, * k 3, p 3 tog; rep from * across until 3 sts rem; end k 3—40 sts.
Row 39: Yo, k across.
Row 40: Yo, k 1, p across.
Row 41: Rep Row 39.
Rows 42 and 43: Rep Row 40.
Row 44: Rep Row 39—46 sts.
Note: Row 45 begins the dec for the second half of the square.
Row 45: Yo, p 2 tog, p across to last 2 sts; p 2 tog—45 sts.
Row 46: Yo, k 2 tog, k across to last 2 sts, k 2 tog.
Rows 47–50: Beg with Row 46, alternately rep rows 46 and 45.
Row 51: Yo, k 2 tog, * k 1, yo, k 2 tog; rep from * until 2 sts rem; k 2 tog.
Rows 52, 53, and 55: Rep Row 46.
Rows 54 and 56: Rep Row 45.
Row 57: Rep Row 51.
Rows 58 and 59: Rep Row 46.
Row 60: Rep Row 45.
Rows 61 and 62: Rep Row 46.
Row 63: Yo, k 2 tog, * k 1, p 1; rep from * until 2 sts rem, k 2 tog.
Row 64: Yo, p 2 tog, * p 1, k 1; rep from * until 2 sts rem, p 2 tog.

Rep rows 63 and 64 until 14 sts rem. With the right side of the square facing you, work a rep of Row 45. Then rep rows 45 and 46 in that order until 3 sts rem. P 3 tog; bind off rem sts.

ASSEMBLY: Join four squares together into a large 15-inch square, placing the leaf motifs in the center. Sew the squares together through the yarn overs at the beginning and end of the alternating rows for an invisible seam.

Assemble 11 more 15-inch squares in the same manner. Sew the 15-inch squares into four horizontal strips, each strip made from three squares. Sew the strips together.

BORDER: With the circular needle, pick up and k 201 sts across one short end of the afghan. Work in garter st (k every row) for 1 inch; bind off sts. Rep border on the opposite end of the afghan.

Pick up and k 279 sts across one long side of the afghan (including the border sts); work in garter st for 1 inch; bind off all sts. Rep on the opposite side.

Lightly block the afghan to shape.

Crocheted Bag

Shown on page 106.
Crocheted bag measures approximately 7 inches long excluding the cord handle and tassel.

MATERIALS

Krcinik 8-ply Ombres (300-meter ball): 2 balls of misty rainbow (No. 1500)
Size 7 steel crochet hook
18-inch square each of rose velvet and acetate lining fabric
Matching rose sewing thread
3 yards of light rose satin cording
Hot-glue gun and glue sticks

Abbreviations: See page 99.

INSTRUCTIONS

Beg at center, ch 5, join with sl st to form ring.

Rnd 1: Ch 5, dc in ring, (ch 2, dc in ring) 6 times; ch 2, join with sl st to third ch of beg ch-5.

Rnd 2: Sl st into ch-2 sp, ch 3, 3 dc in same sp; * 4 dc in next ch-2 sp; rep from * around; join to top of beg ch-3.

Rnd 3: Ch 1, sc in same st as join; * ch 4, sk dc, sc in next dc; rep from * 14 times more; end ch 2, join with dc in beg sc.

Rnd 4: Ch 3, in lp just made work 3 dc, ch 1; * 4 dc in next lp, ch 1; rep from * around; end ch 1, join to top of beg ch-3.

Rnd 5: Ch 3, dc in next 3 dc, ch 2; * dc in next 4 dc, ch 2; rep from * around; join to top of beg ch-3.

Rnd 6: Sl st in next 3 dc; * in next ch-2 sp work sc, ch 3, and sc; ch 5; rep from * around; end ch 5, join with sl st to beg sc; fasten off.

Rnd 7: Join thread in any ch-5 lp, **ch 3, in same lp work dc, ch 2, and 2 dc—beg shell made;** * ch 4, in next ch-5 lp work **2 dc, ch 2, 2 dc—shell made;** rep from * around; end ch 4, join to top of beg ch-3.

Rnd 8: Sl st in next dc and into ch-2 sp, work beg shell. (*Note:* Rnds 9–25 begin this way and read "sl st and work beg shell.") * Ch 5, shell in ch-2 sp of shell; rep from * around; end ch 5, join to top of beg ch-3.

Rnd 9: Sl st and work beg shell; * ch 2, dc in center ch of ch-5 lp, ch 2, shell in ch-2 sp of shell; rep from * around; end ch 2, join with sl st to top of beg ch-3. (*Note:* Rnds 10–26 end this way and read "end ch 2, join.")

Rnd 10: Sl st and work beg shell; * ch 2, sk 2 dc of shell, 3 dc in next dc, ch 2, shell in ch-2 sp of next shell; rep from * around; end ch 2, join.

Rnd 11: Sl st and work beg shell; * ch 2, 2 dc in first dc of 3-dc grp, dc in next dc, 2 dc in next dc, ch 2, shell in ch-2 sp of shell; rep from * around; end ch 2, join.

Rnd 12: Sl st and work beg shell; * ch 2, dc in each of first 2 dc of 5-dc grp, ch 2, sk dc, dc in next 2 dc, ch 2, shell in ch-2 sp of shell; rep from * around; end ch 2, join.

Rnd 13: Sl st and work beg shell; * ch 2, sk 2 dc of shell, dc in each of next 2 dc, 3 dc in ch-2 sp, dc in next 2 dc, ch 2, shell in ch-2 sp of shell; rep from * around; end ch 2, join.

Rnd 14: Sl st and work beg shell; * ch 2, dc in first 3 dc of 7-dc grp, ch 2, sk dc, dc in next 3 dc, ch 2, shell in ch-2 sp of shell; rep from * around; end ch 2, join.

Rnd 15: Sl st and work beg shell; * ch 2, sk 2 dc of shell, dc in next 3 dc, 3 dc in ch-2 sp, dc in next 3 dc, ch 2, shell in ch-2 sp of shell; rep from * around; end ch 2, join.

Rnd 16: Sl st and work beg shell; * ch 2, dc in first 4 dc of 9-dc grp, ch 2, sk dc, dc in next 4 dc, ch 2, shell in ch-2 sp of shell; rep from * around; end ch 2, join.

Rnd 17: Sl st and work beg shell; * ch 2, sk 2 dc of shell, dc in next 4 dc, 3 dc in ch-2 sp, dc in next 4 dc, ch 2, shell in ch-2 sp of next shell; rep from * around; end ch 2, join.

Rnd 18: Sl st and work beg shell; * ch 2, sk 2 dc of shell, (dc in next 3 dc, ch 1, sk dc) 2 times, dc in next 3 dc, ch 2, shell in ch-2 sp of next shell; rep from * around; end ch 2, join.

Rnd 19: Sl st and work beg shell; * ch 2, sk 2 dc of shell, dc in next 3 dc, 2 dc in ch-1 sp, ch 3, sk 3 dc, 2 dc in next ch-1 sp, dc in next 3 dc, ch 2, shell in ch-2 sp of next shell; rep from * around; end ch 2, join.

Rnd 20: Sl st and work beg shell; * ch 2, dc in first 3 dc of 5-dc grp, ch 2, sk dc, dc in next dc, 3 dc in ch-3 lp, dc in next dc, ch 2, sk dc, dc in next 3 dc, ch 2, shell in ch-2 sp of next shell; rep from * around; end ch 2, join.

Rnd 21: Sl st and work beg shell; * ch 2, sk 2 dc of shell, dc in next 3 dc, ch 2, dc in next dc, ch 3, sk 3 dc, dc in next dc, ch 2, dc in next 3 dc, ch 2, shell in ch-2 sp of next shell; rep from * around; end ch 2, join.

Rnd 22: Sl st and work beg shell; * ch 2, sk 2 dc of shell, dc in next 3 dc, ch 2, dc in next dc, 4 dc in ch-3 lp, dc in dc, ch 2, dc in next 3 dc, ch 2, shell in ch-2 sp of next shell; rep from * around; end ch 2, join.

Rnd 23: Sl st and work beg shell; * ch 2, sk 2 dc of shell, dc in next 3 dc, 2 dc in ch-2 sp, dc in next 2 dc, ch 3, sk 2 dc, dc in next 2 dc, 2 dc in next ch-2 sp, dc in next 3 dc, ch 2, shell in ch-2 sp of next shell; rep from * around; end ch 2, join.

Rnd 24: Sl st and work beg shell; * ch 2, sk 2 dc of shell, dc in next 3 dc, ch 2, sk 2 dc, dc in next 2 dc, 4 dc in ch-3 sp, dc in next 2 dc, ch 2, sk 2 dc, dc in next 3 dc, ch 2, shell in ch-2 sp of next shell; rep from * around; end ch 2, join.

Rnd 25: Sl st and work beg shell; * ch 2, sk 2 dc of shell, dc in next 3 dc, ch 2, dc in next dc, ch 2, sk dc, dc in next dc, ch 3, sk 2 dc, dc in next dc, ch 2, sk dc, dc in next dc, ch 2, dc in next 3 dc, ch 2, shell in ch-2 sp of next shell; rep from * around; end ch 2, join.

Note: To work trc-cl in next three rounds, work as follows: **Holding back last lp of each trc, work 2 trc in sp or st, then yo and draw through all 3 lps on hook—trc-cl made.**

continued

Rnd 26: Sl st in next dc and into ch-2 sp, ch 3, in same sp work 5 dc; * ch 2, sk 2 dc of shell, sc in next 3 dc, ch 3, sk 2 ch-2 sp; in ch-3 lp work (trc-cl, ch 2) 2 times and trc-cl; ch 3, sk 2 ch-2 sp, sc in next 3 dc, ch 2, 6 dc in ch-2 sp of next shell; rep from * around; end ch 2, join.

Rnd 27: Sc in next dc, * (ch 3, sk dc, sc in next dc) 2 times; ch 3, sc in center sc of 3-sc grp, ch 4, trc-cl in first cl, ch 2; in next trc-cl work (trc-cl, ch 2) 2 times and trc-cl; ch 2, trc-cl in next trc-cl; ch 4, sc in center sc of 3-sc grp; ch 3, sk first dc of dc-grp, sc in next dc; rep from * around; end ch 3, join to beg sc.

Rnd 28: Sl st in next ch of ch-3 lp, sc in same lp; ch 3, sc in next lp, ch 3, * (in top of next cl work trc-cl, ch 2, and trc-cl; ch 2) 4 times; in top of next cl work trc-cl, ch 2, and trc-cl; ch 3, sk next 2 lps, sc in next lp, ch 3, sc in next lp, ch 3; rep from * around; end ch 3, join to beg sc.

Rnd 29: Sl st into ch-3 lp, ch 1, sc in same lp; **ch 3, sc in third ch from hook—picot made;** sc in same lp; * 4 sc in next lp; (in next ch-2 sp work sc, picot, and sc) 9 times, 4 sc in next lp, in next lp work sc, picot, and sc; rep from * around; join with sl st to beg sc. Fasten off.

PURSE LINING: Cut one circle of velvet and one circle of lining fabric the same diameter as the crocheted circle of Rnd 25.

With the wrong sides of both fabric pieces together, zigzag-stitch around the edge of the fabric circles with the rose-color thread.

With the velvet centered against the wrong side of the crocheted circle, hand- or machine-sew the lining in place.

HANDLES: Cut two 42-inch-long pieces of cording. Pass one cord over and under the mesh openings of Rnd 25 until the cord ends meet. On the direct opposite side of that same rnd, pass the second cord over and under the open holes until those ends meet. Tie the cord ends together with overhand knots. Trim the ends close to the knots.

When you pull the handles, they pull the sides of the bag in and close the bag.

TASSELS: Make a 4-inch-long tassel with the misty rainbow thread following the tassel instructions on page 42.

Sew the tassel securely to the bottom of the crocheted circle in the center of the beginning ring.

Make two 2-inch-long tassels using the misty rainbow thread. Sew the finished tassels into the overhand knots of the cord; add hot glue to secure the tassels to the knots.

FILET CROCHET GRAPE BEDSPREAD

Shown on page 106.
Spread measures approximately 100x124 inches.

MATERIALS

Coats & Clark 3-cord crochet cotton (500-yard ball): 35 balls of ecru
3 yards of 36-inch-wide muslin fabric to match crochet cotton
Ecru sewing thread; sewing needle
Size 13 steel crochet hook

Abbreviations: See page 99.
Gauge: 11 sp = 2 inches; 11 rows = 2 inches.

INSTRUCTIONS

See page 157 for information on the filet crochet technique.

GRAPE FILET PANEL (make four): Beg at bottom, ch 213.

Note: The panel on the spread shown on page 106 has 11 grape motifs. Work the rep bet rows 8–63 for the length you desire.

Row 1: Dc in fourth ch from hook and in next 2 ch; * ch 2, sk 2 ch, dc in next ch; rep from * across until 3 ch rem; dc in last 3 ch—68 sp made; ch 3, turn.

Row 2: Sk first dc, dc in next 3 dc; (ch 2, dc in next dc) 29 times; (2 dc in ch-2 sp, dc in next dc) twice; (ch 2, dc in next dc) 37 times; dc in next 2 dc; dc in top of turning ch; ch 3, turn.

Rows 3–63: Referring to the chart, *opposite, bottom,* work in filet crochet.

Rep rows 8–63 nine times more. Rep rows 8–57, then work only the stem portion of the design on rows 58–63. Do not rep the grape design. Fasten off.

GRAPE LEAF BORDER: Beg at one end, ch 77.

Row 1: Dc in eighth ch from hook, (ch 2, sk 2 ch, dc in next ch) 22 times, dc in last 3 ch—23 sp and 1 bl made; ch 10, turn.

Row 2: **Dc in eighth ch from hook, dc in next 2 ch, dc in next dc—sp and bl made; ch 2, sk 2 dc, dc in next dc—sp over bl made, 2 dc in next ch-2 sp, dc in next dc—bl over sp made;** (ch 2, dc in next dc) 21 times; ch 2, end dc in third ch of beg ch-5; ch 5, turn.

Note: In the following rows, the term mesh indicates the number of squares on the chart. These squares could be sp or bls; follow the chart.

Row 3: Follow border chart, *opposite, upper right,* across 22 mesh, ch 3, trc in next ch-2 sp, ch 3, bl over last sp; ch 10, turn.

Row 4: Make sp and bl; ch 4, sk bl, sk 2 ch of ch-3, sc in first ch of ch-3, sc in trc, sc in next ch, ch 4, bl over next ch-2 sp, follow chart to end; ch 5, turn.

Row 5: Follow chart across 20 mesh; ch 4, sk bl, sk 3 ch, sc in next ch, sc in next 3 sc, sc in next ch, ch 4, bl over last sp; ch 10, turn.

Row 6: Sp and bl, ch 2, sk bl, bl over next sp, ch 3, sk next sc, sc in next 3 sc, ch 3, follow chart to end; ch 5, turn.

Row 7: Follow chart across 22 mesh; ch 3, trc in center sc, ch 3, bl over next ch-3 sp, ch 3, bl over next sp, ch 3, trc in next sp, ch 3, bl over last sp, ch 10, turn.

Rows 8–36: Work following the border chart.

Rep rows 5–36 for pat. End last rep on Row 32; fasten off. The bedspread shown has 74 grape leaves going around it.

continued

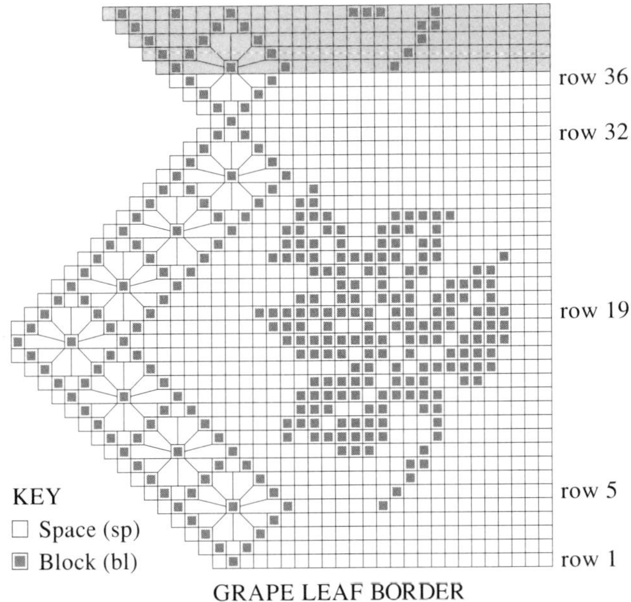

GRAPE LEAF BORDER

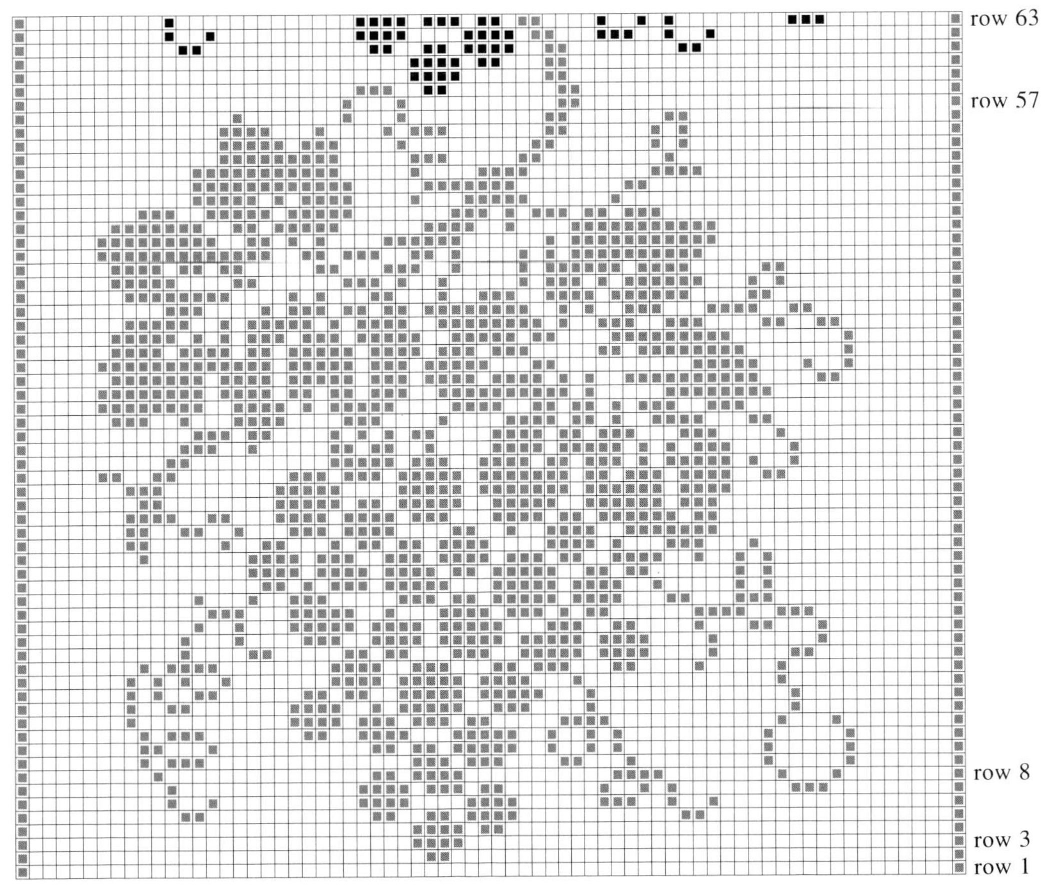

GRAPE PANEL

FILET CROCHET GRAPE BEDSPREAD PATTERNS

INSIDE BORDER EDGING: Join the thread in the first sp on the straight edge of the border.

Row 1: Ch 3, sk sp, dc in next sp, ch 8, **yo hook four times, in same sp draw up lp, yo and draw through 2 lps twice, yo hook twice, sk sp, in next sp draw up lp, yo and draw through 2 lps six times—Y-st made;** (ch 5, Y-st) to end; turn.

Row 2: * **Ch 3, sc in third ch from hook—picot made,** sc in sp, picot, sc in top of Y-st; rep from * across; fasten off.

OUTSIDE BORDER EDGING: Join thread around dc at end of Row 1 of border; ch 1, sc in next ch-sp , * ch 3, trc in same sp, picot, **(holding back last lp on hook, work 2 trc in same sp, yo and draw through 3 lps on hook—joint-trc made,** picot) twice in same sp, joint-trc in same sp, ch 1, sc in next sp; rep from * across—3 joint-trc and 4 picots in each ch-sp; end sc around dc of last bl; fasten off. Whipstitch first and last rows together.

FINISHING: Cut fabric into three panels, each 12x106 inches (or the length to fit your grape panels). Fold over ¼-inch hem twice and machine-stitch along all four sides of each fabric panel.

Hand- or machine-stitch the filet panels to the fabric panels. Sew the hemmed long edge of the fabric panel to the dc on the side edge of the filet panel. Assemble the spread in the following order: filet, fabric, filet, fabric, filet, fabric, and filet.

Stitch picot edge of border over edges of the assembled spread, positioning the center of a leaf motif at the corners. Form an inverted pleat at each side of the corners, sewing four Y-sts over four Y-sts on each side of the corner Y-st. There will be one leaf motif in the pleat at each corner, 16 motifs across each end, and 19 motifs on each side. Sew the last row of the grape leaf border to the border foundation chain with invisible stitches.

COOKIE CUTTER SACHETS

Shown on page 107.

MATERIALS
For one sachet

Cookie cutter; potpourri
Nonpermanent fabric marker
Matching thread; sewing needle
Two pieces of satin fabric slightly larger than the cookie cutter
One piece of lace fabric slightly larger than the cookie cutter
One piece of satin or cotton braid slightly longer than the outline of the cookie cutter
6 inches *each* of ⅛-, ¼-, and ⅜-inch-wide satin ribbons
Buttons, lace, and ribbon rosettes for trim (optional)

INSTRUCTIONS

Place cookie cutter on the right side of one piece of satin fabric; draw around the outside of the cookie cutter with the nonpermanent fabric marker. *Do not cut out.*

With wrong sides together, place the fabric with the design drawn on it on top of the second piece of satin fabric. Place the lace fabric atop the drawn design. The outline of the design will show through the lace. Pin the three layers of fabric together.

Machine-stitch through all three fabric layers along the marked outline of the design, leaving an opening for stuffing with potpourri.

Cut around the design leaving a ¼-inch seam allowance. Stuff the potpourri between the satin and lace, and hand-stitch the opening closed.

Hand-stitch the braided edging around the shape covering the raw edges.

Decorating the sachet

To make a ribbon bouquet, use the ⅛-, ¼-, and ⅜-inch ribbons. Form both the ⅛- and ¼-inch ribbons into bow shapes (without the knot) and fold the ⅜-inch ribbon in half to form a single loop (the hanger); combine the three ribbons so the single ribbon loop sticks up 2 inches beyond the bow shapes. Sew a button or ribbon rosette to the center of the bow shapes and then to the sachet.

Refer to the photograph on page 107 for other ideas to trim your sachet.

SQUARE CROCHETED TABLE CENTERPIECE

Shown on page 109.
The triangular edging measures 11½ inches along the longest side.

MATERIALS

Anchor Mercer crochet cotton, Size 20 (84-yard ball): 8 balls of white
Size 10 steel crochet hook
15-inch square of white cotton fabric

Abbreviations: See page 99.
Gauge: 15 dc = 1 inch; 6 rows = 1 inch.

INSTRUCTIONS

TRIANGLE EDGING (make four): Ch 157.

Row 1: Dc in seventh ch from hook, ch 3, dc in same ch; (ch 2, sk 3 ch, **in next ch work dc, ch 3, and dc—V-st made)** four times, ch 2; * sk 3 ch, dc in next 10 ch, ch 1, sk 2 ch, dc in next 10 ch; (ch 2, sk 3 ch, V-st in next ch) 5 times, ** ch 2; rep from * 2 times more; end last rep at **, ch 3, turn.

Row 2: (In next ch-3 lp make 2 dc, ch 2, and 2 dc; ch 1) 5 times; * dc in next 8 dc; ch 1, sk dc, (dc in next dc, ch 1) twice; sk next dc, dc in next 8 dc, ch 1; **(in next ch-3 lp make 2 dc, ch 2, and 2 dc—shell made,** ** ch 1) 5 times; rep from * 2 times more; end last rep at **; ch 3, turn.

Row 3: * (V-st in next ch-2 sp, ch 2) 5 times; dc in next 6 dc; ch 1, sk dc, dc in next dc, (ch 1, dc in next dc) 3 times, ch 1, sk dc, dc in next 6 dc, ch 2; rep from * 2 times more; end with (V-st in ch-2 sp, ch 2) 4 times, V-st in ch-2 sp; ch 3, turn.

Row 4: * (Shell in next ch-3 lp, ch 1) 5

times; dc in 4 dc, ch 1, sk dc, dc in next dc, (ch 1, dc in next dc) 5 times, ch 1, sk dc, dc in next 4 dc, ch 1; rep from * 2 times more; end with (shell in next ch-3 lp, ch 1) 4 times, shell in ch-3 lp; ch 3, turn.

Row 5: * (V-st in next ch-2 sp, ch 2) 5 times; dc in next 2 dc; ch 1, sk dc, dc in next dc, (ch 1, dc in next dc) 7 times; ch 1, sk dc, dc in next 2 dc, ch 2; rep from * 2 times more; end with (V-st in next ch-2 sp, ch 2) 4 times, V-st in ch-2 sp; ch 3, turn.

Row 6: * (Shell in next ch-3 lp, ch 1) 5 times; dc in next 2 dc, dc in next sp, dc in dc; (ch 1, dc in next dc) 7 times; dc in next sp, dc in next 2 dc, ch 1; rep from * 2 times more; end with (shell in next ch-3 lp, ch 1) 4 times, shell in ch-3 lp; ch 3, turn.

Row 7: * (V-st in next ch-2 sp, ch 2) 5 times; dc in 4 dc, dc in next sp; dc in dc; (ch 1, dc in next dc) 5 times, dc in next sp, dc in next 4 dc, ch 2; rep from * 2 times more; end with (V-st in next ch-2 sp, ch 2) 4 times, V-st in ch-2 sp; ch 3, turn.

Row 8: * (Shell in next ch-3 lp, ch 1) 5 times; dc in next 6 dc, dc in next sp, dc in dc; (ch 1, dc in next dc) 3 times; dc in sp, dc in next 6 dc, ch 1; rep from * 2 times more; end with (shell in next ch-3 lp, ch 1) 4 times, shell in ch-3 lp; ch 3, turn.

Row 9: * (V-st in next ch-2 sp, ch 2) 5 times; dc in next 8 dc, dc in next sp, dc in dc; ch 1, dc in dc, dc in sp, dc in next 8 dc, ch 2; rep from * 2 times more; end with (V-st in next ch-2 sp, ch 2) 4 times, V-st in ch-2 sp; fasten off.

Row 10: Sk one complete bl pat; join thread in first dc of second bl pat, ch 6, dc in same dc; * ch 2, sk 4 dc, V-st in next dc; ch 2, sk 4 dc, V-st in next ch-1 sp; (ch 2, sk 4 dc, V-st in next dc) twice, ch 2; (dc in next dc, dc in next sp) 4 times, dc in same sp, dc in next dc, ch 1, sk ch-3 sp, dc in next dc, 2 dc in next sp; (dc in next dc, dc in next sp) 3 times, dc in next dc; ch 2, in first dc of next pat bl make a V-st; rep from * once; end with ch 2, sk 4 dc, V-st in next dc; ch 2, sk 4 dc, V-st in ch-1 sp; ch 2, sk 4 dc, V-st in next dc; ch 2, sk 4 dc, V-st in last dc; ch 3, turn.

Row 11: * (Shell in next ch-3 lp, ch 1) 5 times; dc in next 8 dc; ch 1, sk dc, dc in next dc; ch 1, dc in next dc; ch 1, sk dc, dc in next 8 dc, ch 1; rep from * once; end with (shell in next ch-3 lp, ch 1) 4 times, shell in ch-3 lp; ch 3, turn.

Row 12: * (V-st in next ch-2 sp, ch 2) 5 times; dc in next 6 dc; ch 1, sk dc, dc in next dc; (ch 1, dc in next dc) 3 times; ch 1, sk dc, dc in next 6 dc, ch 2; rep from * once; end with (V-st in next ch-2 sp, ch 2) 4 times, V-st in ch-2 sp; ch 3, turn.

Row 13: * (Shell in next ch-3 lp, ch 1) 5 times; dc in next 4 dc, ch 1, sk dc, dc in next dc; (ch 1, dc in next dc) 5 times; ch 1, sk dc, dc in next 4 dc, ch 1; rep from * once; end with (shell in next ch-3 lp, ch 1) 4 times, shell in ch-3 lp; ch 3, turn.

Row 14: * (V-st in next ch-2 sp, ch 2) 5 times; dc in next 2 dc; ch 1, sk dc, dc in next dc; (ch 1, dc in next dc) 7 times; ch 1, sk dc, dc in next 2 dc, ch 2; rep from * once; end with (V-st in next ch-2 sp, ch 2) 4 times, V-st in ch-2 sp; ch 3, turn.

Row 15: * (Shell in next ch-3 lp, ch 1) 5 times; dc in next 2 dc, dc in sp, dc in dc; (ch 1, dc in next dc) 7 times; dc in sp, dc in next 2 dc, ch 1; rep from * once; end with (shell in next ch-3 lp, ch 1) 4 times, shell in ch-3 lp; ch 3, turn.

Row 16: * (V-st in next ch-2 sp, ch 2) 5 times; dc in next 4 dc, dc in sp, dc in dc; (ch 1, dc in next dc) 5 times, dc in sp, dc in next 4 dc, ch 2; rep from * once; end with (V-st in next ch-2 sp, ch 2) 4 times, V-st in ch-2 sp; ch 3, turn.

Row 17: * (Shell in next ch-3 lp, ch 1) 5 times; dc in next 6 dc, dc in sp, dc in dc; (ch 1, dc in next dc) 3 times, dc in sp, dc in next 6 dc, ch 1; rep from * once; (shell in next ch-3 lp, ch 1) 4 times, shell in ch-3 lp; ch 3, turn.

Row 18: * (V-st in next ch-2 sp, ch 2) 5 times; dc in next 8 dc, dc in sp, dc in dc; ch 1, dc in dc, dc in sp, dc in next 8 dc, ch 2; rep from * once; (V-st in next ch-2 sp, ch 2) 4 times, V-st in ch-2 sp; fasten off.

Row 19: Sk one complete bl pat; join thread in first dc of second bl pat, ch 6, dc in same dc; * ch 2, sk 4 dc, V-st in next dc; ch 2, sk 4 dc, V-st in next ch-1 sp; (ch 2, sk 4 dc, V-st in next dc) twice **, ch 2; (dc in next dc, dc in next sp) 4 times, dc in same sp, dc in next dc, ch 1, sk ch-3 sp, dc in next dc, 2 dc in next sp; (dc in next dc, dc in next sp) 3 times, dc in next dc; ch 2, in first dc of next pat bl make a V-st; rep from * to ** once; ch 3, turn.

Row 20: (Shell in next ch-3 lp, ch 1) 5 times; dc in next 8 dc; ch 1, sk dc, dc in next dc, ch 1, dc in dc, ch 1, sk dc, dc in next 8 dc, ch 1; (shell in next ch-3 lp, ch 1) 4 times, shell in ch-3 lp; ch 3, turn.

Row 21: (V-st in next ch-2 sp, ch 2) 5 times; dc in next 6 dc; ch 1, sk dc, dc in next dc, (ch 1, dc in next dc) 3 times, ch 1, sk dc, dc in next 6 dc, ch 2; (V-st in next ch-2 sp, ch 2) 4 times, V-st in ch-2 sp; ch 3, turn.

Row 22: (Shell in next ch-3 lp, ch 1) 5 times; dc in next 4 dc; ch 1, sk dc, dc in dc; (ch 1, dc in next dc) 5 times, ch 1, sk dc, dc in next 4 dc; ch 1, (shell in next ch-3 lp, ch 1) 4 times, shell in ch-3 lp; ch 3, turn.

Row 23: (V-st in next ch-2 sp, ch 2) 5 times, dc in next 2 dc, ch 1, sk dc, dc in dc, (ch 1, dc in next dc) 7 times; ch 1, sk dc, dc in next 2 dc; ch 2, (V-st in next ch-2 sp, ch 2) 4 times, V-st in ch-2 sp; ch 3, turn.

Row 24: (Shell in next ch-3 lp, ch 1) 5 times; dc in next 2 dc, dc in sp, dc in dc; (ch 1, dc) 7 times; dc in sp, dc in next 2 dc, ch 1; (shell in next ch-3 lp, ch 1) 4 times, shell in ch-3 lp; ch 3, turn.

Row 25: (V-st in next ch-2 sp, ch 2) 5 times; dc in next 4 dc, dc in sp, dc in dc; (ch 1, dc in next dc) 5 times; dc in sp, dc in next 4 dc, ch 2; (V-st in next ch-2 sp, ch 2) 4 times, V-st in ch-2 sp; ch 3, turn.

Row 26: (Shell in next ch-3 lp, ch 1) 5 times; dc in next 6 dc, dc in sp, dc in dc; (ch 1, dc in next dc) 3 times, dc in sp, dc in next 6 dc, ch 1; (shell in next ch-3 lp, ch 1) 4 times, shell in ch-3 lp; ch 3, turn.

Row 27: (V-st in next ch-2 sp, ch 2) 5 times; dc in next 8 dc, dc in sp, dc in dc; ch 1, dc in dc, dc in sp; dc in next 8 dc, ch 2; (V-st in next ch-2 sp, ch 2) 4 times, V-st in ch-2 sp; fasten off.

Row 28: Sk one complete bl pat; join thread in first dc of second bl pat, ch 6, dc in same dc; ch 2, sk 4 dc, V-st in next dc; ch 2, sk 4 dc, V-st in next ch-1 sp; (ch 2, sk 4 dc, V-st in next dc) twice; ch 3, turn.

continued

Row 29: (Shell in next ch-3 lp, ch 1) 4 times, shell in ch-3 lp; ch 3, turn.

Row 30: (V-st in next ch-2 sp, ch 2) 4 times, V-st in ch-2 sp; ch 3, turn.

Rows 31–35: Rep rows 29 and 30.

FINISHING: Block the four triangular pieces. Cut the fabric square 2½ inches larger than the length of the crocheted edging. Turn under each side of the fabric ¼ inch once, then 1 inch once, and press. Hem the fabric. Hand-sew the triangles onto all four sides of the fabric square.

CROCHETED EDGING: Join thread in last shell of Row 35 on one triangle edging; turn, ch 5, sc in ch-2 sp, (ch 5, sc in same sp) twice; * ch 2, sc in next ch-2 sp, (ch 5, sc in same sp) 3 times; rep from * to corner; ** working in the side of sts, ch 2, sc in ch-3 lp; (ch 5, sc in same lp) 3 times; rep from ** to next corner. Rep from first * around; join; fasten off.

CREWEL PANSY PICTURE MAT

Shown on page 108.
The center opening in the mat is 3⅞x5½ inches.

MATERIALS

Two 18x20-inch pieces of ecru linen
One skein *each* of DMC Médicis 2-ply wool yarn in the following colors: purple (No. 7794), medium purple (No. 7895), light purple (No. 7896), periwinkle blue (No. 8333), light periwinkle (No. 8332), dark avocado (No. 8403), avocado (No. 8418), light avocado (No. 8411), yellow (No. 7725), orange (No. 7742), light yellow (No. 8328), and black
No. 4 crewel needle
Embroidery hoop; tracing paper
Nonpermanent fabric marker
Gold cording; gold thread
Fleece batting; sewing thread to match linen; fusible interfacing
14x15-inch piece of mat board

continued

PICTURE MAT PATTERN

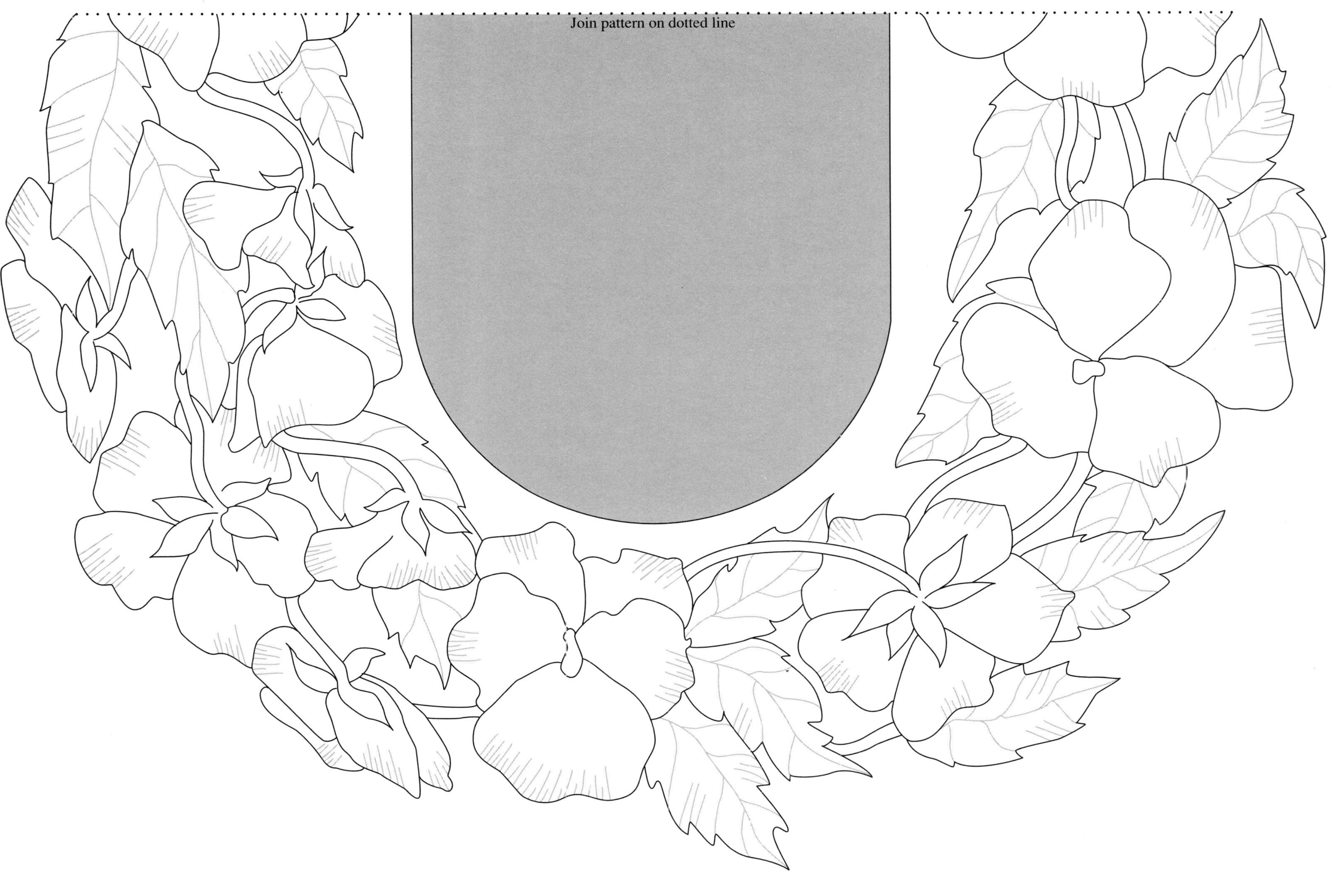
Join pattern on dotted line

INSTRUCTIONS

TO TRANSFER THE DESIGN: The pattern for the picture mat is on pages 126 and 127. Trace the pattern onto tracing paper, joining the two portions on the dotted lines to make one pattern. Retrace the drawing with a black marker to darken the lines. Trace onto the linen using the fabric marker.

WORKING THE DESIGN: Place the fabric in an embroidery hoop. Refer to the photograph on page 108 for ideas in shading the flowers and leaves. Refer to pages 69 and 79 for diagrams that illustrate how to work the stitches used in this picture mat.

Using one strand of yarn, work long-and-short stitches to shade each pansy with two or three colors of the purple and blue yarns. Work an orange satin stitch square in the center of the pansies, then make yellow and black straight stitches radiating out from the centers.

Shade the leaves and stems with the three colors of avocado green. Use outline stitches for the stems and satin stitch or long-and-short stitch for the leaves.

FINISHING: Lightly press the wrong side of the finished crewel piece. Following the manufacturer's instructions, fuse the interfacing to the wrong side of the center oval of the crewel piece, fusing it just beyond the stitching line but not into the embroidery. Baste a contrasting thread along the marked stitching line. Place the fleece batting and the second piece of linen atop the right side of the stitched piece. Turn over the layered pieces and machine-stitch around the basted line of the oval. Cut out the center, leaving a ¼-inch seam allowance next to the stitching; clip the curves around the opening. Turn the crewel piece right side out. Using gold thread, whipstitch gold cording around the edge of the opening.

Cut the piece of mat board to fit your frame. Cut an oval opening in the center of the mat board a little larger than the crewel opening. Insert the mat board between the fleece batting and the back piece of linen. Mat and frame as desired.

FILET CROCHET FORGET-ME-NOT SHUTTER PANELS

Shown on page 109.
Each panel fits a 10x24-inch fabric shutter frame.

MATERIALS
For four panels

J. & P. Coats Knit-Cro-Sheen (225-yard ball): 6 balls of ecru
Size 7 steel crochet hook
Four 10x24-inch fabric shutter frames
Tapestry needle

Abbreviations: See page 99.
Gauge: 4 sp = 1 inch; 4½ rows = 1 inch.

INSTRUCTIONS

The design for the crocheted panels can be adapted to fit any size shutter frame. Add or subtract the open mesh background squares along the sides of the design to narrow or widen the panel. Repeat the flower design or end the design earlier to increase or decrease the length of the panel.

Read the chart, *below,* from right to left for odd-numbered rows and from left to right for even-numbered rows. For best results, a new ball of thread should be tied on at the beginning or end of a row. See page 157 for more information on the filet crochet technique.

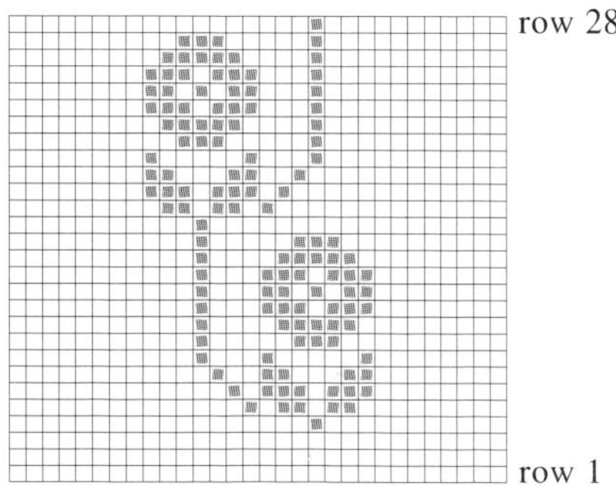

SHUTTER PANELS PATTERN

Ch 95.

Row 1: Dc in eighth ch from hook; * ch 2, sk 2 ch, dc in next ch; rep from * across, ch 5, turn—30 sp.

Rows 2 and 3: Sk first dc, dc in next dc; * ch 2, dc in next dc—sp over sp made; rep from * across to last sp, end with ch 2, sk 2 sts of turning ch, dc in next ch, ch 5, turn.

Row 4: Work 18 sp over sp, 2 dc in next sp, dc in next dc—bl over sp made; work 11 sp to finish row; ch 5, turn.

Row 5: Work 9 sp, (2 dc in next sp, dc in next dc) twice—2 bls made; ch 2, sk 2 dc, dc in next dc—sp over bl made; (2 dc in next sp, dc in next dc) twice, ch 2, dc in next dc, 2 dc in sp, dc in next dc, make 14 sp to finish row; ch 5, turn.

Row 6: Work 13 sp, complete row following chart from left to right; ch 5, turn.

Rows 7–28: Work bl and sp design as shown on chart. All sp consist of 2 dc with ch 2 bet, and all bls have 2 dc in place of the ch 2. Make ch 5 to turn at end of each row.

Rows 29–76: Rep rows 5–28 two times more.

Rows 77–79: Work 3 rows plain sp. *Do not* ch 5 or turn at end of last row.

Final rnd: Ch 1, sc in corner of last row, work 2 more sc over side of last dc made; cont working around panel by working 2 sc in each ch-2 sp along outer edges, and 2 sc in each corner; end 2 sc in last sp, join with sl st; fasten off.

FINISHING: Block the panels to shape; starch if desired.

Note: The panel is made slightly smaller than the frame opening and stretched into the shutter frame.

Lace the panels onto the rods at the bottom and top of the shutter frames using the tapestry needle and crochet thread.

Needlepoint Tips and Techniques

Yarns and threads

There are no limits when it comes to choosing yarns and threads for needlepoint as long as you can thread the fiber through the eye of a blunt-end needle. Refer to the chart, *below,* for a quick guide to the number of yarn strands for the different canvas gauges. This chart is based on continental and basket-weave stitches. For other stitches, you may have to add a strand or two of yarn.

Wool is the most popular yarn for traditional needlepoint. Of the many types available, Persian wool is the most widely used because it wears well, is easy to work with, and is available in more than 300 colors. It can be purchased in 1-yard lengths or by the skein. Persian wool is made of three strands loosely plied together so they can be separated and used individually.

Tapestry wool is a single-strand yarn that can be used in place of three strands of Persian wool. It is nondivisible so its use is limited to 10- and 12-count canvas.

Crewel yarn, used for embroidery, is a finer, single-strand yarn. It is especially nice for working petit point stitches.

When purchasing yarn, try to buy enough for the entire project so you can be sure the colors match. Also, look for colorfast yarns so you don't ruin a beautiful piece of handwork in the blocking stage.

Needles

For stitching needlepoint, use tapestry needles with blunt tips and large, elongated eyes. Blunt tips help you avoid splitting the yarns or threads of the canvas, and an elongated eye won't put undue stress on the yarn in the needle. The eye of the needle should be large enough to hold the thread easily, but narrow enough to pass through the canvas without distorting the threads.

Refer to the chart, *below,* for the correct needle sizes to use on the different counts of canvas.

Stitching techniques

Cut yarn or thread into workable lengths so it won't look worn from being pulled through the canvas too often. For best results, cut floss or pearl cotton into 36-inch lengths and wool strands into 18-inch lengths. Silk and metallic threads should be cut into 12- or 14-inch lengths.

To create smoother-looking stitches and to give the yarn or floss more loft, separate the strands of Persian wool and embroidery floss. Then thread the needle with the required number of strands to fill the canvas. This minimizes the amount of twist in the yarn and makes the stitches lie flatter.

Knots tied on the back of the canvas can cause unsightly bumps in the design. To avoid this, weave the ends of the yarn into the back of the work, or begin with waste knots. To make a waste knot, knot the end of the yarn and insert the needle into the canvas from front to back 10 stitches from the point where you will begin to stitch (the knot will be on top of the work). As you stitch, you will stitch over the yarn on the back side, securing it. Clip the knot and pull the end of the yarn to the back side of the canvas.

Try to maintain a uniform tension as you stitch. It makes the stitches look better and you will be less apt to distort the canvas.

When stitching background areas that need to be adjusted to fit a particular item (a footstool, for example), you can determine the amount of yarn you need to purchase using the following method. First figure in inches the length and width of the finished stitched canvas; multiply these two figures. Then measure the approximate length and width of the design image; multiply these two figures. Subtract the image measurement from the finished stitched canvas measurement to determine the number of background inches to be stitched.

Beginning with one 36-inch length of the yarn you are using for the project, stitch one square inch of the canvas, keeping track of the number of yards to complete the square inch. Multiply the number of yards per square inch times the number of background inches to determine the amount of yarn needed to complete the project.

Needle and Yarn Guide

Canvas Gauge	Needle Size	Persian Strands	Floss Strands	Pearl Cotton
10-mesh	#16	3	10–14	—
12-mesh	#18	3	8–11	Size 3
14-mesh	#20 or 22	2	6–9	Size 3
16-mesh	#22	2	4–7	Size 5
18-mesh	#22 or 24	1	3–5	Size 5

The Children's Corner

In the idealized landscape of the Victorian home, children, too, had their own special niche—the nursery. In the nursery, youngsters romped amongst toys and books and cheerful furnishings, all carefully arranged for their comfort and delight. Doted on by nannies, parents, and elder siblings, the youngest members of the family were considered its dearest treasures—"living poems" Longfellow called them, "better than all the ballads that were ever sung or said."

JACK
JACK
be nimble
be quick
Little Bo-peep
her sheep
MOTHER GOOSE

YOUNG AMERICA
YACH
ON
PRATTLER
RAGS AND
TATTE
"Just a
little salty"
ISCUIT
Beda Bak
YL
BOAT

aily printed paper adorned the walls, gorgeously printed books filled the shelves, and a marvelous array of store-bought toys filled every nook and cranny of the typical Victorian nursery. But then as now, the most treasured mementos of childhood were often the simplest things—an overstuffed pillow, a cozy coverlet, or a worn cloth doll.

Pictorial quilts and pillow tops, embroidered in simple red outline stitch on muslin, were especially popular for nursery decor. By the late 1880s, redwork designs copied from Kate Greenaway's illustrations, or depicting familiar nursery rhyme characters (like Jack Be Nimble and Little Bo-peep on page 131), were standard fixtures in most playrooms across the country. The colorful afghan-stitch coverlet, also pictured on page 131, is a crocheted version of another late 19th-century fad—the crazy quilt. Strewn with embroidered figures of butterflies, flowers, and whimsical animals, it is guaranteed to capture the heart of any child.

While store-bought dolls from England, France, and Germany were widely available in the United States by mid-century, homemade dolls still were favorites in the nursery. In the days when every young man donned a sailor suit for dress-up occasions, the little sailor doll, *opposite,* would have made an especially appealing playmate. For present-day collectors, tea-dyed fabrics give his costume an old-fashioned flavor.

Finally, the cross-stitched silhouette picture, *below,* is reminiscent of the hand-stitched pictures and samplers that crowded the walls of Victorian nurseries. Measuring 9x12 inches, this pretty design would be equally suitable for a small album top or a pillow front.

Instructions for these projects begin on page 136.

THEATRE

Playacting and games of imagination delighted Victorians of all ages, and amateur theatricals were among the most popular of family amusements. Puppet shows in particular were a favorite pastime, and none was more beloved than the venerable Punch and Judy shows of English tradition. The entire family often became involved in such productions, crafting beautifully detailed hand puppets like the pair pictured here, building elaborate theaters out of boxes and bed sheets, devising scripts, and acting out all the characters.

According to *The Young Folks Cyclopedia of Games and Sports*, published in 1890, "The chief characters are always Punch and his wife Judy, but many others are usually introduced, generally including a baby, a doctor, a policeman . . . and a hangman."

The rascally Punch is described in some detail: "Punch has a hooked nose and chin, pointing toward each other." Traditionally, his chief prop is a large stick, with which he gleefully pummels the other characters, as "his whole body rocks forward." Further, Punch "always speaks in a peculiar squeaking voice and gives a sort of squeal of joy at the discomfiture of his enemies."

The moment-to-moment action of the drama depends on the ingenuity of the puppeteer, of course, but the traditional plot line is oddly reminiscent of today's Saturday morning cartoons: "The play begins with an argument between Punch and Judy, and concludes with much shouting and flailing about, which is sure to delight the children." Patterns and instructions for the Punch and Judy puppets begin on page 150.

REDWORK NURSERY RHYME PILLOWS

Shown on page 131.
Design area measures approximately 9x12¾ inches.

MATERIALS
For one pillow

15x18-inch piece of muslin for embroidery (pillow front)
Two skeins of DMC red (No. 321) embroidery floss
Embroidery needle; embroidery hoop
Tracing paper; pencil
Nonpermanent fabric marker
Additional fabric and polyester filling for finishing the pillow as desired

INSTRUCTIONS

These designs are embroidered with one simple stitch—the outline or stem stitch. See the stitch diagram on page 79.

The outline stitch is flexible enough to follow any line or curve. The loop of the stitch can be above or below the needle, whichever is more comfortable for you. To create neat lines of stitches, however, work all loops in the same way and in the same direction. For smooth curves, make shorter stitches on the curved lines.

TO TRANSFER THE DESIGN: The patterns for the embroidery designs are given in two parts, *right* and *opposite* and on pages 138 and 139. Trace the patterns onto tracing paper, joining them on the dotted lines to make one pattern for each design. On a hard surface, retrace the drawing to darken the lines.

Center the muslin atop the traced drawing. Using a nonpermanent fabric marker, trace the design onto the fabric.

WORKING THE DESIGN: Place the fabric in an embroidery hoop. Using three strands of floss, work the design in outline stitches. When all embroidery is completed, remove all markings. Press the wrong side of the fabric.

Finish pillow as desired.

REDWORK PILLOW

Join pattern on dotted line
k
k
be
nimble
be
quick

REDWORK PILLOW

Join pattern on dotted line
has lost her sheep

VICTORIAN BABY AFGHAN

Shown on page 131.
The finished afghan is 38 inches square.

MATERIALS

Brunswick Germantown Knitting Worsted (3½-ounce skein): 3 skeins purple (No. 4141), 2 skeins *each* of red (No. 424) and yellow (No. 403), and 1 skein *each* of green (No. 467), violet (No. 497), and blue (No. 484)
18 to 20 skeins of Paternayan Persian wool (8-yard skein) in assorted colors, including at least four shades of green for stems, leaves, and other embroidery
Size H aluminum afghan hook
Size H crochet hook
Tapestry needle
6-inch square of cardboard

Abbreviations: See page 99.
Gauge: With H hook in afghan st:
4 sts = 1 inch; 8 rows = 1 inch.

INSTRUCTIONS

This afghan is stitched in five vertical strips. Each strip has five repeats of the square shown in Figure 1, *right, top,* with each square worked in different colors.

Before beginning, note the labeling (A, B, C, and D) on each side of the Figure 1 square. As you crochet each strip, rotate the illustration so that A, B, C, or D is at the bottom as indicated in the following instructions. Figure 2, *right, bottom,* shows the colors used in each square. The first square in Strip 1 is positioned as shown in Figure 1 with A at the bottom.

Starting Strip 1

Each strip is stitched from the bottom in afghan stitch. The right side of the work always should face you—never turn the work unless you are directed otherwise in the instructions.

With red yarn and afghan hook, ch 29.

Row 1 (first half): Insert hook in the top lp of second ch from hook, yo (wrap the yarn around the hook), draw the yarn through the ch and leave the lp on the hook—2 lps on the hook; * insert the hook in the top lp of the *next* ch, yo, draw the yarn through the ch and leave the lp on the hook; rep from the * across the row—29 lps on hook.

Row 1 (second half): Working from left to right, yo, draw the yarn through the *first* lp on the hook. * Yo, draw the yarn through 2 lps on hook; rep from * across the row until 1 lp rem on hook. The last lp is the first st of the next row. The upright bars formed in the completed row are the foundation for working pat sts in subsequent rows.

Row 2 (first half): Sk the first upright bar; * insert the hook behind the *front* lp

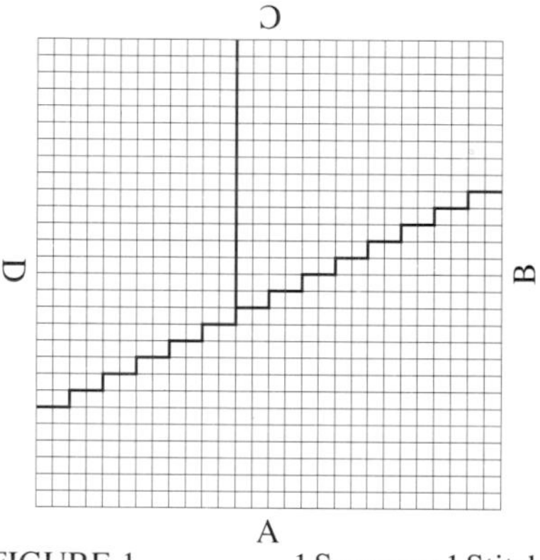

FIGURE 1 1 Square = 1 Stitch

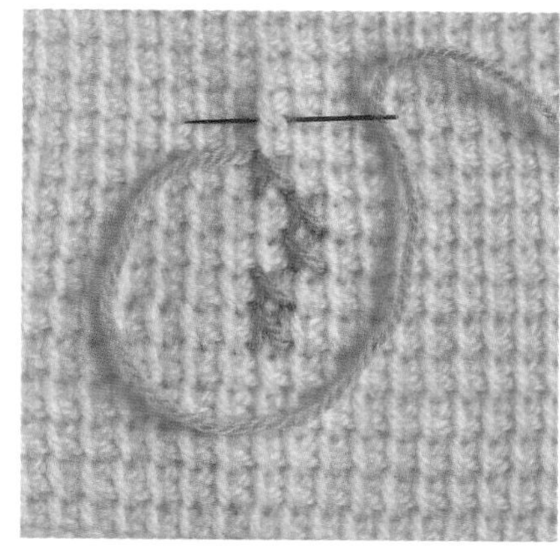

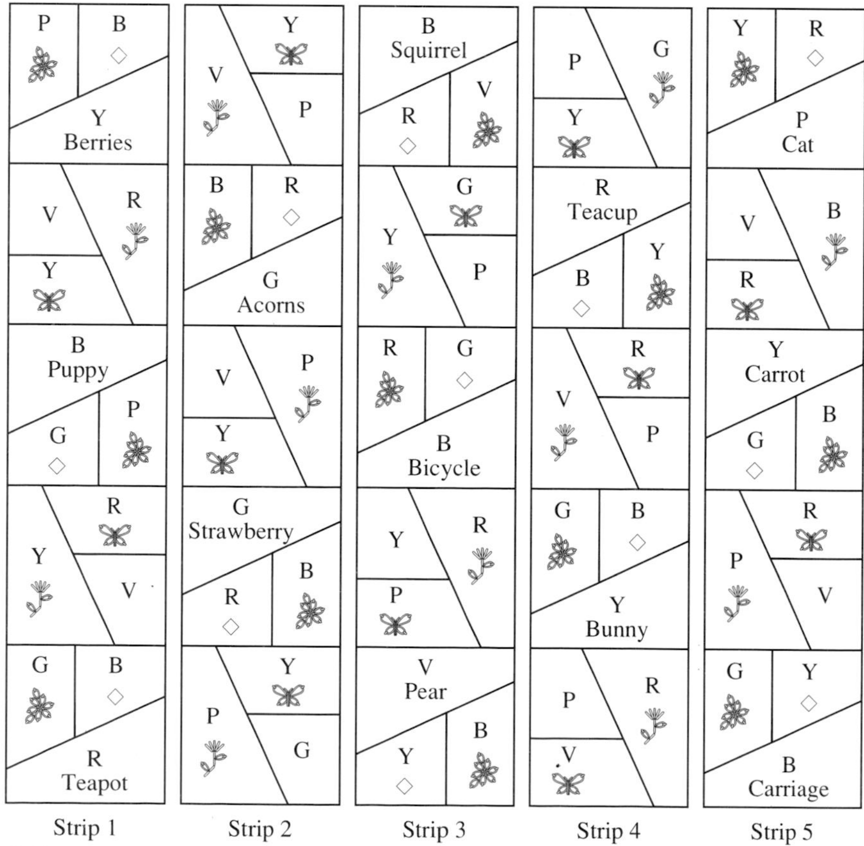

KEY P = Purple V = Violet R = Red Y = Yellow G = Green B = Blue
◇ = Cross-Stitch Diamond = Butterfly
= Straight Stitch Flower = Lazy Daisy Flower

FIGURE 2

of the next upright bar, yo, draw the yarn through the bar and leave the lp on the hook; rep from * across the row until 28 lps on hook; draw up lp in next bar and in lp behind last st—29 lps on hook.

Row 2 (second half): Rep the second half of Row 1.

Rows 3–6: Rep Row 2 (first and second halves).

CHANGING YARN COLORS: When changing colors in the middle of a row, work across the first half of the row using the first color and pick up the required number of stitches, referring to Figure 1 as you work. Drop the yarn in use to the back of the work. Pick up the required number of stitches with the next color.

On the second half of the row, take loops off the hook until one loop before the next color remains on the hook; drop yarn to back of work. Then, with the next color on the hook, take the two different-colored loops from the hook. Remove the loops in that color until one loop remains before the next color change. Continue across the row in this manner until one loop remains on the hook.

Row 7: With red yarn, pick up 27 lps on the hook; drop red yarn to back of work. With green yarn, pick up the 2 rem lps in the row. Work off first lp in green, then switch back to red to work across the row.

Rows 8–29: Referring to Figure 1, work red, green, and blue yarns to complete the square as shown.

Rows 30–59: Rotate Figure 1 so that B is at the bottom. Referring to Figure 2 for colors, cont working crochet following the st count in Figure 1.

Rows 60–149: Rotate Figure 1 so that C is at the bottom to work rows 60–89. Then turn the illustration to put D at the bottom. Return Figure 1 to the A position to crochet the last 29 rows.

Last row (bind-off row): Sk the first upright bar, * insert hook in front of the next bar, yo, draw the yarn through the bar and through the lp on the hook—sl st made and 1 lp on hook; rep from the * across the row, matching yarn colors as you come to them; fasten off.

Working remaining strips

Strip 2 begins with Figure 1 in the B position and progresses with C, D, A, and B. Strip 3 is C, D, A, B, and C, Strip 4 is D, A, B, C, and D, and Strip 5 is A, B, C, D, and A. Refer to Figure 2 for color changes.

When beginning strips 2, 3, and 4, make the starting ch in two colors to correspond with the first row.

EMBROIDERY: Cross-stitch and embroidery designs are given *below.* Work designs using two strands of Persian yarn. Referring to Figure 2 for placement, stitch designs right side up, upside down, and sideways on the block segments to fit the space. Refer to the cross-stitch photograph, *opposite,* to work cross-stitches on top of the afghan-stitch panels.

continued

LAZY DAISY FLOWER (FRENCH KNOT CENTER)

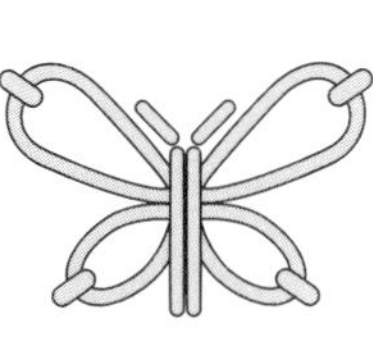

BUTTERFLY

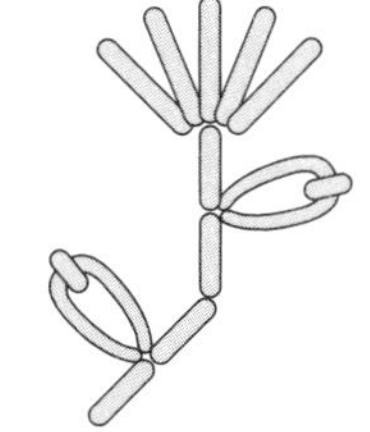

STRAIGHT STITCH FLOWER

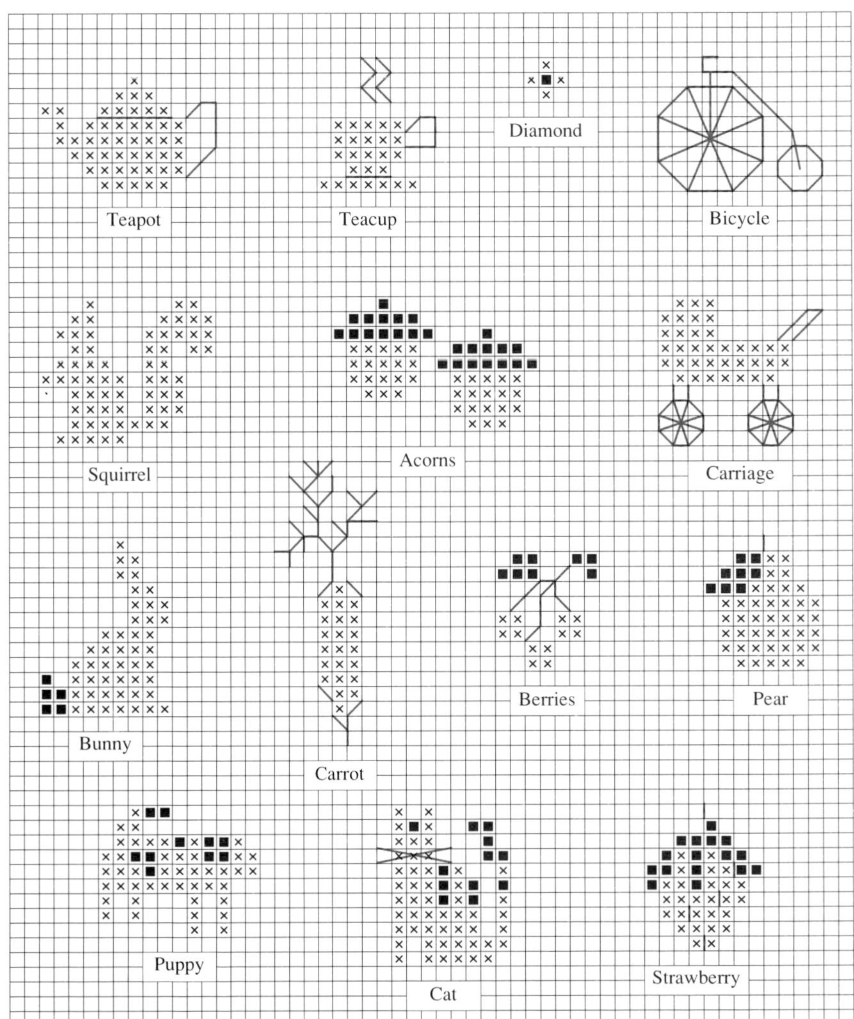

CROSS-STITCH AND EMBROIDERY DESIGNS FOR VICTORIAN BABY AFGHAN

ASSEMBLY: Sew strips 1 and 2 together using yarn scraps and matching colors. On both strips, embroider around each color shape using two strands of Persian yarn. See pages 69 and 79 for embroidery stitch diagrams. Stitches such as herringbone, running, cross, and chain are ideal for the look of a Victorian crazy quilt. Combine yarn colors for unusual effects in the embroidery.

Sew Strip 3 onto Strip 2; embroider as before. Repeat for strips 4 and 5.

FINISHING: With purple yarn, work 3 rnds of sc around the afghan edge, working 3 sc in each corner. Work 2 rnds of red, then 2 more rnds of purple.

Cont with purple yarn to make the picot edging. * Work 3 sl st, ch 3, sl st in same st as last sl st, rep from * around the afghan; join to beg sl st; fasten off.

MAKING TASSELS: Wind purple yarn around the cardboard approximately 40 times. Pass a 15-inch piece of matching yarn under the loops at one end; tie securely, leaving the ends of the tie free. Slide the yarn off the cardboard.

Cut a 12-inch strand of matching yarn. Positioning it at the top of the yarn bundle, wrap it five times around the bundle approximately 1¼ inches from the top; tie the strand. Make three more tassels in the same manner.

Tie the loose ends of the ties at the top of each tassel to the corners of the afghan. Pass any remaining loose ends of the ties through the tassels.

Cut the loops at the bottom of each tassel and trim evenly.

SAILOR DOLL

Shown on page 132.
The finished doll measures approximately 18¼ inches tall.

MATERIALS

For the doll

- ¾ yard of flesh-color felt
- 4½x8 inches of short-napped imitation fur for hair
- Scraps of white and brown felt for eyes
- Black carpet or buttonhole thread
- Sewing thread; sewing needle
- Polyester fiberfill
- Powder rouge
- White crafts glue
- Tracing paper; pencil; ruler

For the doll's clothes

- ⅓ yard of antique dollmaker's muslin
- ⅓ yard of blue fabric
- 28 inches of white middy tape
- One ¾-inch-diameter red pom-pom
- 6x12-inch rectangle of black lightweight vinyl for shoes
- 24 inches of narrow string for trouser drawstring
- 7 inches of ⅜-inch-wide blue grosgrain ribbon for hat
- 5½-inch square of heavyweight iron-on interfacing
- Rubber cement
- Scraps of lightweight cardboard

INSTRUCTIONS

Note: Add ¼-inch seam allowances when cutting the pieces from fabric.

Making patterns

Trace the full-size patterns *below, opposite,* and on pages 144–146. Place folded tracing paper atop the patterns that have center folds, matching the pattern fold lines with the tracing paper folds; trace the patterns. Cut out a completed paper pattern for each shape. The arm, leg, shoe, and sole are complete patterns.

Making the doll body

From one corner of the flesh-color felt, cut a 4½x8-inch rectangle for the head. Cut the remaining felt in half.

On one layer of the felt, draw around the patterns to mark one body piece, two arms, and two legs.

With the marked piece of felt on top and the unmarked piece underneath, machine-stitch through both layers on the marked lines, leaving openings in the stitching as indicated on the patterns. Cut out each shape.

ARMS: On the arm pieces, clip curves and turn each piece right side out. Stuff arms to within ½ inch of the top edge, then sew the open ends closed.

Insert the stuffed arms into the side openings of the body piece, aligning the top (shoulder) of each arm with the top of the opening. Machine-stitch through all layers to secure the arms and close the openings. Turn the body right side out through the bottom opening.

continued

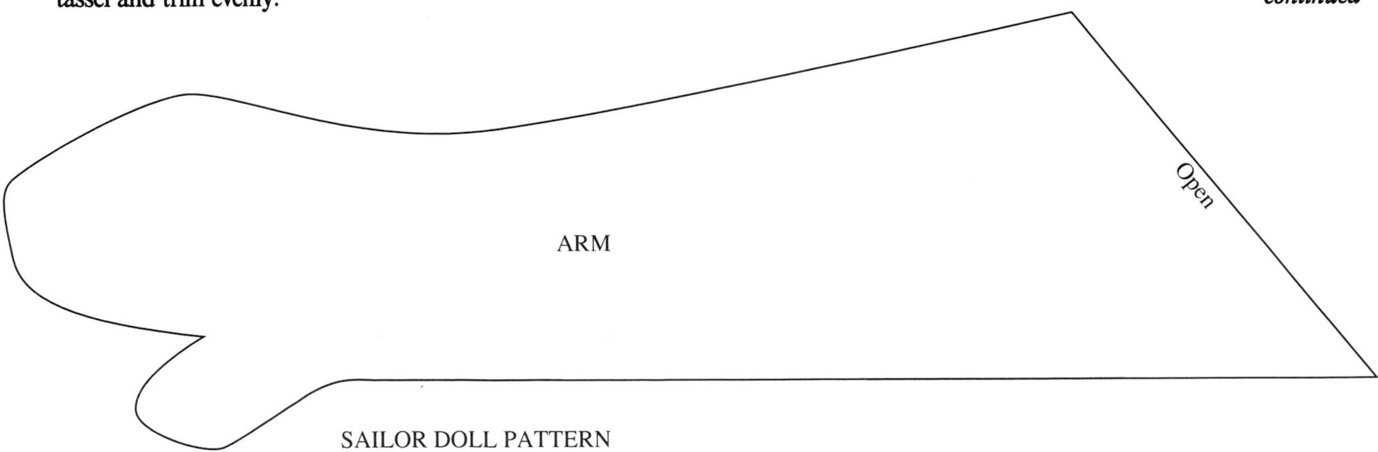

SAILOR DOLL PATTERN

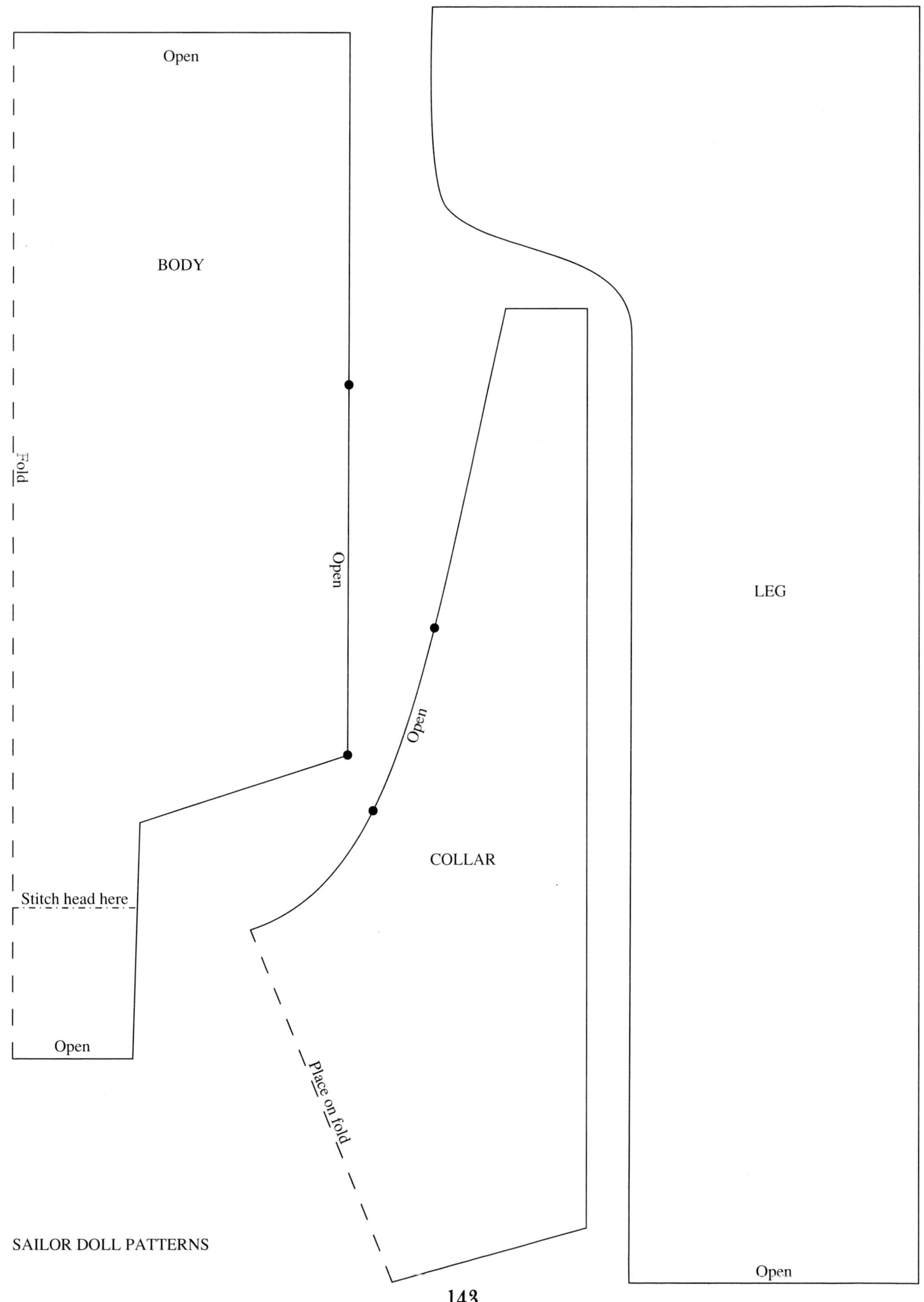

SAILOR DOLL PATTERNS

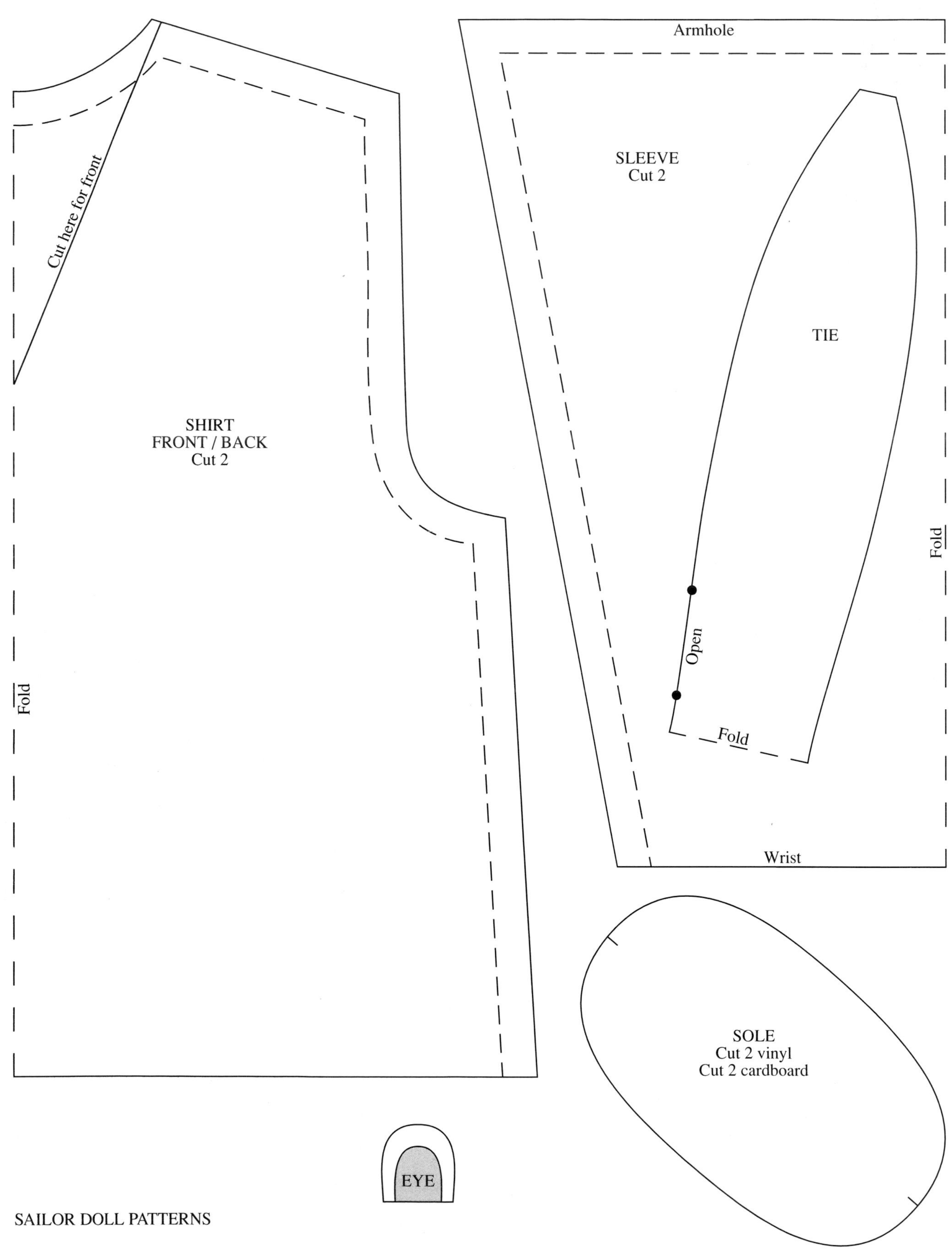

SAILOR DOLL PATTERNS

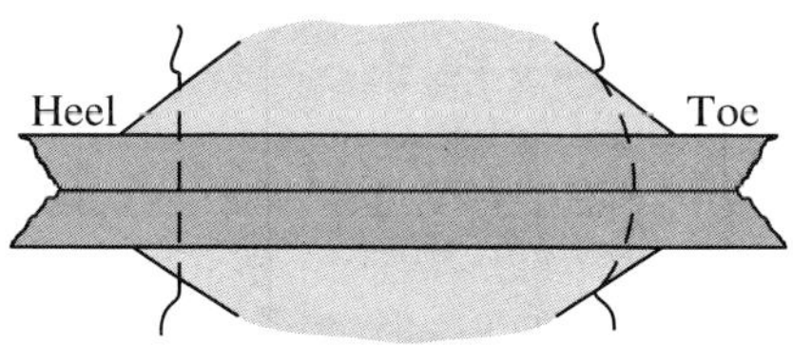

FIGURE 1

LEGS: Clip the seam allowances in the curve of each leg piece. Refer to Figure 1, *above,* to make the toe and heel gussets that shape the bottom of the foot. To make the gussets, first finger-press the seam allowances open on each leg.

Then align the seam at the bottom of the foot with the center front seam at the toe, bringing the toe to a point as shown in Figure 1. Machine-stitch through all layers, including seam allowances, approximately ½ inch from the point. Align the seams at the heel in the same manner and stitch.

Trim excess fabric close to the stitching at each gusset. Turn both legs right side out, pulling out the points of the toe with a pin or the tip of a seam ripper.

Stuff each foot and leg to within ½ inch of the top edge, stuffing the lower portion of the leg more firmly than the top. Stitch the open ends closed.

Insert the legs into the bottom opening of the body. Stitch across the bottom edge of the body, securing the legs. Stuff the body through the neck opening.

HEAD: Seam the short ends of the 4½x8-inch rectangle together; turn right side out. Turn under a ¼-inch hem along one edge and loosely hand-baste.

Slip the basted edge over the neck, centering the head seam at the back. Gather the basting thread until the head fits snugly around the neck. Hand-sew the bottom edge of the head to the neck.

Firmly stuff the head through the top opening. Close the opening with a gathering thread.

WIG: Fold the fur rectangle in half, with right sides together, so it measures 4x4½ inches. Stitch one 4-inch-long edge, widening the seam allowance from ¼ inch at the top of the seam to ¾ inch at the

continued

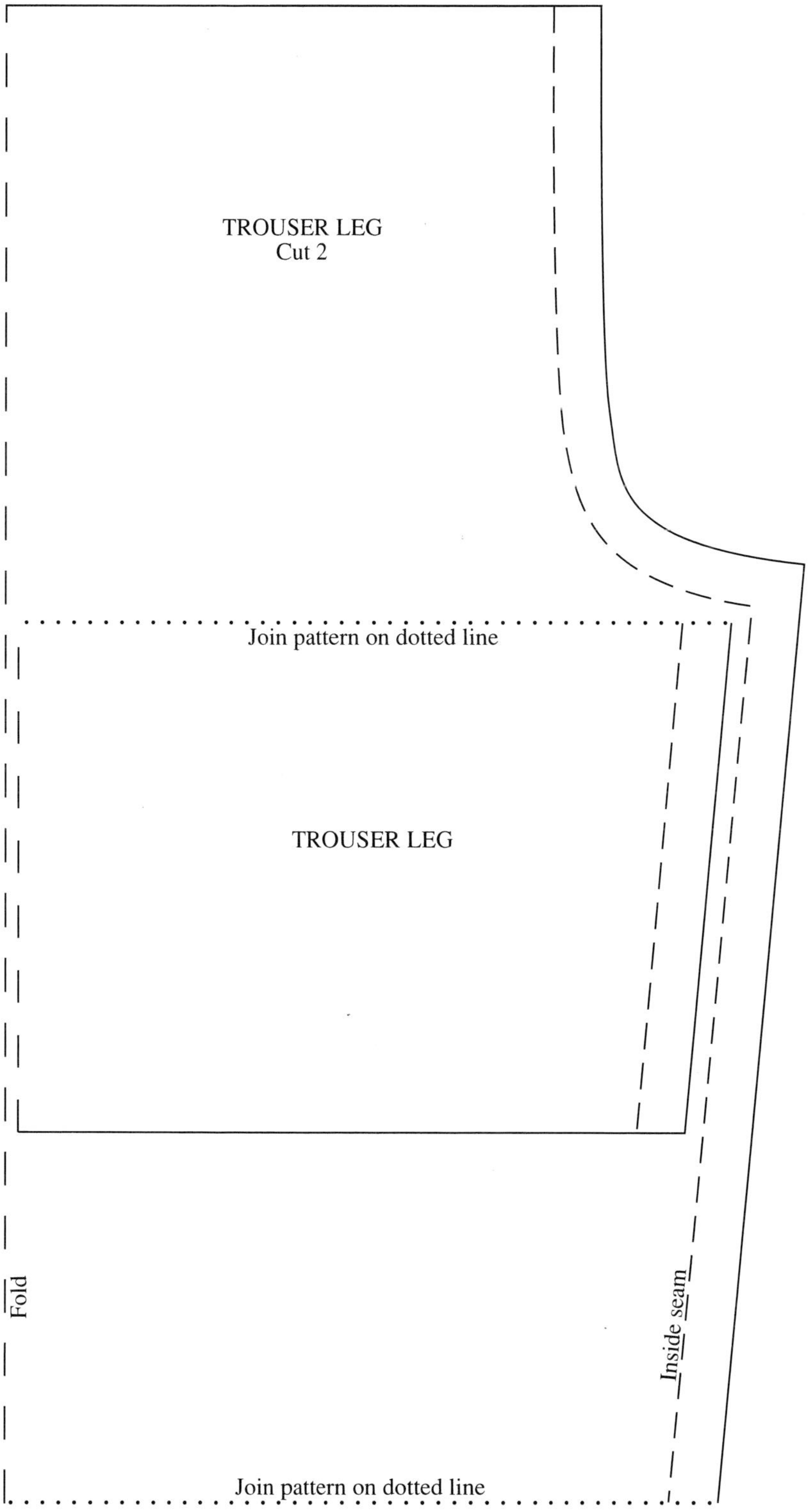

TROUSER LEG
Cut 2

Join pattern on dotted line

TROUSER LEG

Fold

Inside seam

Join pattern on dotted line

SAILOR DOLL PATTERNS

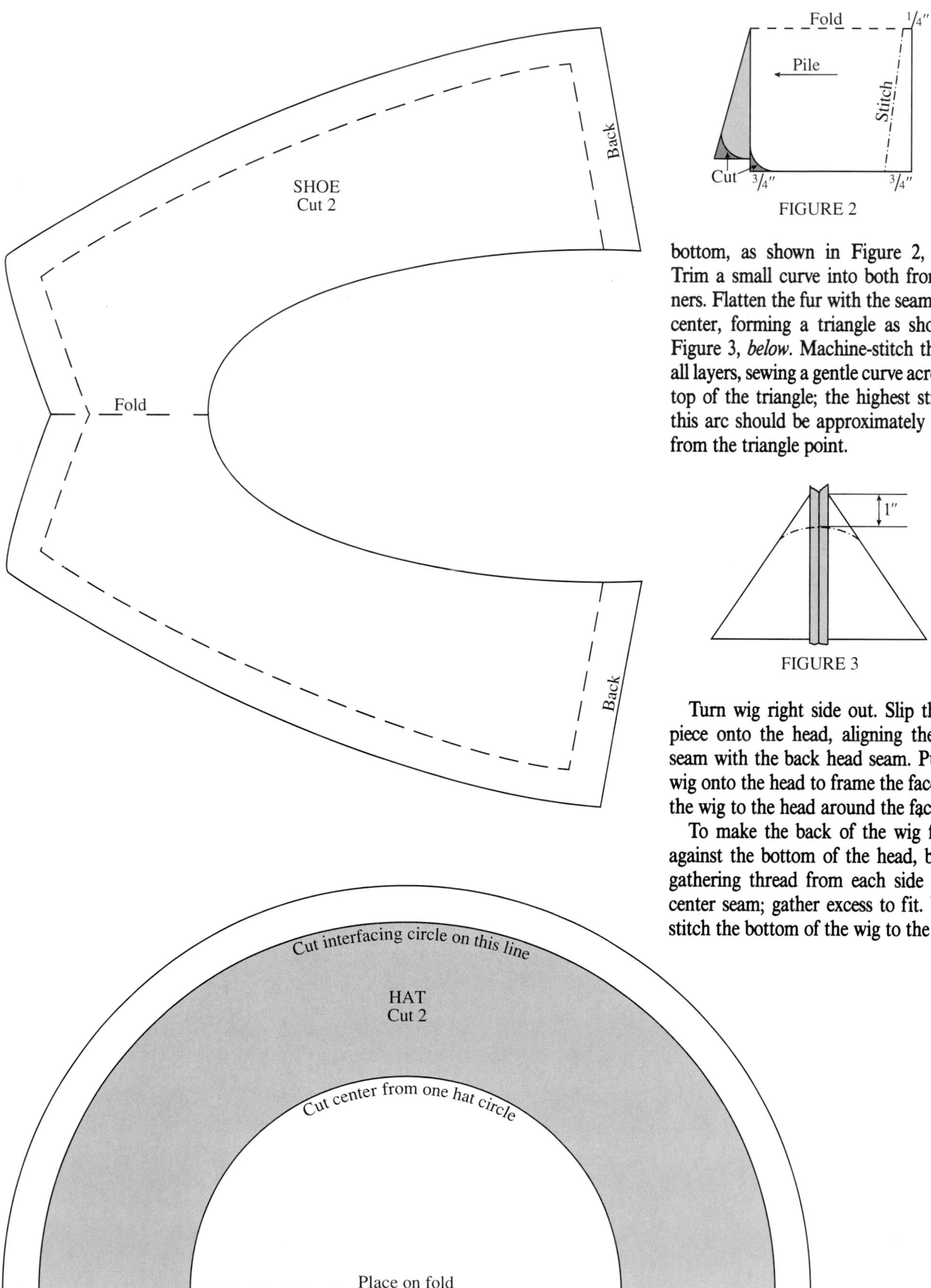

FIGURE 2

FIGURE 3

SAILOR DOLL PATTERNS

bottom, as shown in Figure 2, *above*. Trim a small curve into both front corners. Flatten the fur with the seam in the center, forming a triangle as shown in Figure 3, *below*. Machine-stitch through all layers, sewing a gentle curve across the top of the triangle; the highest stitch in this arc should be approximately 1 inch from the triangle point.

Turn wig right side out. Slip the wig piece onto the head, aligning the back seam with the back head seam. Pull the wig onto the head to frame the face; glue the wig to the head around the face.

To make the back of the wig fit flat against the bottom of the head, baste a gathering thread from each side to the center seam; gather excess to fit. Whipstitch the bottom of the wig to the head.

FACE: Cut two eyes from white felt and two pupils from brown felt; glue to the face. For definition, glue a strand of black carpet thread around the outside curve of the white eye.

Refer to the photo on page 132 for guidance on placing facial details. Using one strand of black sewing thread, make straight stitches for the nose and eyebrows; work the mouth in outline stitch (see page 79 for stitch diagram). Apply powder rouge for rosy cheeks.

Making the doll's clothing

You can use the antique dollmaker's muslin or dye regular muslin with strong tea and coffee to give it the mottled appearance of an antique.

To dye plain muslin, steep two tea bags in 4 cups of boiling water until the tea is dark brown. Pour the hot tea over premoistened muslin; let it soak for 30 minutes. Rinse in cold water.

Next, mix 1 tablespoon of instant coffee in ¼ cup of hot water. On a cookie sheet, loosely crumple the fabric. Use a basting brush to dribble the coffee over the folds. This creates dark, mottled areas on the fabric. Spread the muslin out and let it dry overnight.

SHIRT: Cut two sleeves, one shirt front, and one shirt back from muslin. Trim the neckline of the front piece as indicated on the shirt pattern on page 144. Sew the front and back together at the shoulders. Press the seam allowances open.

Stay-stitch around the neck opening, ¼ inch from the edge. Turn the fabric to the inside along the stitching; topstitch the hem in place.

With right sides together, sew one sleeve into each armhole opening. Hand-baste a gathering thread along the wrist edge of each sleeve.

From the blue fabric, cut two 1½x4¼-inch strips for the shirt cuffs. Adjust the gathers in the sleeve to fit the long edge of each cuff. Stitch a cuff to the bottom edge of each sleeve.

On each side of the shirt, stitch one continuous seam from the bottom edge of the shirt to the cuff. Turn under the raw edge of each cuff and hand-stitch a hem, covering the cuff seam allowance to make a ½-inch cuff. Turn the shirt right side out. Stitch or glue middy tape around each cuff.

Cut a 2x11½-inch blue strip for the waistband. Sew the short ends together. Gather the bottom edge of the shirt to fit the waistband. With right sides facing, sew one edge of the waistband to the bottom of the shirt, adjusting the gathers to fit. Turn the waistband over the raw edge and hand-stitch a hem. Pull the shirt onto the doll.

COLLAR: Fold the remaining blue fabric in half. On the top layer, trace the completed collar pattern and the completed tie pattern. Stitch on the drawn lines through both layers, leaving openings as indicated on the patterns. Cut out both pieces. Clip curves and turn right side out; press. With matching thread, topstitch around all edges of the collar. Sew or glue middy tape to the collar ⅛ inch from the outer edge.

Place the collar around the doll's neck. Cross the narrow ends at the front and tack them together. Tie an overhand knot in the center of the tie piece. Tack the tie in place over the collar ends.

For the front shirt insert, cut a small triangle from the selvage of the muslin. At the neckline, tuck the fabric between the shirt and the body with the selvage edge on top.

TROUSERS: Cut two trouser legs from the remaining muslin. Stitch the inside seams of each leg. Turn one leg right side out and slip it inside the second leg, so right sides are together and the curved edges are aligned. Starting at the top edge of the curve, stitch the seam to within 2 inches of the opposite edge. Turn the trousers right side out; press the unsewn seam allowances open at the center front and topstitch along the open seam.

Stay-stitch the top edge of the trousers. Turn this edge in ⅜ inch and topstitch to make a casing. Thread the drawstring on a blunt needle and ease it through the casing. Turn under the bottom edge of each trouser leg ¼ inch twice to make the hems; hand-sew the hems in place.

SHOES: Cut two of the shoe pattern from black vinyl. *Do not* add seam allowances to the shoe or sole patterns.

With right sides together, fold each shoe in half. Stitch the ends together at the toe and the back edge. Trim the toe seam close to the stitching, then turn shoe right side out. Use rubber cement to glue the back seam allowances open. Clip notches around the bottom ¼-inch edge of the shoe.

Cut two soles each from the vinyl and the lightweight cardboard. Pin a cardboard sole inside each shoe at the center of the toe and heel. With rubber cement, glue the bottom notched edges of the shoes to the bottom of the cardboard soles; let dry.

Glue a vinyl sole to the bottom of each cardboard sole. Glue black carpet thread around the bottom edges of the shoes, outlining the vinyl soles. When the glue is dry, slip the shoes onto the doll.

HAT: From the remaining blue fabric, cut two of the hat pattern and one 2x10-inch strip for the hatband.

Cut the inside circle from one hat piece as indicated on the hat pattern. Seam the short ends of the hatband. With right sides together, sew the hatband to the inside circle of the hat piece.

Fold the hatband in half to the inside, then fold it over again, covering the seam allowance. Hem the edge of the hatband in place.

Cut one circle of interfacing. Center it on the uncut fabric circle, matching the fusible side of the interfacing with the wrong side of the fabric; press.

With right sides together, stitch the two hat circles together around the outer edge. Turn hat right side out through center opening; press.

Cut a V-shaped notch in each end of the grosgrain ribbon. Fold the ribbon in half and glue the fold over the hatband seam. Glue the pom-pom to the top of the finished hat.

SILHOUETTE SAMPLER

	DMC
●●	312 navy blue - lt
Backstitch:	
⌐	312 everything

Instructions are on page 150.

Cross-Stitch Silhouette Sampler

Shown on page 133.
Design area as shown measures approximately 11¾x9 inches. Design is 165x126 stitches.

MATERIALS

15x18-inch piece of 28-count Tea-Dyed Linen by Charles Craft
Eight skeins of DMC blue (No. 312) embroidery floss or color of your choice
Size 24 or 26 tapestry needle
White paper tape
Embroidery hoop

INSTRUCTIONS

The chart for the sampler is given in two sections on pages 148 and 149. The shaded row of stitches on page 149 is repeated from page 148 and is used only as a guide in moving from one pattern section to the other. Do not rework this row of stitches.

Tape the raw edges of the fabric to prevent the threads from raveling.

Measure 3 inches down from the top edge of the fabric and 9 inches in from the side; begin stitching the top left border here. Use three strands of floss and work all cross-stitches over two threads of fabric. When the cross-stitch is complete, work the backstitches with one strand of floss.

Lightly press the finished stitchery on the back side. Frame as desired.

Punch and Judy Puppets

Shown on pages 134 and 135.
The finished puppets measure approximately 20½ inches tall.

MATERIALS

For both puppets

¼ yard of ivory velour
Scraps of fusible interfacing
1¼-inch-diameter paper towel tube
Polyester fiberfill
Fine-point permanent black marker
Red fabric paint (squeeze tube)
Powder rouge
White crafts glue
Tracing paper; pencil; ruler

For Punch puppet

¼ yard *each* of red fabric for shirt and striped fabric for pantaloons and hat
⅓ yard of green fabric for coat and hat
12-inch square of knit-backed gold lamé
⅓ yard of 2½-inch-wide flat ecru lace (both edges finished) for neck ruffle
⅔ yard of 1½-inch-wide flat ecru lace for sleeves and pantaloons
⅓ yard of 1-inch-wide brocade ribbon for sleeve trim
2 yards of narrow, flat, gold trim
½ yard *each* of ¼-inch-wide satin ribbon in three coordinating colors
One 12-mm-diameter gold bell for hat
Six 10-mm-diameter colored bells
Two ¼-inch-diameter beads for eyes
Twelve 6-mm-diameter gold beads for shoes and hat brim

For Judy puppet

⅓ yard of fabric for dress
12-inch square of black fabric for boots
10-inch square of white fabric for hat
1 yard of ¾-inch-wide white gathered lace for hat
1x11-inch strip of long-fibered crafts fur
1 yard of 1-inch-wide ribbon for bow
⅜ yard *each* of 1½-inch-wide lace and ¼-inch-wide black ribbon for boots
¼ yard of 1-inch-wide lace for cuffs
Two ⅜-inch-diameter shank buttons for eyes; black sewing thread

INSTRUCTIONS

Note: Use a ¼-inch seam allowance throughout the construction of the puppets and their clothing.

Making patterns

Trace each of the puppet patterns *opposite* and on pages 152–156, making one complete tracing for each shape. Cut out a paper pattern for each piece.

Making the puppet heads and hands

Cut the velour fabric in half. On the wrong side of one piece, trace the outlines of both head patterns. Trace four of the hand pattern. Leave at least ½ inch of space between tracings.

Layer the two pieces of velour with right sides together. Machine-stitch through both layers on the marked lines, leaving openings in the stitching as indicated on the respective patterns. Cut out each shape, leaving a scant ¼-inch seam allowance around the stitching. Clip curves; turn each piece right side out.

Lightly stuff each hand. Using a backstitch, hand-sew finger divisions as indicated on the hand pattern.

Stuff each head with fiberfill until firm. Force filling into the cheeks to contour the face, stretching the velour.

Cut a 2½-inch-long piece of cardboard tube for each puppet. Smear glue onto one side of each tube; keeping the glued side toward the back, push a tube into the neck of each head. Let glue dry. If necessary, push additional filling into the chin areas. Glue the front of each tube to the front neck fabric, pulling the fabric down to the edge of the cardboard.

Sew beads or buttons in place for eyes. Make eyelashes for Judy with straight stitches of black sewing thread. Use rouge to make rosy cheeks.

For each mouth, cut two squares of interfacing slightly larger than the pattern; fuse the two squares together. Using black permanent marker, trace the mouths on the interfacing. Squeeze fabric paint around the mouth outlines; let dry. Carefully cut out each mouth; glue in place on the puppet heads.

Wrap the strip of crafts fur around Judy's head, overlapping the ends at the back of her head. Whipstitch the hair onto the head around the face; tack the strip at the back. Brush the long fibers of the fur forward.

Making Punch's clothes

HAT: Cut two 5x7-inch pieces of green fabric. On the wrong side of one piece, trace the outline of the hat pattern. Layer the two pieces with right sides together; stitch on the drawn lines through both layers. Cut out hat; clip curves and turn right side out. Turn under the raw edge at the bottom of the hat; hand-baste the hem in place.

Slip the hat onto Punch's head, centering front and back seams. Baste edge of hat to head, easing fullness at each side.

Measure 6 inches along the vertical stripe of the striped fabric and cut a 6x9-inch piece for the brim. With right sides together, fold the piece in half lengthwise so it measures 3x9 inches. Trace the brim pattern on one side. Stitch on the drawn line, leaving the opening as indicated on pattern.

Cut out the brim. Trim all points and clip the seam allowance at each V; turn right side out and press. Hand-stitch the opening closed.

Sew a gold bead to each point. Wrap the brim around the hat, matching the bottom edges; whipstitch the brim in place. Glue gold trim around the bottom edge. Sew the gold bell to the hat tip.

SHIRT: From the dark red fabric, cut one shirt front and two backs.

Starting at the top edge, stitch 1½ inches of the center back seam. Press the seam allowances open; topstitch the seam allowances in place along both sides of the back opening.

Sew back to front at shoulders, leaving a neckline opening between the dots shown on the shirt pattern; press seam allowances open. Stitch side/underarm seam at both sides; clip seam allowance at underarms.

Position a hand in each sleeve, matching right sides and raw edges. Stitch across the sleeve ends, enclosing the hands. Do not turn shirt to right side yet.

continued

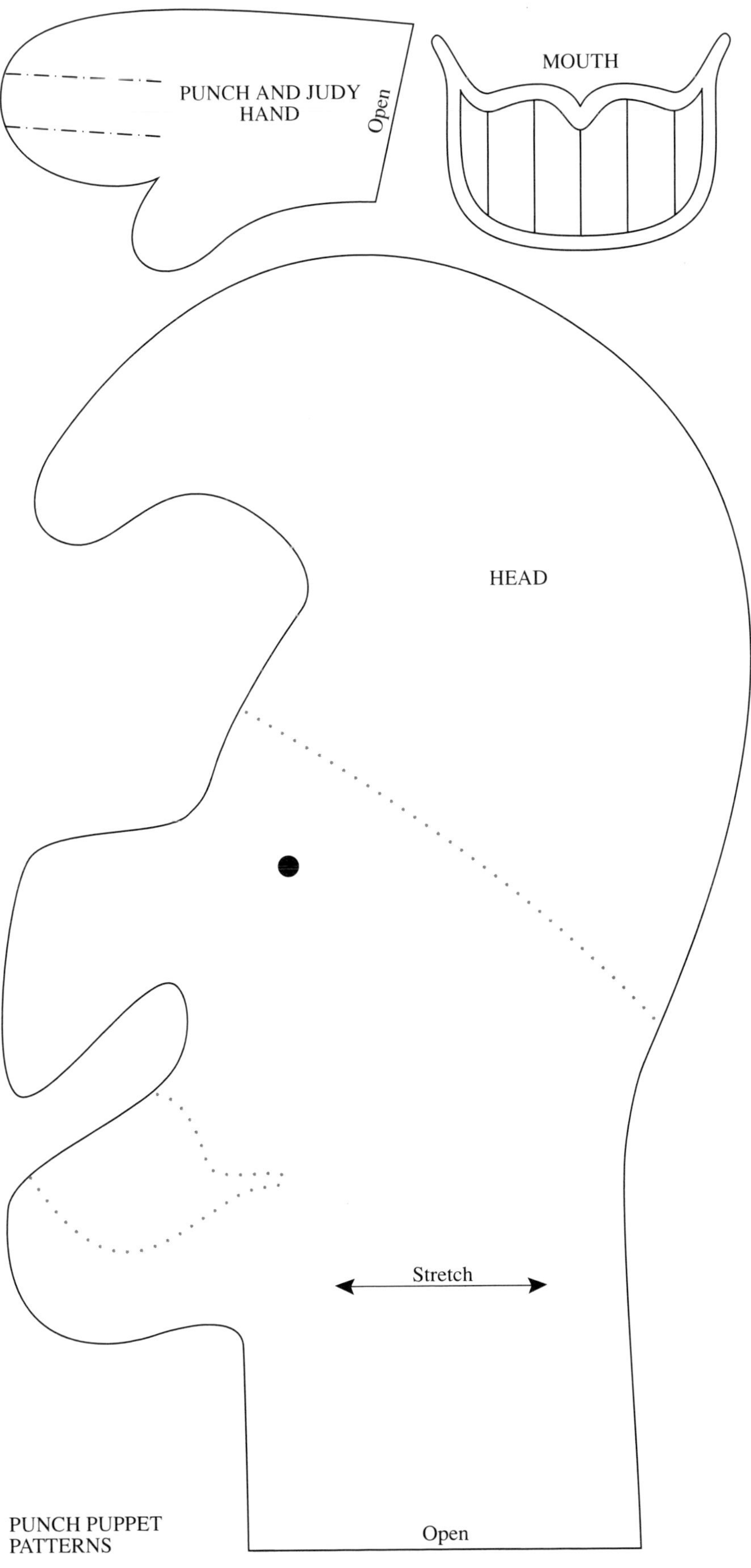

PUNCH PUPPET PATTERNS

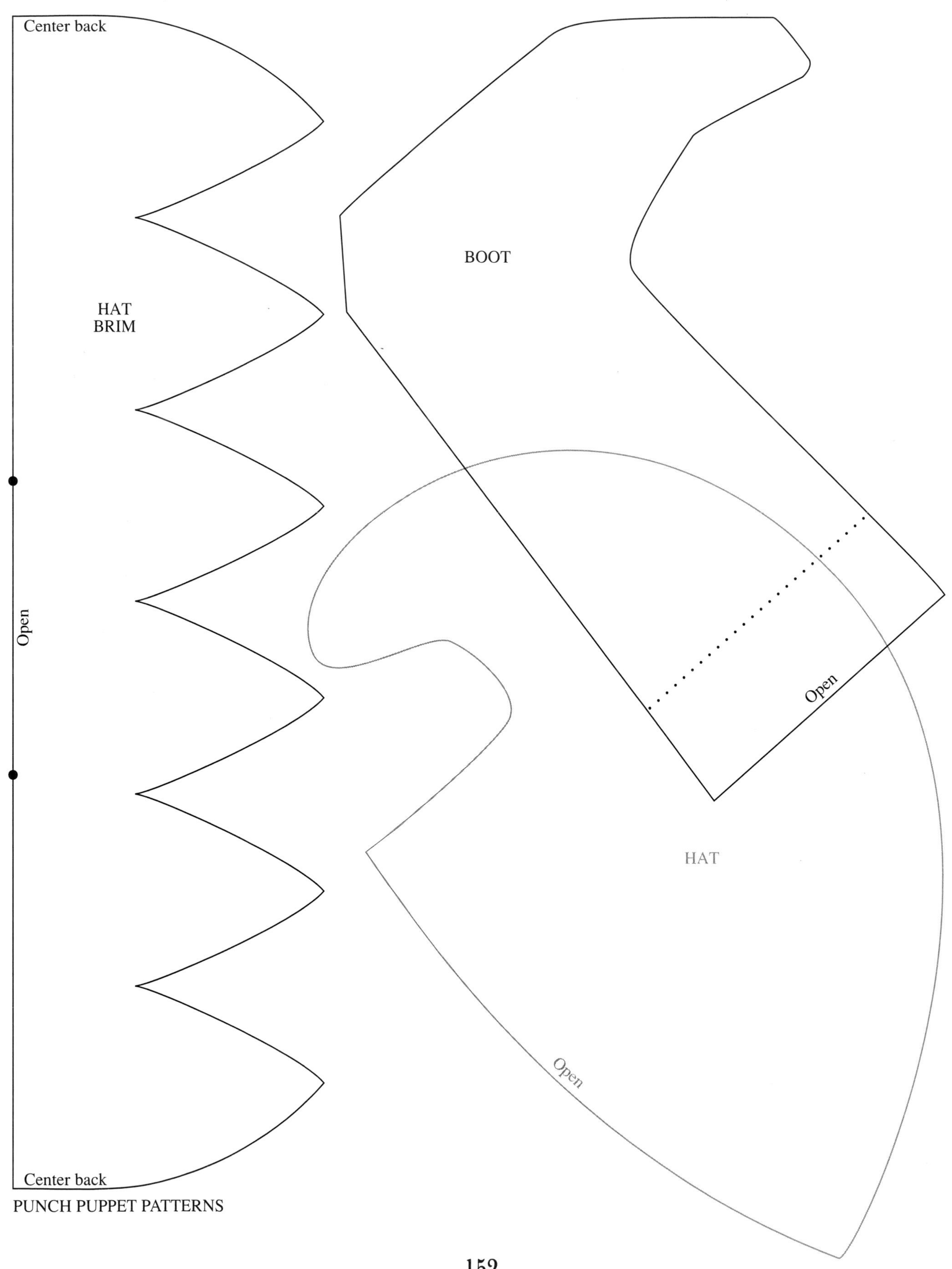

PUNCH PUPPET PATTERNS

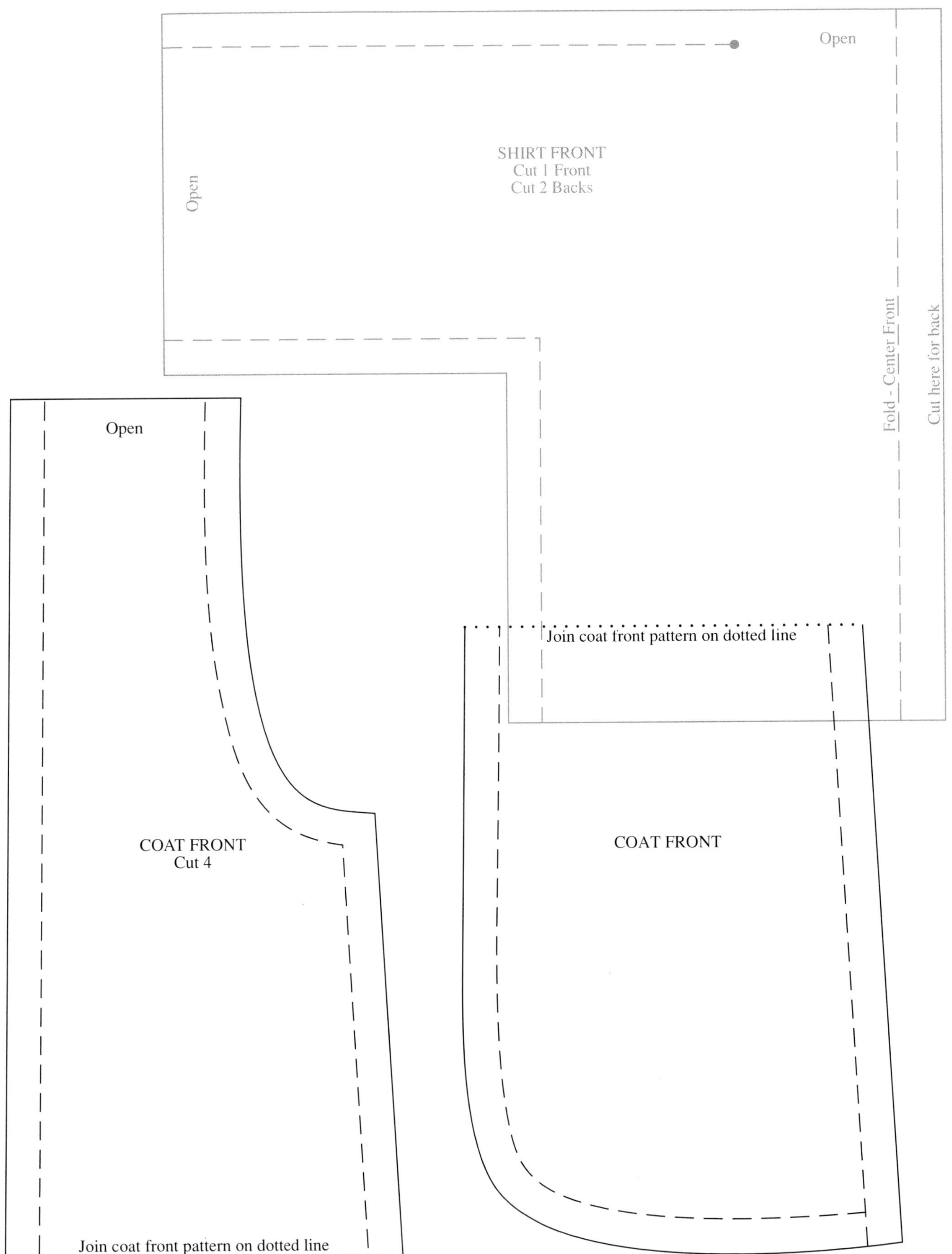
Open
SHIRT FRONT
Cut 1 Front
Cut 2 Backs
Open
Fold - Center Front
Cut here for back
Open
COAT FRONT
Cut 4
Join coat front pattern on dotted line
Join coat front pattern on dotted line
COAT FRONT

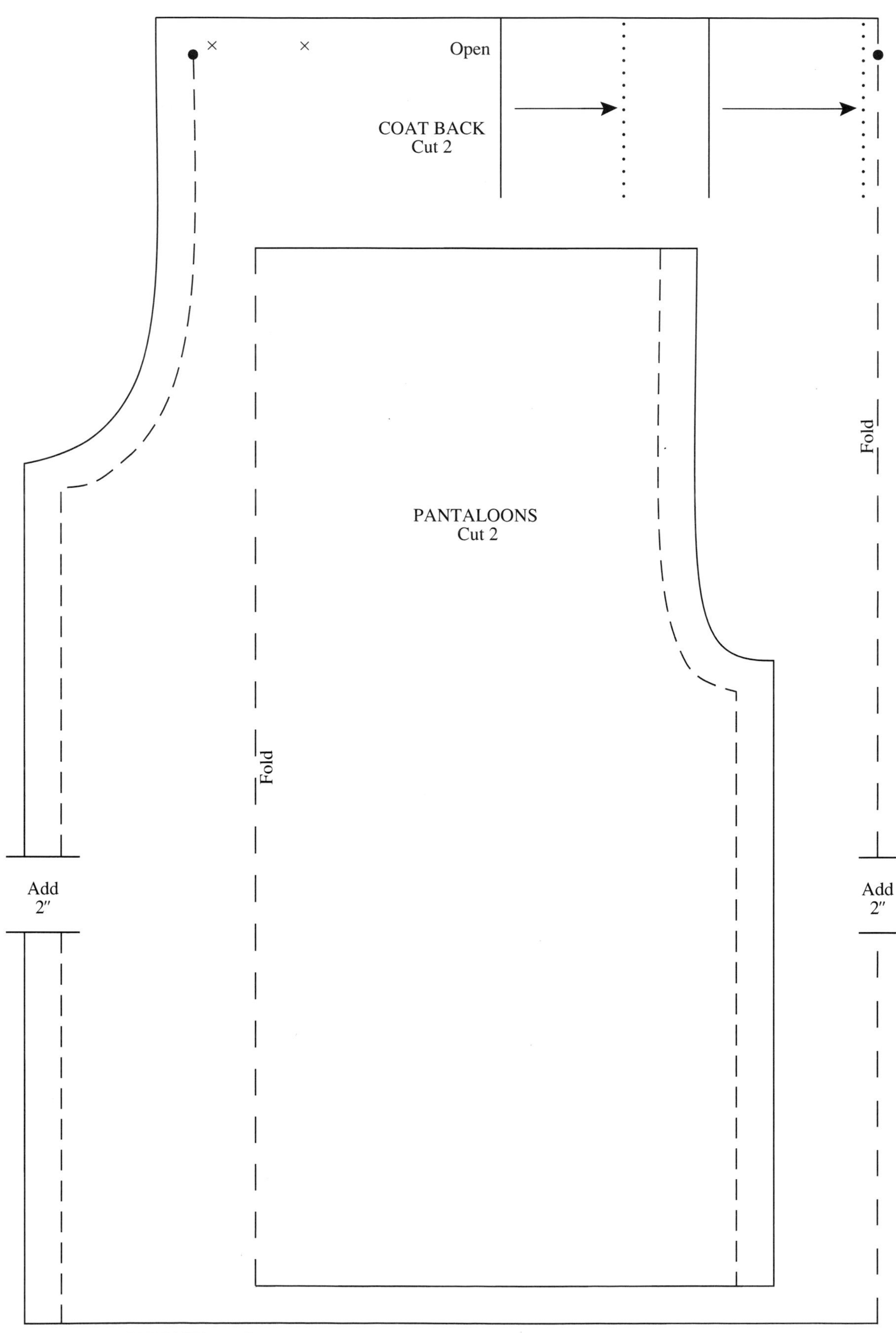

PUNCH PUPPET PATTERNS

PANTALOONS: Cut two pantaloons pieces from the striped fabric, positioning the pattern fold line parallel to the stripes. With right sides together, stitch the straight seam of each leg.

Turn one leg right side out and slip it inside the second leg so right sides are together and the curved edges are aligned. Starting at the top edge of the curve, stitch the seam to within 2½ inches of the opposite edge. Turn the pantaloons right side out; press seam allowances open. Topstitch the unsewn seam allowances at the center back.

With right sides together, sew the top edge of the pantaloons to the bottom edge of the shirt. Align side seams and back openings. Turn right side out.

BOOTS: Fold the gold lamé in half, right sides together. Trace two of the boot pattern onto the wrong side of the fabric. Stitch on the drawn lines through both layers. Cut out two boots; clip corners and turn each boot right side out.

Stuff boots until firm. Hand-baste a gathering stitch at the top of each boot to close the opening. Insert boots into pants legs up to the dashed line indicated on boot pattern. Gather a pants leg around each boot; whipstitch legs to boots.

Cut 8 inches of 1½-inch-wide lace for each leg. Gather top edge of lace; hand-baste it in place to cover the raw edge of each pants leg. Glue gold trim over the top edge of the lace. Sew three gold beads atop the center seam of each foot.

Insert Punch's head through the shirt opening. Whipstitch neck of shirt to puppet's neck.

Cut the brocade ribbon and the remaining 1½-inch-wide lace in half. Stitch the top edge of the lace around the bottom edge of each sleeve. Gather the ribbon to fit the wrist; topstitch the ruffle in place over the lace.

COAT: From the green fabric, cut four of the coat front pattern and two of the back pattern. Stitch front pieces to both sides of each back. With right sides together, sew lining to coat around the outside and armhole edges; leave top edges open as indicated on patterns. Clip armhole curves; turn right side out and press.

Turn under a ¼-inch hem around the back neckline. Insert the shoulder edge of each front piece between the front and back linings; pin each shoulder in place between the two Xs shown at the top of the coat back pattern. Topstitch ⅛ inch from the edge of the back neckline, encasing the front shoulder edges.

Make two pleats on either side of the center back as indicated on the coat back pattern, folding the fabric at the point indicated by the solid line and bringing the fold over to the dotted line. Fold each pleat toward the center back. Topstitch the four pleats in place.

Glue gold trim around front and bottom edges of coat; slip coat onto puppet.

Seam the short ends of the 2½-inch-wide lace. Baste a gathering stitch ¾ inch from one edge. Slip the lace over the puppet's head with the narrower section of lace at the top. Gather lace tightly around neck; secure thread.

Tie satin ribbons around neck as desired. Thread colored bells onto ribbons.

continued

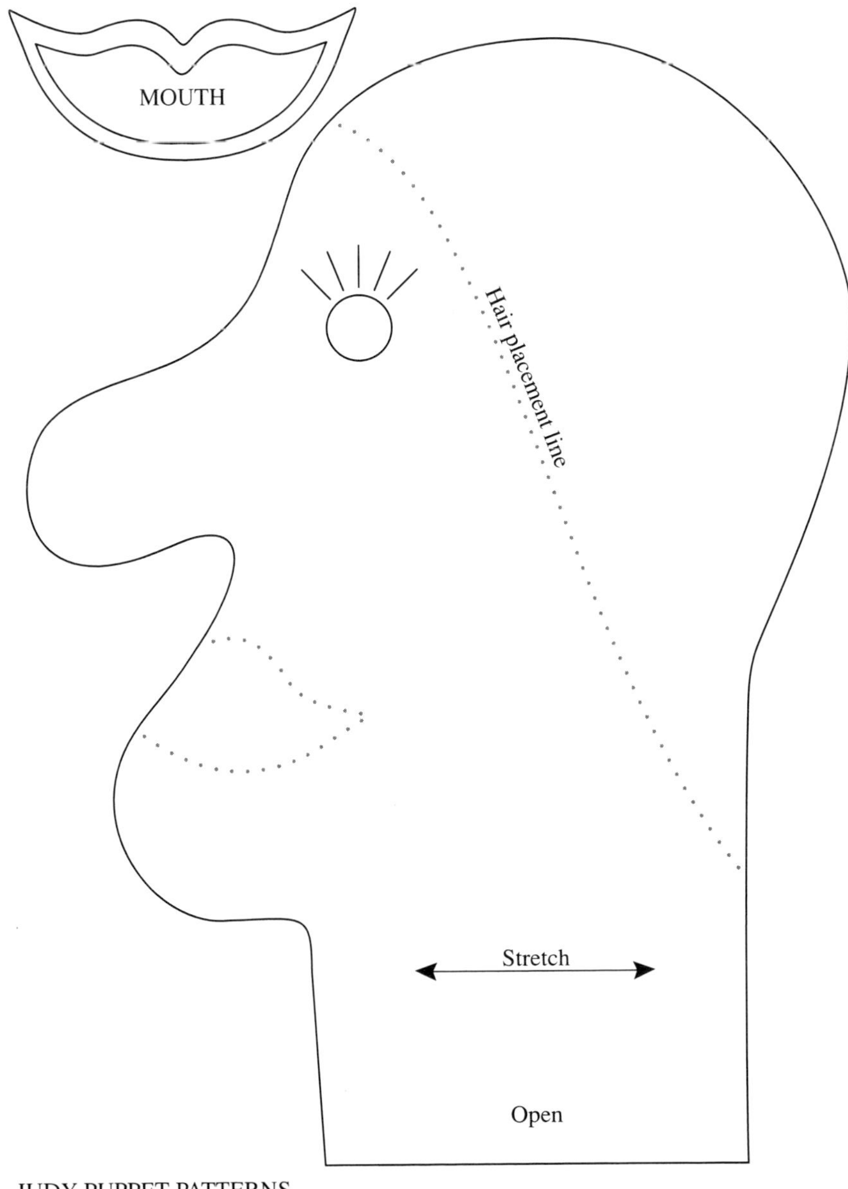

JUDY PUPPET PATTERNS

Making Judy's clothes

DRESS: From the dress fabric, cut two of the bodice pattern and one 11x26-inch rectangle for the skirt.

With right sides together, stitch bodice shoulder seams; leave an opening between dots as indicated on the pattern. Press the seam allowances open. Stitch the side/underarm seam at each side.

Insert hands into sleeves, matching right sides and raw edges. Machine-stitch across the end of each sleeve, encasing the hands. Turn bodice right side out. Add lace trim to each sleeve.

Seam the short ends of the skirt rectangle. Turn under a ¾-inch-wide hem along one edge; press. Machine-baste a gathering stitch ½ inch from the top edge. Gather skirt to fit the bottom edge of the bodice.

Pin skirt to bodice, placing the skirt gathering line approximately ½ inch from the raw edge of the bodice. Topstitch the skirt in place. Make a 1-inch hem at the skirt's bottom edge.

Insert Judy's head through dress neck opening. Whipstitch dress neck to puppet neck. Tie ribbon bow around neck.

BOOTS: Trace two of the boot pattern on the wrong side of the black fabric. Stitch on the drawn line through two layers of fabric. Trim excess fabric; clip corners. Turn boots right side out.

Stuff each foot until firm, using less stuffing in the upper leg. Machine-stitch across the top of each boot.

Cut the lace and ribbon in half. Baste a lace cuff around the top of each boot, placing the top edge of the lace approximately ¼ inch from the top of the boot. Tie ribbon bows; tack a bow at the top of each foot.

Position the boots under the dress front. Hand-stitch boots to skirt hem.

HAT: Cut a 9½-inch-diameter circle from the hat fabric. Stitch lace around the outer edge. Hand-stitch a gathering thread around the circle approximately 1¼ inches from the edge.

Place hat on Judy's head; adjust gathers to fit. Secure gathering thread. Tack hat onto head.

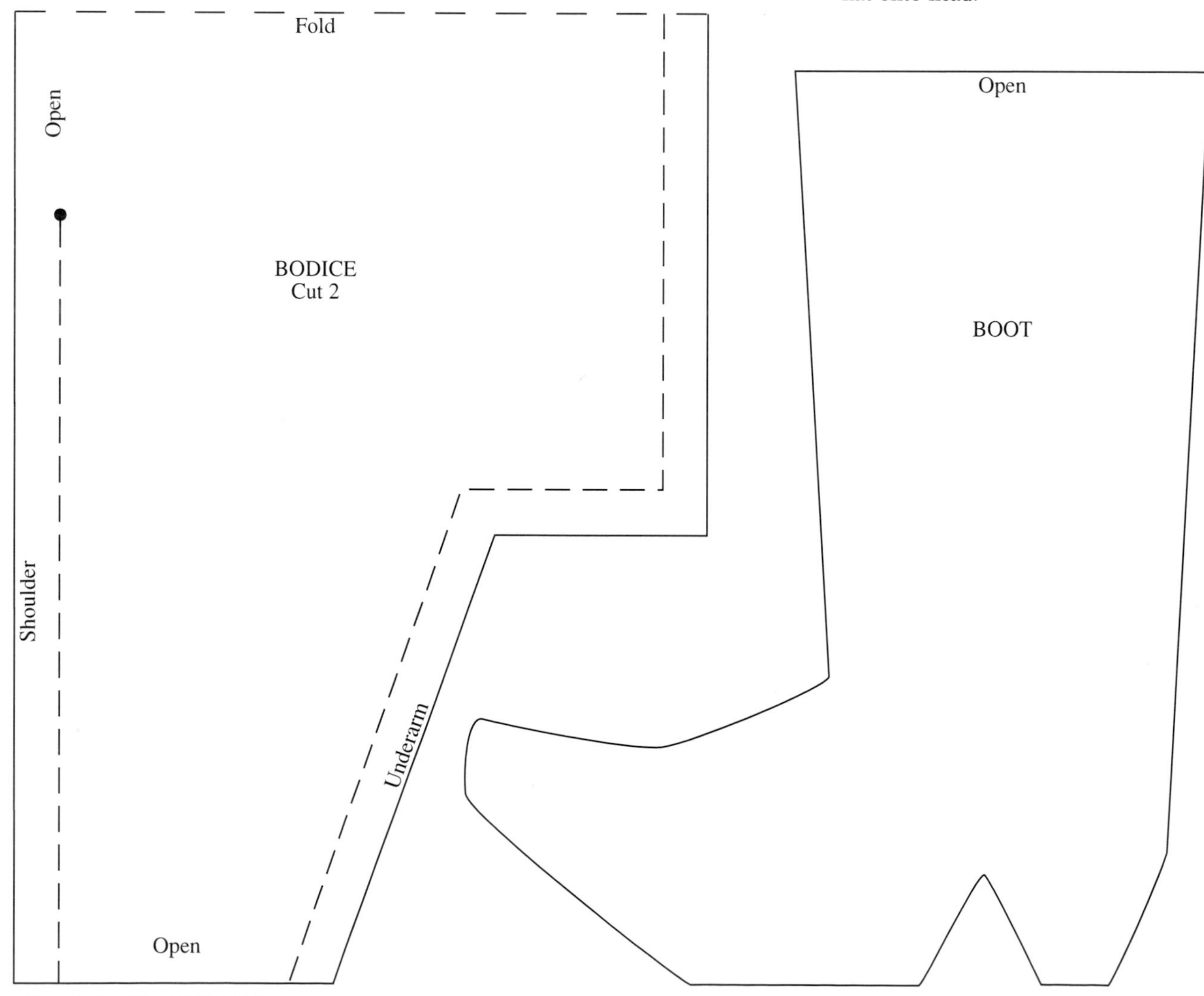

JUDY PUPPET PATTERNS

WORKING FILET CROCHET DESIGNS

Perhaps the easiest crochet patterns to stitch are filet crochet designs. These exquisite and often intricate designs are worked from charts that are filled with blocks and spaces that create the pattern and allow the crocheter to turn thread into lovely lacy fabric. The designs in this book that are created using the filet crochet technique are on pages 32, 52–55, 71, 95, 104–106, and 109.

Stitching the designs

Filet patterns are worked in rows and produced by stitching an open "net" background where filled-in spaces, called blocks, form the design. The spaces are made by working a chain-2 loop between 2 double crochets. When you build a pattern of blocks within these spaces, you create the design.

To begin a filet pattern, crochet a foundation chain upon which the first row of the design begins. For ease in remembering the block and space sequence, keep in mind that each block or space is equal to 3 stitches *plus 1 more stitch*. For example, 1 block is 4 double crochets (1x3 plus 1); 2 side-by-side blocks are 7 double crochets (2x3 plus 1); 3 side-by-side blocks are 10 double crochets (3x3 plus 1).

The patterns are worked from charts in which 1 square equals 1 filet space or 1 filet block.

When working from a chart, read the odd-numbered rows from right to left and the even-numbered rows from left to right, unless the instructions specify otherwise.

Working a space over a space

Double crochet in the double crochet in the row below, work 2 chains, then double crochet in the next double crochet in the row below.

Working a space over a block

Double crochet in the first stitch of the block of the previous row, work 2 chains, skip 2 double crochets, then double crochet in the next double crochet in the row below.

Working a block over a space

Double crochet in the double crochet before the space in the row below, work 2 double crochets in the chain-2 space; work a double crochet in the next double crochet in the row below.

Working block over block

Double crochet in each of the 4 double crochets of the previous row.

Working scalloped edges

Many filet patterns have scalloped edges that require you to increase or decrease the number of blocks or spaces at the beginning or end of a row. The patterns in this book cite the directions for making increases and decreases at the ends of the rows when called for in the design.

Working turning chains

When working along the straight edges at the ends of rows, you'll need to chain to turn the work and begin the next row. When the pattern begins with a block, chain 3 to turn and to count as the first double crochet.

When the pattern begins with a space, chain 5 to turn and count as the first double crochet and the first chain-2 space.

Other stitch patterns in filet crochet

Many patterns use other combinations of stitches to form interesting backgrounds for filet designs. For example, the hand towel edging on page 32 has lacet and chain-5 loops separating block patterns. The directions for this "netting" and any other open mesh background follow the same mathematical sequence (3 plus 1) as the basic filet crochet technique.

Working mitered corners

We recommend that only an advanced crocheter attempt the filet designs that incorporate the design in a mitered corner. The corner areas are shaded in our patterns for ease in working. To keep the work lying flat and to maintain the design, it is necessary to work short rows and join these rows to the existing work with either slip stitches, double crochets, or chain stitches. The crocheter needs to determine which stitch works best to begin the next row.

Creating your own designs

Use graph paper to chart your own filet crochet designs. Inspirations can come from cross-stitch designs such as the sampler on page 133, or you can chart your own ideas from a drawing.

Shade the squares for blocks and leave them blank for the chain-2 spaces, or white out the vertical line between two squares for the chain-5 spaces or lacets.

To figure the foundation chain, count the number of squares across the bottom of the chart and subtract 1 for the first square. Multiply that number by 3. Then if the first row begins with a block, add 6 to the total number of chains and work a double crochet in the fourth chain from the hook and the next two chains (if there's only one block). If the piece begins with a space, add 8 to the total number of chains and work a double crochet in the sixth chain from the hook. And if the piece begins with a lacet, add 12 to the total number of chains and work a single crochet in the ninth chain from the hook; chain 3, skip 2 chains, and double in the next chain.

We express our gratitude and appreciation to the many people who helped with this book.

Our heartfelt thanks to the following designers who contributed material that was developed especially for this book, to the photographers for their creative talents, to the companies who generously shared their products with us, and to all those who in some other way contributed to the production of this book.

DESIGNERS

Lori Birmingham for DMC—51

Stephani Bishop—107

Coats & Clark, Inc.—31, crocheted pulls; 32, knitted edgings; 56–57; 103, doily

Laura Holtorf Collins—10–11

Sue Cornelison—29, monograms; 131, redwork designs

DMC Corporation—7, tatted pincushion

Susan Z. Douglas—131, afghan

Cheryl Drivdahl—53, cross-stitch picture

Phyllis Dunstan—132; 134–135

Marlene Ehrhart—7, needlepoint pincushion

Dixie Falls—7, fan pincushion; 8–9; 30; 103, heart pincushion, beaded box; 133

Diane Hayes—72, picture mat; 74

JAMESA—77; 94, footstool cover

Gail Kinkead—109, crocheted shutter panels

Joyce Nordstrom—76, afghan

Nancy Reames—7, crocheted pincushion; 31, tassels; 93; 104, redwork pillow design; 106, purse; 108

Sue Rogers—29, Battenberg pillow

Helene Rush—94, afghan; 104, afghan

Margaret Sindelar—7, crazy-quilt pincushion; 34–35

Dee Wittmack—75; 76, pillow

For their technical skills, we thank:
Donna Glas
Marylou K. Helt
Margaret Sindelar
Marian Sprecher
Mary Vermie
Elaine K. Wichman
Pat Wilens
Dee Wittmack

PHOTOGRAPHERS

Scott Little—8; 30; 51–52; 54; 56; 75–76; 94; 104; 132

Lyne Neymeyer—7; 9–11; 31; 33; 53; 55 (small photo); 57; 73–74; 77; 95; 107–108; 133–135; backgrounds on 6–7, 28–29, 50–51, 70–71, 92–93, 102–103, and 130–131

Perry Struse—29; 32; 34–35; 71–72; 93; 103; 105–106; 109; 131

ACKNOWLEDGMENTS

Evlyn M. Anderson

Jeanne Anthony

Anne Brinkley Designs
21 Ransom Road
Newton Centre, MA 02159

Brunswick Yarns
P.O. Box 276
Pickens, SC 29671

Charles Craft, Inc.
P.O. Box 1049
Laurinburg, NC 28352

Coats & Clark, Inc.
Dept. CS
P.O. Box 1010
Toccoa, GA 30577

DMC Corporation
Port Kearny Building No. 10
South Kearny, NJ 07032

Dot's Frame Shoppe
4521 Fleur Drive
Des Moines, IA 50321

Harry and Sally Downing

Heritage Imports, Inc.
P.O. Box 328
Pella, IA 50219

Ellen S. Holt
1013 Slocum Street
Dallas, TX 75207
for fringe on footstool
(to the trade only)

Angie Hoogensen

Kreinik Mfg. Co. Inc.
P.O. Box 1966
Parkersburg, WV 26102

Laird Macdonald

Sheila Mauck

C.M. Offray & Son, Inc.
261 Madison Avenue
New York, NY 10016

Paternayan Yarns
Johnson Creative Arts
445 Main Street
West Townsend, MA 01474

Mark and Susan Pennington

Anne Powell, Ltd.
P.O. Box 3060
Stuart, FL 34995

Smith & Hawken
25 Corte Madera
Mill Valley, CA 94941

Dave and Carol Thomason

William Unger & Co., Inc.
P.O. Box 1621
2478 E. Main Street
Bridgeport, CT 06601

Waverly Fabrics and Wall Coverings
Division of Schumacher & Co.
79 Madison Avenue
New York, NY 10016

Wichelt Imports, Inc.
R.R. 1
Stoddard, WI 54658

Zweigart Fabrics and Canvas
Rose Gardens
P.O. Box 261
Madison, TN 37115

Page numbers in **bold** *type refer to photographs; other page numbers refer to how-to instructions.*

A-B

C-D

E-M

N-R

S-Z